DON'T STOP BELIEVIN'
THE UNTOLD STORY OF
JOURNEY

For Emma Kilgannon…

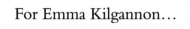

DON'T STOP BELIEVIN'
THE UNTOLD STORY OF
JOURNEY

NEIL DANIELS

OMNIBUS PRESS
London / New York / Paris / Sydney / Copenhagen / Berlin / Madrid / Tokyo

Exclusive Distributors
Music Sales Limited,
14/15 Berners Street,
London, W1T 3LJ.

Music Sales Corporation,
257 Park Avenue South,
New York, NY 10010, USA.

Macmillan Distribution Services,
56 Parkwest Drive
Derrimut, Vic 3030,
Australia.

Every effort has been made to trace the copyright holders of the photographs in this book but one
or two were unreachable. We would be grateful if the photographers concerned would contact us.

Typeset by Phoenix Photosetting, Chatham, Kent
Printed in the E.U.

A catalogue record for this book is available from the British Library.

Visit Omnibus Press on the web at www.omnibuspress.com

Contents

Foreword

BY ANDREW McNIECE
of melodicrock.com

"There's quite a bit of musicianship and variety that makes up Journey."
Ross Valory[1]

When you think Journey – you think of the songs. They seem to have taken on a life of their own and for many the songs are all they know. There is no knowledge of the personalities behind them, nor the years of hard work, endless touring and paying dues that it took to make these songs classics.

Those that are better educated know that beneath the surface lies one of the most fascinating, complicated and dysfunctional histories of any rock band of the modern era.

A myriad of individuals have been part of the Journey machine over the years, from the various members of the band who have come and gone, to those that guided their way and the various crews that kept them on the road.

Journey have always engaged tough management. In the early days Herbie Herbert was a pioneer, a groundbreaking hands-on manager. No one ever said no to Herbie, and decisions he made then still influence the music world today. In more recent times the equally infamous Irving Azoff has guided the band and kept them going when many other bands would not have made it.

At the core of Journey is guitarist Neal Schon – the founding member. And together with Herbie Herbert and later keyboardist Jonathan Cain and Azoff, he made a number of tough calls over the years. These key moments are numerous. The decision to hire a full-time lead vocalist in Steve Perry saw the band lose its early progressive fans for the new commercial direction. As Perry gained more control he brought in his own rhythm section for the *Raised On Radio* album and tour. Perry then departed and the band disappeared for ten years, only to reunite for *Trial By Fire* in 1996. Perry was unable to commit to touring due to the need for hip surgery, leaving the band with their toughest call of all. And this time they didn't hesitate – they made the hardest call in their history and replaced Perry. These were all momentous decisions. Any one of them could have killed the band; but, in hindsight, each decision seems only to have added to the legacy of the group and allowed them to be where they are now – still creating new music, still touring and still playing those beloved classics.

And that is what it is all about – the songs. These are the songs that bring thousands out of their homes each summer as the band tours year in, year out. They are the songs that appear in countless movies and TV shows each year. They are the songs that inspire an unprecedented number of tribute bands, each adopting a song title as a moniker of their own. And Journey have written some brilliant songs that have stood the test of time. The fact that 'Don't Stop Believin'' is the most downloaded song of all time only proves that.

And one cannot forget this band's fans – some of the most dedicated, passionate, loving (and at times crazy) people that anyone could wish to meet. The band are their adopted family and they will at times duel to the death to protect their favourite members. It is all part of the energy that envelops this band and everything they do.

Most of the band's most memorable and popular songs came from the Steve Perry years. The chemistry between vocalist Perry, guitarist Neal Schon and keyboardist Jonathan Cain was undeniable. Despite the dysfunctional nature of their personal relationships with each other, or perhaps because of that creative tension, the trio created a legacy that lives on today, more than thirty years since 'Don't Stop Believin'' was committed to vinyl. This book details some of the personalities behind the band and some of the countless stories that make up everything that is Journey.

Andrew J McNeice
October 2010
www.melodicrock.com

Introduction

"They [critics] were critical of Journey being corporate and the money orientation and so forth; shit, try that nowadays. Nowadays, if you're not making money you're just not hip."

Herbie Herbert[2]

In 2009, a quirky musical comedy set in a high school called *Glee* aired in the United States, and before long the show's critical and commercial success spread around the world. The format takes well-known popular songs – often classic rock tracks – and reworks them according to the premise of the show. Without question, *Glee*'s most popular and widely-travelled song is 'Don't Stop Believin'', from Journey's classic mega-selling 1981 album *Escape*. The song – both the *Glee* version and the original Journey cut – became significant chart successes the world over and Journey, a band barely known among British teenagers, became popular all over again. The song took on a life of its own: not only was a version played on *Glee*, but also on the UK talent contest *The X Factor*, run by the music mogul Simon Cowell, and Channel Five in the UK even took the big step of naming a TV show after the song. Once "rock dinosaurs", Journey quickly became anything but "has-beens". Indeed, *Journey's Greatest Hits* – surely one of the finest collections of rock tracks ever assembled on one disc – re-entered the charts in both their native

America and many foreign territories, including the UK where their career has often been haphazard.

The enormous success of *Glee* was perfect timing for the band. In late 2007, Journey hired a new singer from the Philippines named Arnel Pineda after guitarist and co-founder Neal Schon had seen him perform Journey tracks on YouTube. So impressed was Schon with Pineda's vocal abilities that he had the singer flown out to San Francisco to audition for the band. The band had experienced years of relative obscurity following the second – and ultimately final – departure of Steve Perry, Journey's most iconic singer. It had hired (and fired) two singers, Steve Augeri and Jeff Scott Soto, who, although popular with long-term Journey enthusiasts, brought the band no closer to the mainstream success which had eluded them for years.

In many ways the hiring of the diminutive Pineda would either make or break the band. Ticket and albums sales were down on their early Eighties heyday, a fact most put down to Steve Perry's absence. In the event, though, the hiring of a frontman from a foreign country turned out to be a masterstroke, since it gave them more publicity than they had had since Perry reunited with them for the *Trial By Fire* album in the mid-Nineties. In many ways it echoed Judas Priest's hiring of former Priest tribute singer Tim Owens after the departure of Rob Halford.

With Arnel Pineda, Journey released their thirteenth studio album *Revelation*, which became their biggest selling album since *Trial By Fire*. Suddenly, Journey were popular again and their success spread over to the UK where they played sold out tours in 2008 and 2009. Journey's appeal in the UK has never been as high-profile as in the US or Japan, where they can walk on water, and, prior to their short UK tour in 2006, the band hadn't played a concert in England since 1980. Journey fans were so keen to have the band tour the UK again that a petition was launched on www.journey.co.uk to entice promoters to invest in a Journey headlining road jaunt. It certainly helped as the band played the UK (with different singers) in 2007 through to 2009 before taking a year off from the road.

The hiring of Arnel Pineda has begun a new epoch in the band's career and has seen their name rocket to international status for the first time in well over a decade. They have been seen regularly on major American TV shows and are featured in the popular press. Nevertheless, though Robert Flesichman, Steve Augeri, Jeff Scott Soto and Arnel Pineda are excellent singers in their own right, nobody has ever – or indeed will ever – better the vocal perfection of Steve Perry. *Rolling Stone* included him in their '100 Greatest Singers Of All Time' poll for a reason.

At the time of writing, in mid-2010, as the band are working on their fourteenth studio album with producer Kevin Shirley, there is not a single book on Journey despite their having sold over seventy million albums worldwide and having broken the record for the most downloaded song in the history of iTunes with 'Don't Stop Believin''. The only book published on the band was by Robyn Flans back in 1985.

Unfortunately for biographers, most members of Journey, past and present, are believed to have signed confidentiality agreements that prohibit them from giving interviews for 'unofficial' books or any other publication without the consent of their management. In other words, like former employees of celebrities such as David and Victoria Beckham, many musicians who feature in Journey's story have signed contracts with "gagging" clauses. This level of control by Journey's management is exceptional in rock, and seems to contradict the notion of free speech that the United States proudly upholds as the First Amendment of its Constitution. Isn't effectively banning musicians from talking about their own experiences with Journey something more associated with dictators in the Middle East or former communist countries? For God's sake, it's meant to be rock 'n' roll.

However, what this means is that those writers who go down the other route, which is to produce an unofficial book such as this, can offer a complete perspective on the band's history without prejudice. That's one reason why there is not a major biography of the band currently sitting on bookshelves in retail stores.

'Don't Stop Believin" is not only Journey's signature song but also a motto they have lived by, and it has taken them through some hard times. This biography begins in 1973 when the band was hastily assembled in San Francisco, California and takes the reader through the early jazz fusion years, the dramatic change in sound to AOR/melodic rock, the numerous line-up changes, the hiring and firing of the band's first frontman Robert Flesichman and, of course, the enormous success they would achieve with Steve Perry, as well as those years following Perry's first and second departures.

The Untold Story Of Journey follows their career as they formed, matured, flourished, succeeded and failed. Their story is by no means straightforward: there are obvious lulls in their career like the periods between the release of *Frontiers* in 1983 and *Raised On Radio* in 1986 and of course, the massive gap between that album and 1996's *Trial By Fire*; and then there was yet another lull while the band were waiting on Steve Perry to decide if he could (or wanted to) go on tour in support of *Trial By Fire*, their disappointing so-called reunion album. In the end, of course, the band hired another singer so Journey and Perry went their separate ways for the final time. For a band that formed way back in the early 1970s they have been far from prolific. Why is that? Was it down to internal politics?

It is interesting to learn what went in the creation of a back catalogue filled to the brim with beautiful, dulcet songs. The behind-the-scenes arguments and divisions between certain members – always common in rock bands – may startle some readers, as will the ego clashes of some very powerful personalities, and the stories of greed and deceit and the baggage that inevitably comes with superstardom.

The question is: do fans really want to know how the songs that have entertained them for years were actually crafted? Do fans truly want to know the stories behind those songs? It is never easy to learn that one of your idols is perhaps not as endearing as you have been led to believe. Journey's career certainly is not as controversial or as drug-crazed or booze-soaked as the careers of other American rock bands, but neither has it been an easy ride. If you look deep enough there is still some bitterness, heartache and anger there. This is the story of the band that gave the world songs such as 'Wheel In The Sky', 'Ask The Lonely' and 'Lights' and whose career became synonymous with the term 'stadium rock'.

Neil Daniels
November 2010
www.neildaniels.com

CHAPTER 1

The Journey Begins:
The Early Years
(1973–1976)

"I would say it was … fusion rock with vocals. It was different. There was a lot of soloing, but the songs were good. The soloing was the thing that really drove it very, very high but we did write songs but they went through a lot of changes."

Gregg Rolie[3]

On November 5 and 6, 1981, Journey played two of their most celebrated concerts ever at The Summit in Houston, Texas. Filmed for MTV, Journey took the opportunity to cement their status as one of the biggest selling and touring rock bands in the United States. They were on fine form as they promoted their mega-selling *Escape* album in front of 20,000 fans and churned out soon-to-be classics like 'Wheel In The Sky', 'Don't Stop Believin'', 'Who's Crying Now' and 'Any Way You Want It'. They were at the peak of their career, but getting to that point had been no easy ride. In fact, in the beginning there was a different band name, a different line-up and an altogether different sound…

The journey began in the unlikeliest of places and under the moniker Golden Gate Rhythm Section. The hastily assembled line-up featured former Santana guitarist Neal Schon and his bandmate, keyboardist/organist/vocalist Gregg Rolie, with bassist Pete Sears and drummer Gregg Errico. Though Journey are known the world over as an AOR/melodic rock band, famous for immaculately produced rock anthems and power ballads, their roots were, in fact, firmly planted in the Latin American rock of Santana, the San Francisco group named after their charismatic guitarist Carlos.

Thanks in no small way to an acclaimed set at the 1969 Woodstock Festival, *Santana*, their debut album, was a smash hit when it was initially released that same year. Alongside Carlos, it featured the talents of Gregg Rolie who sings lead vocals on the track 'Evil Ways' and plays an electrifying Hammond organ solo in the song's middle section. Born on June 17, 1947 in Seattle, Washington, Rolie formed the Santana Blues Band with guitarist Carlos in 1966 after he quit an unknown early outfit called William Penn & His Pals. Joining Santana and Rolie in the first line-up of the band was vocalist and guitarist Tom Fraser, drummer Rod Harper, percussionist Michael Carabello and bassist David Brown. The band soaked up the hazy sounds of liberal San Francisco, becoming deeply imbedded in the dope-smoking hippie lifestyle of the mid- to late sixties. But getting the band to life was far from easy.

Former Santana road manager Walter James Herbert II, better known as Herbie, explains: "When they signed their deal with Columbia, finally some sort of really low deal with It's A Beautiful Day, Columbia took the two acts almost on one contract and they went into the studio… and finished the album and sent it to Columbia Records and it was rejected. When it was rejected, I guess that's when they decided, 'Well, I guess we really have to change this all around. It's probably the best record that we can make with this kind of line-up and we need to change.'"

A radical realignment was clearly necessary, so Rolie and Santana set about making changes. Herbert: "We had a conga player named Marcus Malone that was very Afro. He wasn't Latin really at all. He was into the mesmerising trans-dance kind of sound and [Harper's replacement drummer] Doc Livingstone really had one beat and this one particular type of drum solo that he played, and it seemed like every song became the same when he played it. They made those changes: they went back to an earlier conga player that had played with the band even before I knew them – Michael Carabello. And Michael Carabello met this young Nicaraguan that didn't even speak any English at all down at Aquatic Park in San Francisco, and his name was Jose Areas [nicknamed Chepito] so Michael brought Chepito into the band. Even way back in the early, early days it was Michael Carabello [who] suggested they call the band Santana after Carlos' last name. I don't believe it was ever because he was the leader *per se* especially back in those days… That was something that evolved over time. They changed the band and got Michael Shrieve – the young nineteen-year-old drummer – Chepito and Carabello, and took the live engineer Brent Dangerfield from the Straight Theatre, and went in and tried to make a record with him, and that is the first Santana album that the world is so familiar with."[4]

"Santana was a phenomenon, a melting pot of ideas and people from different walks of life when nobody else did it," Gregg Rolie explained. "That part I'm extremely proud of. We just played as hard as we could and created a music no one had done before. If you want to talk about crossing borders, we crossed so many of them… It never got in the way. The only thing that ever got in the way was the music. When we disagreed on the music, that's when it changed. As far as developing that style of music – that was done by the original six people."[5]

That Santana was a different kind of rock band to the norm was apparent at Woodstock, where their fusion of a startling array of musical styles, Latin rock, blues, salsa, African beats and rhythms and jazz – grabbed everyone's attention. Nevertheless, Gregg Rolie remained unmoved by the attention: "When people tried to explain what Santana music is… it's not Latin rock. I hate that term. It's really focused around guitar, organ and percussion. To explain it simply, the organ is huge in it. It carries a lot of the rhythms."[6]

The West Coast city of San Francisco was a cultural hotbed from the mid-sixties to the end of the decade, the focus of an alternative society that coalesced around mind-expanding drugs, a sexually liberated lifestyle and free concerts by groups whose music resolutely rejected the limitations of the pop charts. Its heart was where Haight Street intersected with Ashbury, a neighbourhood where the Grateful Dead, Jefferson Airplane and Janis Joplin settled and which in 1967 – the Summer of Love – attracted thousands of wayward college drop-outs, the first wave of hippies.

"I went up to San Francisco [and] purely because of the music I moved into the city," said Rolie. "This was the summer of love, and we were really into the music, and wanted to be an international band. It was our driving force. It was a great place to get that across. San Francisco at that time, you could draw an equivalency to what Seattle became in the nineties. It was the same kind of ideal, when the music scene totally changed. It was a very experimental type of music that was based upon blues that all of a sudden was miraculously found by everyone from FM radio."[7]

Santana's second album, *Abraxas*, featuring a notable cover of Fleetwood Mac's 'Black Magic Woman', sold over four million copies and hit number one in the *Billboard* Top 200 album charts, as did their third, *Santana III*, on which new guitarist Neal Schon joined Santana in a twin-lead attack. However, tension was mounting within the ranks, especially after Chepito Areas had an almost fatal brain hemorrhage. Schon gave the band a powerful, rock-driven stamp but this was increasingly at odds with Carlos's vision for a more spiritual, ethereal sound in keeping with his deepening interest in meditation and the teachings of Indian philosopher Sri Chinmoy.

Neal Schon was born on February 27, 1954 on Tinker Air Force Base in Oklahoma. His father was a jazz saxophonist who encouraged his son to learn the guitar from an early age, and both parents even backed their son when he made the life-altering decision to pursue his musical ambitions and drop out of high school (Aragon High in San Mateo, California) before graduating.

"I picked up my first guitar when I was ten years old and practised all the time," he said. "When other kids were playing sports, I was playing guitar – it was an obsession. I dedicated all of my time to learning and was addicted to guitars. By the time I was twelve I was getting around the guitar pretty well. I never got into sports at all until I was in my early twenties and after my music career got going."[8]

Predictably, Schon's earliest musical influences were the American blues pioneers Robert Johnson, Muddy Waters. John Lee Hooker, B.B. King and Albert King, but perhaps more importantly he learned his technique from the British electric blues players of the sixties, Jeff Beck, Eric Clapton, Jimmy Page and Peter Green. The earth-shattering white electric English blues of that era really grabbed his attention, and he devoured albums by the Yardbirds, Fleetwood Mac, Cream and, later, Led Zeppelin. Jeff Beck's *Truth*, with Rod Stewart on vocals, was regularly played on his turntable at home. Those British artists still inspire Schon to this day.

Eric Clapton made a surprise appearance in Schon's life on the eve of his joining Santana. "Clapton was a fan of Carlos and the band, and while I was jamming with them at the Wally Heider Studio in Berkeley, Eric dropped by," he recalled. "This was before I joined Santana. That night we met again and jammed some more. Eric said 'Goodnight' to everyone and the next morning I had this note from him saying he wanted me to sit in with him. Later that day he asked me to join his band, Derek & The Dominos. That was the day before Carlos asked me to join him… I went with Carlos."[9]

Schon came to the attention of Santana after Gregg Rolie and drummer Michael Shrieve saw him play at a local club called the Poppycock in Palo Alto about 35 miles south of San Francisco - and even got up on stage to jam with the teenage guitarist. Up to that point Schon had performed only with local bands after his family had relocated and settled in the Bay Area. Schon's adopted home had an enormous influence on the young guitarist and his playing. He said: "San Francisco had a lot of influence on me… when I was younger. When I was about 15 playing in the clubs, the scene was hot. If I got out early enough I could see three different acts. There was a lot of jazz clubs and I would sit in with Gabor Szabo and then take off and play Latin music with some others guys."[10]

What Rolie and Shrieve witnessed that night at the Poppycock club impressed them enough to ask the young guitarist to join Santana. He wouldn't make a great deal of money in the band but it was certainly more than delivering newspapers for a local store or working Saturday jobs at movie theatres. Plus Schon – only 16 years old at the time of joining the band – was getting an incredible amount of experience and first-hand knowledge of what it is like being in a successful band.

Schon explained: "It was a pretty amazing experience, very much an eye opener for me. We were travelling all over the world, playing in Africa, South America, all over Europe, experiencing the different audiences all over the world. The band was one of the biggest in the world at that time. I loved playing with Carlos and the rest of the guys. Musically, they opened me up to many different types of music that I was unaware of at that point – Latin music, Cuban rhythms, African rhythms – the band was a melting pot of all different kinds of music. The most I got out of playing with Carlos was how melodic he was. He rubbed off on me definitely, and I think vice versa too, when we were playing together. I became much more of a melodic guitar player."[11]

After yet more changes to the line-up – largely different approaches in musical styles which resulted in divisions between some members – *Santana III* was recorded between January and July of 1971 at Columbia Studios in San Francisco, marking the recording debut of the teenage guitar prodigy and the first sessions that teamed Neal Schon with Gregg Rolie. The album's sound was given more meat by the addition of the horn section from the Bay Area group Tower Of Power, as well as a number of extra percussionists and background vocalists. *Santana III* was a big success with two hit singles, 'Everybody's Everything' and 'No One To Depend On', both of which featured solo spots by Schon. In many ways, that album was the end of an era for Santana, although it sold a healthy two million copies and like its predecessor peaked at number one on the *Billboard* charts.

In January 1972 Neal Schon joined Carlos Santana, Santana percussionist Thomas 'Coke' Escovedo and former Band Of Gypsy's drummer Buddy Miles for a concert at the Diamond Head Crater in Honolulu, Hawaii. The concert resulted in the live album *Carlos Santana-Buddy Miles Live* though it was far from a stellar performance. Indeed, despite the towering success of Santana's first three albums, behind the scenes there was an abundance of drug use, bitterness and arguments, especially between Carlos and Michael Carabello, and the latter left before the recording of their fourth album *Caravanserai* between February and May of 1972.

Neal Schon explained: "It was kind of just falling apart at that point. There was a lot of tension in the band. Gregg and I were the only members left besides Michael [Shrieve]. Carlos was wanting to play a certain kind of music and we wanted to play rock and continue with what we had. And we weren't into Carlos' new direction. It was pretty much that nobody could agree on what they wanted to play."[12]

Along with Carlos, Shrieve, Rolie and Schon, *Caravanserai* featured some external musicians: bassists Tom Rutley and Doug Rauch replaced David Brown, and Michael Carabello was replaced by percussionists Armando Peraza and James Mingo Lewis. To make matters worse, Gregg Rolie even had support on the keyboards from Wendy Hass and Tom Coster. The growing tensions between Rolie and Carlos over the band's musical direction resulted in Rolie being replaced on select tracks. Despite some notable changes to the line-up in the past, Santana was shifting towards jazz fusion, and prior to the completion of the record, both Schon and Rolie decided to quit the band. Indeed, Rolie moved back to Seattle to open up a restaurant with his father, which proved unsuccessful.

Herbie Herbert: "It was in early '72 when I was touring with Steve Miller in Europe and the band [Santana] was making their fourth album and were having lots of problems. [They] were not really talking to each other in a civil way, and going into the studio independently, hardly ever any two members at the same time… and I thought that there was likelihood that the band might be imploding. It was devastating to consider what my vibe was, and we had been to Europe several times and Steve Miller was a really close friend and wanted me to take him to Europe in January and February of '72 for his first European tour.

"During that tour, John [Villanueva] and Jack [Villanueva] – my other partners in crime, the other two roadies for Santana – called me and said: 'Hey, the band has decided to break up. They told us. We did nothing. They can't afford to pay us what they owe us. We pick up our last cheque on Friday and you better come home and fix this'… so [I] flew home. We had a few days left to go on the Steve Miller tour. [We] tried to negotiate a settlement, which we did, and part of that settlement was we use the sound and production for Santana should they ever reform or tour again..."[13]

Caravanserai was the final Santana album to feature Gregg Rolie and Neal Schon. It was a critical success and made it in to the top ten in the *Billboard* album charts but the drastic change in sound probably damaged sales. Certainly Columbia Records head Clive Davis feared that if the band continued to pursue their new musical direction they would lose their commercial appeal and prominent status in the US and abroad. The album featured many lengthy jazz influenced instrumentals and the complex nature of the music probably distanced even the most enthusiastic and broad-minded Santana fan.

Around November and December of each year Santana had traditionally flown to Hawaii to play shows at the HIC – now called the Blaisdell Arena – as well as a New Year's Eve gig at the Otani Mansion on Diamond Head, and then they would perform inside the Diamond Head Crater for free on New Year's Day. Importantly, it was this tradition – and the lead up to those proposed shows in 1972 after the departures of Schon and Rolie – that would have an impact on the creation of the Golden Gate Rhythm Section and thus create the foundation for the band Journey.

Herbie Herbert describes the haphazard beginnings of the Golden Gate Rhythm Section in detail: "Let's say summer of '72: Carlos approaches me and wants me to manage him once he's got a whole new band together. We have a conversation, I say, 'Well, I love Gregg Rolie and Neal Schon.' And he said: 'Well, they're really part of my past.' And so we went on what we called the *Caravanserai* tour on September 1, 1972...

"The band was coming off their first three albums and doing sell-out arena business [like] two nights at the Forum in LA. All of a sudden on this tour it became two nights at the Long Beach Arena with maybe 5,000 people a night. Faster than Rolls could tell Royce something, the whole world knew that this version of Santana was basically instrumentals only, progressive, kind of fusion-jazz. Nobody was playing or singing any of the old hits, 'Evil Ways,' 'Black Magic Woman,' 'Jingo,' none of that stuff, 'Oye Como Va', and the ticket business was very soft everywhere. We get to Hawaii and we play two nights at the Blaisdell Arena, a small crowd [of] 3,000 a night and the place holds 8-9,000. Carlos meets with me the following morning and gets all up in my face about the reason he's doing such bad business at the Blaisdell Arena is because everybody knows that Santana is gonna play the free show in the Crater, which is my pet project, and so he was telling me how that was fucking him up and why should people pay to see the band if they're gonna get to see him play for free. My response was: 'Carlos you did bad business coast to coast, border to border in America because there's no Gregg Rolie and no Neal Schon, and nobody's singing the hit songs. You're doing what you wanna do; you're not doing what the audience wants.'

"We had a fight and we decided to part ways, at which point I talked him into staying until the day after Christmas so we could have our Christmas dinner with the whole band and their families and Chepito had his family from Nicaragua there. I said: 'I'll take you to the airport on the day after Christmas on the 26th' which is what I did. I called [promoter] Bill Graham and said: 'Bill, You're going to have to become Carlos' manager. He and I are parting ways. Here's his flight, pick him up at the airport, take care of him; you're the only guy that would even want to bring this guy back. I have no desire.' He thought I was nuts. He said: 'What are you gonna do?' I said: 'As soon as I hang up this phone I'm gonna find Gregg Rolie and Neal Schon and put something together.' He said: 'Well, that could take a long time.' I said: 'I've gotta do it today because I've gotta have someone to play the Crater to replace Santana.' And so I called Gregg Rolie, Neal Schon, Gregg Errico from Sly & The Family Stone, Pete Sears, a British guy that had played in Cooperheard, [who] was a great bass player and keyboardist, so I brought all these guys together and flew 'em to Hawaii and called it the Golden Gate Rhythm Section."[14]

Settled back home in Seattle, Gregg Rolie had been off the road since late 1971. Herbert was more than confident with the keyboardist/organist's talent; his vocals were known to millions on such Santana hits as 'Black Magic Woman' and 'Evil Ways' so to reunite him with Neal Schon was a no-brainer.

9

Herbie Herbert: "Their first and only show was at the Diamond Head Crater which was probably in terms of audience the most successful of all the Crater[s]. I stood there on the stage and watched them perform with Gregg and Neal and no percussion; it was kind of a rock 'n' roll version of Santana when they do a song like 'Black Magic Woman'. I said, 'Hey, this is very cool. Let's put together a rock band' and that's what I proceeded to do immediately... But we didn't have a name yet; we weren't called Journey. It was still the Golden Gate Rhythm Section."[15]

Though they ended up playing only the one show in Hawaii, the Golden Gate Rhythm Section was also conceived as a sort of backing band for artists in the Bay Area. However, the initial line-up of the band with Pete Sears and Gregg Errico was short-lived, as Herbert explains, "We decided no, let's go get Prairie Prince from The Tubes to play drums and Ross Valory, fresh out of the Steve Miller Band, to play bass, and George Tickner was a person I knew that wrote a lot of instrumental material that would be perfect for Neal, so I introduced Neal to all those things."[16]

In March 1973, Herbert created Nightmare Incorporated to service the needs of Journey. It became his music industry empire. "We called it Nightmare because the business tends to be that way, it's not the way we want it to be," he says.[17]

Bassist Ross Valory was born on February 2, 1947 in San Francisco and was a childhood friend of Herbie Herbert. Prior to joining the band that would become Journey, Valory had been schooled in the blues in the same way as Neal Schon and it showed during his tenure in the Steve Miller Band. From 1967 to 1969, Valory played in the Sixties psychedelic rock band Frumious Bandersnatch – a cult outfit in the Bay Area that had supported the Santana Blues Band on a number of occasions. He was joined by guitarist David Denny, drummer Jack King and bassist Bobby Winkelman, all of whom would become members of the Steve Miller Band. In fact it was Jim Nixon, the manager of Frumious Bandersnatch, who would introduce the band's road manager Herbie Herbert to Bill Graham, the famous concert promoter who would have important relationships with both Santana and, later, Journey. Valory's bandmate in Frumious Bandersnatch was the New York-born rhythm guitarist and songwriter George Tickner (born September 8, 1946). Finally, Prairie Prince (born May 7, 1950) relocated to San Francisco from Arizona with some fellow musicians in 1969 and it was there that the two Arizona outfits, The Beans and The Red, White And Blues Band, merged to create The Tubes, a band that caught the attention of Herbie Herbert.

With a line-up that consisted of guitarist Neal Schon, keyboard player and vocalist Gregg Rolie, bassist Ross Valory, rhythm guitarist George Tickner and drummer Prairie Prince, the Golden Gate Rhythm Section opted for a name change almost as soon as they began to work on fresh material. The strongest songwriter of the group at the time, George Tickner, set about writing lyrics and the band recorded some (still unreleased) demos that were influenced by the raw energy of British bands like Led Zeppelin, Deep Purple and the Who. Those recordings were submitted to a radio station in San Francisco named KSAN-FM.

Herbie Herbert: "[Roadie] John Villaneuva was sitting in San Rafeal smoking a joint...We had put a contest out on [the] radio to find a name but the names that were coming back from the fans – hundreds and hundreds of them – were [not] really very good or appropriate. John, one day on the couch, said: 'I think we should call the band Journey.' I said: 'You're right! You've got it!' We claimed that it was a contest winner from the radio station, Toby Pratt, just so the radio station would save face and it wouldn't look like management decided to name the band and blow off the contest. But it was actually John Villaneuva who named the band Journey."

With a new name and some fresh recordings, Journey was born. However, it would take a considerable amount of time and effort for them to find their niche sound. Gregg Rolie: "It was an assumed band, as a matter of fact. I have to say the band really belonged to Neal and Herbie because they started it. They called who they wanted to call and put that together and it turned into a band pretty quickly... I could say I am a founding member of that group, easily. But it really was their brainstorming that started it. It became a band and we started working and then we worked harder, as opposed to Santana. For me, Santana was a phenomenon. We worked hard at it for a few years, when it exploded after Woodstock. Journey was more of an effort. It was three or four years of real hard work."

Journey made their live debut at the Winterland Ballroom in San Francisco on New Year's Eve, 1973, in front of 10,000. The following day they flew to Hawaii to play at the Diamond Head Crater to an even larger crowd. It was obvious that the often complex Santana-type jazz fusion sound with doses of progressive rock had a massive impact on the early sound of Journey.

Herbie Herbert already had in mind the type of band he wanted Journey to be, as he explains: "The idea with Journey was we wanted to be able to play with Santana, play with Weather Report, play with Mahavishnu Orchestra, play with Return To Forever; but then on the very next night [after] you play with Return To Forever... you play with Ted Nugent or Aerosmith... and that absolutely worked. CBS Records in Europe put out a couple [of compilations] albums way back then, progressive pop and progressive rock, and one of the albums was a compilation with Mahavishnu Orchestra, Weather Report and so forth and Journey; and the other was a rock record with Ted Nugent and Aerosmith and Blue Öyster Cult and Journey and all the various CBS rock genre artists and all the various CBS jazz artists. We worked well in both mediums and both genres and would have loved to have made it as that progressive band that made the first three albums but we didn't. That was a very, very tough time."[18]

There was no question about it: Journey was an incredible live band from the get-go. How could they not be? Coming from similar backgrounds – albeit with different tastes in music – each member brought not only their talent, but their individual idiosyncrasies to the band's sound, which was manifested in the early live performances. "There was no Latin percussion, or a Latin feel to it. It was a fusion rock band, with a lot of soloing. It was based on the energy of that at the time. That's why the band always did well when we played live. People were blown away by it," said Rolie.[19]

However, the initial line-up did not last long. Drummer Prairie Prince returned to The Tubes at the start of 1974. "I never made it to their first album, but we wrote all the songs on the demo that got them their first record deal. So I'm on the demo for the first album," Prince said.[20]

Enter Liverpool-born drummer Aynsley Dunbar (born January 10, 1946) who beat 30 fellow hopefuls in getting the job on Journey's drum stool. Dunbar had made a name for himself in the UK playing drums for Jeff Beck, John Mayall's Bluesbreakers and even David Bowie on his seventh album, *Pin-Ups*, in 1973. But what grabbed Herbie Herbert's attention was Dunbar's work with Frank Zappa and The Mothers Of Invention. Dunbar explained: "Well, I had done some sessions with Neal Schon, and he called me up – or his manager – our manager had called me up… And I never knew who the hell he was till one day I got back, and it said Neal Schon wanted to talk to me. So when I saw Neal, I did a couple of sessions with him."[21]

Dunbar became an official member of Journey on February 1, 1974, and though unfamiliar with the work of the individual members of the band was impressed with their chemistry and obvious talent. He was also looking for a more stable job after a career of jumping from one band to another. He said: "That's what I was looking for all the time. But you have to live, and therefore you have to jump around. I didn't want to become a sideman and just get lost in somebody else's situation, so you have to keep jumping around, until the situation's right. Fate. I always believed in fate."[22]

On February 5, Journey performed with Dunbar for the first time at the Great American Music Hall in front of executives from Columbia Records. On the strength of that performance and the band's growing reputation as a sort of Santana-type outfit, Journey were signed to Columbia. They started to build up a name for themselves on the Bay Area live circuit, playing the Oakland Coliseum and the Cow Palace, even venturing back to the Winterland Ballroom where they played support to Robin Trower and Dave Mason.

With producer Roy Halee – known for his collaborations with Simon & Garfunkel – the band entered Studio A at CBS Studios in San Francisco in November to record what would become their self-titled debut album. With the exception of Aynsley Dunbar, the rest of the band had a hand in writing the seven tracks. Even Ross Valory's poet wife,

Diane, shared writing credits on the lengthy 'Mystery Mountain' with Rolie and Tickner.

Released in April 1975, the record hardly set the charts on fire, creeping up to a rather unhealthy number 138 on the *Billboard* albums list though it managed to get to 72 in Japan. Many critics noticed the similarities with *Santana III* and there are influences from Pink Floyd and Frank Zappa, but some have argued that the album was too left field for the mainstream rock audiences yet not inventive enough for the progressive audience. Journey somehow lingered between the two musical camps. Strangely, the album depicted the band dressed in space suits alighting on an alien planet.

Comparisons with Santana soon began to grate as Gregg Rolie said: "Talking about Santana screws up the whole concept of everyone in this band. A lot of people would come to see us and expect conga drums. The last thing I want to see for the rest of my life is conga drums!"[23]

Journey opens with the seven-minute epic 'Of A Lifetime' which features vocals from Gregg Rolie. It is a curious track with hints of jazz fusion, and some of the passages certainly lean towards early Pink Floyd. 'In The Morning' has a stronger vocal presence from Rolie and it holds the album's most distinctive guitar spot; about two minutes into the track a heavy guitar strums into action alongside some pounding drums while the organ is on fire as the band blitz through this passage. The six-and-a-half minute instrumental 'Kohoutek' has since become something of a cult classic amongst Journey enthusiasts. It is a terrific slice of progressive rock with some "spacey" passages, and immediately demonstrated to critics and fans the power of their talents and the obvious chemistry between them. 'To Play Some Music' sees more vocals from Rolie, while the melody is probably the most accessible on the album. There are some vocal effects which add a science-fiction type theme to the song and the organ work adds considerable depth to the track. The album's second and final instrumental, 'Topaz', has hints of Santana's 'Song Of The Wind' about it with some exuberant guitar playing and a dreamy ambience. The five-minute 'In My Lonely Feeling/Conversations' has a powerful one-minute climax where the pace picks up considerably and Schon displays some intricate guitar playing backed up by Tickner's rhythm guitar; it's undoubtedly the main attraction of the song. 'Mystery Mountain', the album's closer, has since become a fan favourite. There is some very complex guitar playing and, predictably, some heavy instrumental spots.

Journey is by no means a perfect album by any stretch of the imagination but each instrumentalist plays his part amid plenty of left-field influences. Though it's mostly an instrumental album, Gregg Rolie does more than a half-decent job on vocals. It is obvious, however, that the vocals – just as they were in Santana – are secondary to the actual musicianship. However, much of the album is self-indulgent and it appears as though the band were jamming just for the sake of jamming. It was merely a taste of things to come...

Following its release, Journey continued to tour heavily to promote their album and to build up a strong fan base. However, the touring became too much for rhythm guitarist and songwriter George Tickner who quit before the release of their second album. Although credited as a co-writer on the tracks 'You're On Your Own' and 'I'm Gonna Leave You', Tickner decided to enroll at Stanford Medical Centre which left the band without a rhythm guitarist. When Schon opted to take on all guitar duties by himself it actually gave the band a tighter, more concise sound.

Journey entered CBS Studios in San Francisco in late '75 and came out with *Look Into The Future.* To promote it they performed a two-hour show at the Paramount Theatre in Seattle, a one-off performance that was aired on FM radio several days later. The album was released in the US in January 1976 and peaked at number 100 in the *Billboard* top 200 album charts, although over in Japan it managed a healthier 58.

Whereas *Journey* seemed like a band that had been jamming in the studio, *Look Into The Future* was more controlled and taut. The less experimental sound probably helped the band climb higher in the album charts than they had with their initial album.

Produced by the band themselves, *Look Into The Future* opens with 'On A Saturday Night'[24], a surprisingly upbeat, poppy song with a bouncing melody helped along by Rolie's piano. Curiously, the next track is a cover of George Harrison's Beatles tune 'It's All Too Much' from their animated film *Yellow Submarine*. Journey's version certainly has some progressive elements to it though it's much less psychedelic than The Beatles' original cut, with Schon's guitar solo undoubtedly the centrepiece. 'Anyway' is a slow, almost sombre bluesy effort in sharp contrast to the previous songs. 'She Makes Me (Feel Alright)' – co-written with the San Francisco singer-songwriter Alex Cash – is probably the album's standout rock track; Schon's guitar playing is surprisingly gritty and Rolie's vocals are more aggressive and dominant than on other songs. 'You're On Your Own' opens with some downbeat keys before the rest of the band join in, and has a more earthly feel than its siblings, with progressive guitar and nifty organ work. 'Look Into The Future' – co-written with Ross' other half, Diane Valory – is an eight-minute track which some critics dubbed Journey's 'Stairway To Heaven' for its length, shifts in tempo, complex melody structure, intricate guitar work and memorable harmonies. Sure, Led Zeppelin had been an enormous influence on Neal Schon and it shows in this single track, but it's by no means easy on the ears and takes several pushes of the repeat button to fully appreciate its ingenious nature. 'Midnight Dreamer' is similar in style and temperament to 'She Makes Me (Feel Alright)'; it's a hard and fast rock song with some angry vocals, no-nonsense guitar work and notable drums. The final track, 'I'm Gonna Leave You', is led by some memorable organ work which was perhaps inspired by early Deep Purple.

Look Into The Future is a sharper, tighter and more enjoyable album than its predecessor. Schon's guitar work is exemplary and Rolie's organ is a joy to hear. It is obvious that the band were heading for a more commercial rock sound, although blues, jazz and prog rock still find their way into the melting pot. While an album like *Journey* was never going to get much airplay, *Look Into The Future* quite literally saw the band look into their own future.

After its release Journey headed off on another road jaunt, beginning on February 23, 1976 and closing on December 31 at the Winterland in San Francisco. During the tour they were already making plans for a third album, as Gregg Rolie indicated not long afterwards: "We were never discouraged because every time we've gone out on the road, there's been growth. We've learned more about each other, the music and the industry. Journey is a democratic situation that will last because everyone is a little older now and more aware and that's the only way a band can work. Everyone has their own musical taste and their own ideas but we've learned how to use them to improve the group."[25]

The music scene had changed dramatically during Journey's short life span, especially in the period up to the recording of their third album. Heavyweights like The Rolling Stones, Led Zeppelin and The Who – though still extremely popular – no longer appealed to many in the next generation of rock fans; nor did glam rockers like Queen, Bowie or Roxy Music. Punk, a new style of rock and a movement that that also encompassed culture and politics, was gaining ground in both the United States and Britain.

Most of the punk rock bands were based in London and New York with The Clash and Sex Pistols most prominent in the UK and The Ramones and Television flying the flag in the US. The punk attitude – anti-establishment and anti-authoritarian – was no different from rock's traditional stance, but in their style of dress and the music they performed, the punk bands were the complete antithesis of bands like Journey and contemporaries like Foreigner, and certainly less musically accomplished. Nevertheless, punk's aggression made it less palatable to radio which vindicated Journey's decision to forge a more accessible, definable and commercial sound on their third album.

They went into His Master's Wheels Studios in San Francisco in May 1976 and came out in October with *Next*. As with *Look Into The Future*, Journey chose to produce it themselves. The release of the album the following year would bring some massive changes to the band's sound – and line-up.

CHAPTER 2

Journey's Evolution: A New Musical Direction (1977–1980)

"I still think some of the stuff we did then was great. Some of it was self-indulgent, just jamming for ourselves, but I also think a lot of other things hurt us in the early days. It took awhile for the politics to sort of shape up."
Neal Schon[26]

Journey began the New Year with a gig at the Sports Arena in San Diego with Lynyrd Skynrd and the Alpha Band. They would continue to tour heavily throughout the year. The third album *Next* was released in February and charted higher in the *Billboard* top 200 than its two predecessors, making it to number 85, and it even charted in Sweden. This was still short of expectations at Columbia, and critical response was unfavourable. In actual fact, although *Next* charted higher than both *Journey* and *Look Into The Future*, their record sales were on the slide and, indeed, had hardly been promising to begin with. The main reason why Columbia didn't drop Journey from their roster was probably because they were a hard-working touring band and were gradually building up a loyal following.

"We toured probably nine, ten months a year, and the other two months we were in the studio making more new music," explained Neal Schon. "We did that for about five years, that grueling schedule. And we ended up making two more records – *Look Into The Future* and then *Next* – and each sold progressively less than the last. But we attained a huger live audience, because new were playing so much."[27]

Their third album was certainly more commercial than *Journey* and *Look Into The Future*, but it retained the jazz fusion and progressive flavourings that were the hallmarks of Journey's roots. Members of the band had even taken singing lessons in an effort to get a more commercial sound that might appeal to FM radio. "Anyone who performs in the recording industry and on most stages is already in the realm of commercial music," said Ross Valory. "So there's no difference except in terms of the number of people your audience is comprised of. How far and to what extent does your music reach the people?"[28]

Next opens with 'Spaceman', a curious song with a touch of the haziness that characterized Pink Floyd, and its rather strange melody no doubt led to it being chosen as the album's only single. 'People', a blues rock stomper with sprinklings of piano and acoustic strumming, seems more suited to Schon than Rolie, and while 'I Would Find You' sees Schon on lead vocals, the instrumentation is the song's primary focus. 'Here We Are', a Rolie-penned track, opens with a dream-like effect before the rest of the band slowly come into play. It's a fairly downbeat song that slows the album down. 'Hustler' opens with a fantastically gritty riff before Rolie's vocals commence. Similar to 'People', 'Hustler' is a Deep Purple-style blues rocker with some terrific organ work. The title-track is speedy rocker that slows down and speeds up, with Dunbar excelling on the drums. The instrumental 'Nickel And Dime', four minutes of ambitious progressive rock, has become a cult favourite among hardcore Journey fans. Finally, 'Karma' is another song where Schon takes over as lead vocalist and does a decent job although, predictably, the song features more instrumentation than singing.

Next has some standout moments but it was obvious the band were in two minds about whether they should head down the Santana route and become more of a instrumental, progressive rock style band or concentrate more on melody and vocals. Hovering between the two camps tainted all three of their albums thus far, which may explain why their record sales were disappointing. Yet their ticket sales remained consistent because the music worked remarkably well on the live stage.

By early 1977 it was getting to a point where it was make or break time for Journey. "I loved that original band and many people did," says Herbie Herbert. "I think the first album in real time sold like 150,000 and the second album sold 250,000 and then the third album did 100,000 or maybe 150,000."[29] Nevertheless, executives at Columbia were losing faith, and growing tired of trying to sell Journey's music to a public uninterested in jazz fusion or progressive rock. With punk creating headlines and critical acclaim, Journey did not seem to fit in anywhere.

Ross Valory: "We toured relentlessly using road cash to keep us going and developed enough of a following that they could count on record sales of about 200,000... We decided to play less and sing more so we wouldn't have to slave for the rest of our lives."[30]

But it wasn't enough. Something else needed to be done to get those record sales up to keep the big-wigs at Columbia happy. Herbie Herbert: "I don't even think that the musicians themselves are even aware of where they were in 1977, but they were basically finished. They were over with. The labels throughout the business, and America, were dropping artists right, left and centre. The music business had changed radically by the end of '77. The disco movement had taken root, and *Saturday Night Fever* was a huge hit... The whole top five was *Grease*, *Saturday Night Fever*, Donna Summer, *Disco Inferno*, that kind of thing. They were standing in the station and they couldn't even see the tail lights on the train that they had missed... already artists had been successful on Journey's back - like Kansas... and Rush... but we were standing in the stations with our dicks in our hands and the train had left."[31]

To tackle Journey's decline in status, poor record sales and a fairly low-key name, manager Herbert had an idea that could change the band's future: "Boston, Foreigner, Styx, REO Speedwagon and Survivor and everybody you could think of had already had their hits and their platinum records. I bet Styx had four platinum records out already. By disco time you're finished. So I went to the label [Columbia] and begged that they not drop the act and they said, 'No, we're gonna drop the act.' I said, 'Well, I'll change to a pop formula and we'll get a lead singer.' And they said, 'No, we don't wanna go forward.' Well, I knew that the head of artists' development at Columbia in New York had a lead singer that was managed by the Denver promoter Barry Fey that he was high on so I tried that angle and said, 'How about we put that singer you're talking about, Robert Flesichman, in Journey?' So he went for it and gave us a stay of execution, a reprieve…"[32]

Some reports have suggested that it was executives at Columbia Records who proposed the band hire a frontman to compete, as it were, with melodic rock heavyweights such as Styx, Kansas and REO Speedwagon, and that if the band failed to sell sufficient units of their fourth album, they'd be dropped for sure. Either way, the band hired a frontman and moved forward in a vastly different musical direction from their first three albums.

Robert Flesichman: "I was going to move out of an apartment and I had my car all loaded up with my stuff and I had forgotten to give the key to the landlady, so I went and knocked on the landlady's door. I heard my phone ringing upstairs so I went up to my empty apartment and I answered the phone. It was a management booking company out of Chicago – they had about four bands and they wanted me to check out these bands and come out and pick a band to play with. I went to Chicago and I played with the band for quite some time and then I got a phone call from a gentleman named Barry Fey, a big promoter in the United States, who asked me if I'd be interested in coming up to Colorado and have a meeting with him to form a band. I left the band in Chicago and I went to Denver, and I did a showcase for Columbia Records. I was there for about a week and I wrote a bunch of songs. I found some players and I did this audition. I just put this band quickly together and everybody came out from Columbia, the East Coast and West Coast, and then a couple of weeks later I got a phone call from Columbia on the West Coast, and they wanted to know if I'd be interested in playing with a band called Journey. I had a meeting with the head of A&R in Los Angeles... They basically told me that they were thinking about getting rid of Journey. At that time Boston and Foreigner and bands with lead singers and that kind of formula were kind of merging, and so that's want they wanted to do. They wanted a frontman in front of the band... I was picked up by Herbie Herbert and his assistant John [Villaneuva] and [we went] to a place called SIR, which is a rehearsal studio, and I met everyone and started playing. It just kind of took off, it was just a great chemistry and we really got along. It was really powerful. I hadn't ever played with a band that was just so tight."[33]

Journey's continued existence could be attributed to Herbie Herbert's foresight. Through his connections and associations in the record industry, his contacts in the radio media and concert market, Herbert had managed to give the band a new lease of life.

The idea was that Fleischman would not only front the band but would share lead vocals with Gregg Rolie. How did Rolie, an original member, react to the new singer? "Gregg was terrific," says Fleischman. "He let me live with him at his house. He was just a really generous person. We spent many times together at his house. He had this really beautiful [Rolls Royce] from 1958 and we were driving into San Francisco – the hills up in San Francisco, they're outrageous – so he stops the car on its angle on this hill and says, 'I have to go in this bank. Drive around the block and I'll be out when you get around.' I had never driven a car like that. The sixth shift was up on the steering column and so I'm driving this unbelievable Rolls Royce up this hill and I have to stop because there's a stop light and I've got cars behind me, and if I roll back I'm going to smash the cars. I'm just so unbelievably nervous, scared to death. Finally I make it to the bank and he's not there so I had to do that like three times. I'm like, 'Just get in this car... Just take over!' He liked me enough to give me his Roll Royce!"[34]

Was the new singer made to feel welcome by the rest of the band?

Fleischman: "Yes, they were very nice to me except when we were on the road, they let me know that I was getting it easy because they had worked so hard to get to where they were at before I joined in the band, so we are staying in nice hotels and all that. It was so great to be in a band that was so well organised. Gregg Rolie was the most generous to me [but] management – that was another story."[35]

Journey had the *Next* album to promote so live dates were arranged with their new singer which they'd hoped would give their songs a more harmonic sound on stage. With Fleischman, the band went on tour at the time of the album's release in February 1977 supporting Black Sabbath and, opening the show, a band called Target, which featured singer Jimi Jamison before he joined Survivor. Jamison remembers Neal Schon from those shows: "He was a very humble guy who played his butt off. Target had two guitars players who each played 1958 Les Pauls through Marshall amps. I remember Neal asking them how they got such a huge sound when he had six amps wired together trying to get it. My guys told him that he was such a great player that he could play through a pignose amp and sound great."[36]

Robert Fleischman remembers one circuit of the tour: "We started our road trip opening up for Judas Priest down in Texas so we did the full Texas circuit and then we went out to the Mid-West; and then later at the end of the tour we got hooked up with Emerson, Lake & Palmer when they were doing the tour with the [70-piece] orchestra at that time. Then they kind of dropped the orchestra because it was just getting too expensive and too hard to book hotel rooms with all the different orchestra people. They decided to go back as a four-piece so we did shows with them in Canada and then in I think we did some shows in Seattle."[37]

What was the reception like from the fans at live shows?

Robert Fleischman: "The band would do about three or four songs then they would introduce me. The front row [was] always diehard Journey fans and they would flip me off and say fuck you. It was hard for them to see a front man in the band so every time I got up on stage that's what I was up against and at the end of the show we won them up over, thank God."[38]

Indeed, during the nine-month tour, Robert Fleischman seemed to fit in with the other members of the band, and almost immediately started to make his mark by coming up with some new music. "Then eventually I started writing songs and... it was just kind of odd because I'd just came there – I'm more of a pop-rock singer-songwriter – I'd basically just rearranged their furniture. It was like now Aynsley had to play four/four instead of all these wild off tempos and stuff. Then it became, 'Oh, we're gonna be playing song structure'. I don't think it was really easy for them. It took a lot of doing for them to get to that point and start thinking in that way. Then we rehearsed for quite some time and wrote and did some recordings and did some demos of 'Wheel In The Sky', 'Anytime', 'Diva', 'Winds Of March' another one called 'All For You' we did in the studio... Basically just put it together there in the studio and then we were talking about producers and I suggested Roy Thomas Baker and they didn't even know who Roy Thomas Baker was. CBS set up a meeting and Roy came to San Francisco and we all met and we talked and then we went on the road [for some more shows]."[39]

Fleischman adds some more background detail to the writings of those songs: "Neal and the band had the music already [for 'Wheel In The Sky']. I came up with the melody and one day [I was] given a poem that was written by Ross Valory's wife so to make everyone happy I plucked the line 'wheel in the sky' and then I wrote the rest. 'Anytime' is a funny song. Gregg and I wrote it at his house on the piano. I thought for some time that we wrote the song together but he had written some of the music with a couple of other people; it looks like an army wrote a song! We recorded that song, also. 'Winds Of March'. It was Neal's music that he wrote with his father and I wrote the lyrics for it except for one half of a verse that Perry wrote who was given credit."[40]

"No, there were no demands," says Fleischman in response to a question about whether they had any specific ideas on the conception of the music, "plus they never played with a lead singer and songwriter before, so I think it was a big education for the both of us. At that time they were the rock fusion band and I was a pop songwriter but it worked... Neal and I have always got along... we wrote some great songs together, so I think that has a lot to say about our relationship. It's a magical one…"[41]

However, the tour would not go as planned for the band's new singer, as Fleischman explains: "After that [Seattle show] we came back – I think we did San Francisco, the Cow Palace, and then we were going to play in Long Beach and that's when I was sort of told it wasn't gonna work out anymore. I didn't know why it was all happening this way. One night Herbie came to me and said, 'Tonight you're singing backgrounds and you're not going to be doing these songs'. I said, 'That's ridiculous'. We were like the five musketeers, you know, I'm the lead singer and all of a sudden that night I'm [playing] tambourine or triangle. That's what kind of happened. During the time that we were playing in front of about just under 100,000 people at Soldier's Field, I was introduced to this guy named Steve [Perry] and he's like hanging out with the road crew and people like that. He was trying to blend in. He watched me from the side for quite a few gigs and kind of got a feel for what was going on, so they got Steve."[42]

Herbie Herbert tells his side of the story: "I went as far as I could with Robert but he was just a pain in the ass. A pampered poodle of a person, just a management nightmare to put up with this guy… I kind of had this guy Steve Perry floating around in my life for ten years by then. I thought I had this notion that he was very good but I had not heard him and then I finally heard him and I loved the band that he had. We got to July 4, Independence Day, and I was gonna manage his band called Alien Project in addition to Journey and really hadn't made the connection that he could be the singer in Journey. That weekend the bass player [Richard Michaels] died in an automobile accident and he [Steve] felt Alien Project was over with, so as a result I said, 'Man, I should put this guy in Journey'. I brought that up to him and he didn't want to do it. Not only did he not want to do it, the band didn't want to hear anything of it. They loved Robert Flesichman so I just forced my will on them."[43]

"I liked Herbie, but later on I found out he didn't like me," Fleischman says. "He thought I was cocky – name me one lead singer that's not a little cocky? – I was always professional but I think he

26

was a great manager. He was ambitious. He put the band on the map. He sold them like [a] candy bar – who wouldn't want a manager like that?"[44]

So, after less than a year with the band, Robert Fleischman was out of the picture. "I wasn't bitter," he says now. "I was just sort of perplexed: how did this all happen and what was going on? Supposedly Herbie had something about me that he didn't like. I guess he felt like I was really pompous and I was conceited or whatever. But it wasn't bad at all. I was scared actually in the very beginning. I had to be really super positive: 'Hey, don't worry it's going to work out great!' I kind of put on that suit. I became misread and I just didn't want to come off like I'm scared. I tried to be a little stronger to show that I can handle this. I can do the job… Neal [Schon] was always protective. He was actually mad and kind of angry when they were told I was no longer in the band. They really didn't want Steve; they thought that he was too much of a crooner. They wanted the more edgy rock [singer] like what we were doing. But Herbie said, 'No, this is what's gonna happen'. Herbie was the one who pull the plug on me and got Steve in there and everybody else kind of had to [say] okay and [went] along with it."[45]

Nevertheless, some of those songs he penned with the band would become important fixtures in Journey's back catalogue with the result that Fleischman did make his mark in rock history. "['All For You'] was written at the time of 'Anytime', 'Winds Of March' and 'Wheel In The Sky'," Fleischman elaborates. "I think we're on the road and Neal and I shared a room, and he was playing his guitar, and then I came up with the melody; then the words came pretty fast. You could say it was one of those ten-minute songs. We recorded it in San Francisco when we split up. They wanted that song but I had already given them 'Wheel In The Sky', 'Anytime' [and] 'Winds Of March' so I decided to keep that one for myself for the *Perfect Stranger* album but the song later ended up on the box set *Time3* and there is a video of us playing it in Hawaii at the Crater Festival. Lots of goofy hair back then…"[46]

Finally, another song that was added to the *Time3* (1992) box set was 'Feeling That Way', originally titled 'Velvet Curtain'. "I remember it was some idea that we were fooling around with during rehearsals but I can't really remember too much about it," says Fleischman, "plus I never heard this song and its final version maybe..."[47]

Steve Perry was born Stephen Ray Perry on January 22, 1949, in Hanford, California of Portuguese descent. "It's near Fresno, it's a small town, a nice town... kind of an *American Graffiti* type of town," he said. "Nice little main street, right in the centre of town."[48]

His parents separated when he was just eight years old. Evidently, the separation had a major impact on their son who became introverted and something of a loner. Prior to moving to Lemoore, also in California, Perry had been struck by the Sam Cooke tune 'Cupid' on his mother's car radio and decided at ten years old that he would follow a career in music. He was also influenced by his parents, both of whom were singers – his father with a big band – and R&B acts like Chuck Berry as well as Motown pioneers Stevie Wonder and Marvin Gaye; and like everyone else his age he was exposed to rock acts like Cream, Janis Joplin and Jimi Hendrix.

In high school, Perry played drums in a marching band and immersed himself in as much music as possible with the support of his mother. He said years later: "I played drums until '71... I was a lead singer/ drummer, like Buddy Miles, or the guy in Rare Earth, or the drummer in the Standells if you want to go back that far. Finally, my voice ended up surpassing my drum technique so I decided to be a singer."[49]

His interest in singing started proper when he attended the College Of The Sequoias, also in California, joining the college choir as a tenor. There were further moves, to Fresno and then Los Angeles, and it was in LA where he made some important contacts and found a job for a couple of years: "I worked as a sound engineer at LA's Crystal Studios. But I was spinning my wheels there."

Life in the City of Angels was tough, a world away from the apple pie life in Hanford or other small Californian towns. He admitted: "I was starving in Los Angeles. I was eating a lot of pork and beans, and having no money for anything else. I went back to my hometown with my gums bleeding. One dentist said I had some strange disease, that I ought to have all my teeth out."[50]

It was around this time – after spells with The Nocturns, Dollar Bills, Sullies and Pieces – that Perry fronted the rock band Alien Project, and when their bassist died just as they were about to sign to CBS, Perry was invited to join Journey. Herbie Herbert had heard Alien Project's demo recording of 'If You Need Me, Call Me' and had his heart set on Perry. He fixed it for band to perform with him on vocals during a soundcheck in Long Beach when Fleischman was elsewhere, a performance that sealed the fate of both singers.

Perry said some years later: "They definitely had a camaraderie going on for years prior to my entrance. That still exists. I think there is a very tight allegiance between Neal and Herbie that will never go – they are like brothers. That will always be there. We do all get along, it's a democracy. The truth is that all groups have their conflicts and they have to rely on the fact that there is some sort of democracy, otherwise it doesn't work."[51]

Steve Perry made his live debut with Journey on October 28, 1977, at the Old Waldorf in San Francisco, though it was obvious to some that there was an issue between certain members. Did Perry get along with the band from the word go? "Well, not instantly but eventually, yes," recalls Herbie Herbert. "I think Neal, who didn't want him, wanted Robert; and then when he realised how good he was, Neal was happy with the change. But it was a struggle. I had to shove him down Neal's throat."[52]

Maybe that was the case at the time but Schon was diplomatic as far as the press was concerned: "Robert was good in helping us decide that having a person out front was the right idea. He just wasn't the right person."[53]

With Fleischman out of the picture, Perry joined Journey as they recorded their fourth album between October and December of 1977 at His Master's Studios in San Francisco, and Cherokee Studios in Los Angeles for overdubs and mixing. Tired of producing themselves after *Look Into The Future* and *Next,* eccentric English producer Roy Thomas Baker, famous for his work with Queen, was invited on board.

Gregg Rolie: "It became a little tedious. There's a lot of work checking things out and it's easier to have someone there who'll tell you when you have to do something again. You can get bogged down with your own work when you produce yourself. You get too close to it."[54]

Not everybody in the Journey camp was happy with Baker, however. Herbie Herbert: "I'm not a big fan of Roy Thomas Baker. He made successful records. I don't wanna take anything away from him. I didn't like the sound that he got. I thought the band's natural sound was infinitely better than his idea. He had done those Queen records and I didn't like producers that seemed to put their mark on bands... marking off territory. That's what I felt he did with that record."[55]

Steve Perry put his own spin on what it was like working with Roy Thomas Baker: "We all know what we want and we all pretty much used him [RTB] as the instrument. He doesn't do nothing really special except multi-track, and Geoff Workman – his right-hand engineer – is a very talented man who needs mentioning beyond any engineer I know. Roy doesn't hang out too much, he just comes and goes. Roy comes in, has a piece of cheese, says, 'I love it' or 'I don't' and he leaves."[56]

Engineer Joe Chiccarelli says, "Even though I did do some slight engineering on the album the credit goes to Geoff Workman who did a brilliant job... The sessions were long but lots of fun. The band was excited to record and very passionate and full of ideas. Roy always kept the atmosphere light, sometimes bordering on total silliness... Roy constantly played tricks on the band. Shooting off fire extinguishers, wear[ing] disguises, etc... But he always managed to get great performances from the band... Roy is one of the most creative and intense people I've ever worked with. I learned immensely from him. His willingness to push the limits and the equipment was mind-blowing to me. He never stopped trying to get the biggest drum sound or the most dynamic mix possible."[57]

What does Chiccarelli recall about the band during those recording sessions?

"Neal was very particular about his sound and his execution of his parts. A true perfectionist... At the time Steve was new to the band so I think everyone was feeling out their space. Steve, even though new to the band, was very much a perfectionist and approached his vocals with

110 per cent commitment… I loved watching Steve sing. He was very intense and a perfectionist regarding his performances… I was quite impressed with Aynsely's drumming as well. So powerful and distinctive for the times."[58]

Herbie Herbert, on the other hand, said: "I just thought he [RTB] did a piss poor job… And you have great songs which is the nucleus, the epicentre of our business, and so they had great songs and they had great performances. What was really bad was the way it was recorded. I remember going to Cherokee and he was playing back the songs and he'd blown up the speakers and I said: 'Please Roy, don't play it back so damned loud.' I want to hear it so I'm insisting that I don't want it to go over 104 DBs."

Despite differences of opinion and personality clashes, the band came out of that period with a strong commercial rock album. "This album is absolutely more accessible," Gregg Rolie said. "That was one of the prime reasons we decided to emphasise vocals, we wanted to broaden our audience but we didn't want to lose the following we already had so the logical choice was a more true-oriented album. We still want to do solos, but the focus is on the songs. Having a lead vocalist join the group was a natural progression for us… Even with Steve in the group, I'm singing just as much now."[59]

Speaking about the final product, Joe Chiccarelli enthuses, "When we were mixing I loved the music but I never imagined it would be so successful… [It's] an absolute classic but musically and from a production standpoint, I'm very honoured to have had a very small part in the process."[60]

Titled *Infinity*, Journey's fourth album was released in January 1978 and peaked at number 21 in *Billboard* in the United States; and it also charted in Sweden and Canada. Without doubt the band's most successful album up to that point, *Infinity* married a drastic change in style with an emphasis on vocals and melody. "You've got to do what you have to do to make them listen," Neal Schon said. "I mean you can only beat an audience over the head for so long with what you know before you realise that it doesn't work and you have to move on to something else. I'm really proud of what we've done. I think we've learned to play a totally different style of music that we would have never probably have tried."[61]

"*Infinity* is the closet thing to a definitive Journey album there is," wrote Susan Ahrens in *Circus*. "Even the album cover reflects the change."

The album's commercial success certainly gave Journey some much-needed confidence and, though there was no hit single, it went on to sell a healthy half-a-million copies right away, and continued to sell as the band hit the road. Though the new sound would be less popular with critics, Journey had faith in themselves. Ross Valory: "Did we ever think about hanging it up? Throwing in the old towel? Not really. We've hung together through thick and thing and that, more than anything else, is why we're successful."[62]

Infinity opens with the Steve Perry track 'Lights', originally written about LA when he was living there. Opening the album with what is essentially a beautifully crafted ballad in the form of a homage to San Francisco certainly drew immediate attention to Journey's new style, and though it was suggested that the song's opening keys sound similar to Queen's 'Somebody To Love', 'Lights' would go on to become a regular fixture in the band's setlist. 'Feeling That Way' opens with Gregg Rolie's vocals before Perry takes over and the pair share vocals throughout. It's a mid-paced track with some steady drumming and some fairly standard guitar work. 'Anytime' has Roy Thomas Baker's stamp all over it and could have fitted on *Queen II*; the vocal harmonies and melody certainly recall classic early to mid-seventies Queen. 'La Do Da' is an excellent rocker with some gritty guitar work, pounding drums, nifty keys and a fast melody. 'Patiently', the album's most pedestrian song, is a relaxed ballad that introduces some much needed guitars midway through before the pace picks up with 'Wheel In The Sky', with its wonderful melody, fine vocal performance from Perry and hugely infectious chorus. 'Somethin' To Hide', a soppy ballad that shows Perry's vocal skill as a "rock crooner", is catchy enough and shows just how competent Journey had become at crafting original ballads. 'Winds Of March', yet another ballad, is not quite as appealing as some of it's siblings, though the joint organ and guitar riff about three minutes into the song injects some much needed life. 'Can Do' is a gritty rocker with a surprisingly aggressive vocal performance from Perry and, again, a Queen comparison can be made with the harmonies that evidently came from Roy Thomas Baker. And finally, 'Opened The Door' closes the album with the way it started – with a ballad.

Infinity has one or two too many ballads, but it did prove that with Steve Perry they could open up their sound and successfully craft contemporary melodic rock with appeal and longevity. More than thirty years later, *Infinity* has stood the test of time and, despite its flaws, it was a giant step in the right direction for the San Francisco rock band.

On January 20, the band hit the road and sales of *Infinity* started to shoot up. Herbie Herbert: "[We] found our initial success, not really on the radio, and certainly not in the traditional way that we would be successful, but I found a way to expose the music that was very unique. We were able to sell four million albums without really being in the top fifty in the 200 *Billboard*. It was like alternate method, lots of live touring..."[63]

On March 3 and through to April, Journey toured with two far heavier rock-based bands: Montrose, with singer Sammy Hagar, and Van Halen. Herbie Herbert: "Of course I love the story of the '78 Journey tour with Montrose and Van Halen. The tour started in Racine, Wisconsin, and I said: 'Hey Neal, be sure to get a look at the opening band [Van Halen]. I want you to go and see them and give me a call.' Then I got out to Chicago, Detroit and Cleveland, the big cities, Pittsburg, Philly; every time I'd say, 'Hey Neal, you seen the opening band yet?', he goes, 'No man, I never get there on time. I'll do it, I'll do it.' When I finally get to New York, I'm sittin' in the lobby, Pat Morrow the road manager brings 'em in. He's taken them out to do radio and the Sam Goody stores and all that and they got just enough time to grab their clothes and maybe a little bit of food and I say, 'Hey Neal, have you seen the opening band', and he goes 'No' and I say, 'Give your room key to Pat. He'll bring your guitars and all your shit. You're going with me right now'. I took him to the theatre. We were sold out 3,500 people and I said, 'Let's just walk in and sit down'. We walk in the front door and sit down and he looks around and says, 'Where's all the people?' I go, 'The people don't come until very late. I mean hardly anybody sees this band'. And even when we were done there was maybe a thousand people out of 3,500 when their set was over. But when they started playing 'Runnin' With The Devil' and 'You Really Got Me' and 'Jamie's Crying' and all that stuff, and all the guitars, Neal was just blown away. He says, 'Man I gotta meet that guy [Eddie Van Halen], I gotta learn that stuff and I mean, you think he'll teach me that shit?' I says, 'Man if you'll teach him some of those melodies you come up with.' He says, 'Whadaya mean?' I go, 'The man can't believe the melodies'. 'You mean he watches me?' I said: 'He watches your every note'. On this whole tour he hasn't missed a note you played and you haven't seen him once. So from then on he never missed a note. And they've become very good friends."[64]

It turned out to be an important tour for Journey in other ways, not least because they were introduced to Montrose's powerhouse drummer Steve Smith, then 25 years old. Some reports have suggested there were tensions between drummer Aynsley Dunbar and the rest of Journey; other reports have alleged that Dunbar was not keen on the new musical direction, a massive shift in gears from the jazz fusion of the early years. Neal Schon elaborated: "We would talk about it, and he'd say he'd be willing to simplify things. But we'd get out there, and after five shows he wasn't doing that at all."[65]

The band flew over to Europe and played at the Pink Pop Festival in Holland which was reviewed in the UK magazine *Sounds* by Geoff Barton. He wrote:"Journey's performance turned out to be so uninspired that I doubt they motivated a single one of the sizeable amount of punters present to go out and buy their new album *Infinity*... which was surely the point of the visit, after all: to sell product."

Barton continued: "Obviously, the band had problems. The travelling had taken its toll, the stage equipment was unfamiliar and the PA sound left much to be desired – but, even accepting these facts, the performance was pretty shallow, all in all... Steve Perry's lead vocal contributions were barely audible. For all the clarity and purity of Perry's chords, he doesn't possess a strong rock 'n' roll voice and this surely should have been taken into account at the mixing desk."

The *Infinity* tour ended on September 2 in their native San Francisco, which was the last time Aynsley Dunbar played with the band. Steve Smith made his first live appearance in November at Super Jam II in San Francisco. Herbie Herbert: "I love Aynsley by the way, a dear friend. I had to fire him. He had started playing erratically, if I take the band's word for it, and talking derogatorily about the other members of the band…"[66]

Of Dunbar's performance at the Pink Pop Festival, Geoff Barton had written in *Sounds*: "His solo was clumsy and so boring it made the bumbling efforts of the roadies trying to hand a flashing 'Thin Lizzy' logo from the scaffolding on an adjacent stage seem like compulsive entertainment at the time."

Did Dunbar and Perry get along? "Perry didn't get along with anybody," says Herbert. "Find somebody that says, 'Oh, I'm best friends with Steve Perry. I love the guy…' Find that! Well, somebody lied to you or you're a liar."[67]

Steve Perry: "Steve Smith was a fusion drummer who was with Montrose… that's where we saw him play every night and I turned to Neal and said: 'This is the guy we should have in our band. This is what we need.' I admit I was making trouble, but I had a gut level… that we had to look at making a change."[68]

Ultimately, Perry and Dunbar only lasted one album together. Herbie Herbert: "He [Perry] was afraid of Aynsley Dunbar not having a groove, being too white, a British drummer with very minimal exposure to soul or R&B and not strong on the backbeat."[69]

Even Ross Valory – the reserved Charlie Watts type figure of the band – commented on Dunbar's sacking: "Unfortunately those musical problems became personal ones and it became impossible to remain unified from set to set… The situation doesn't leave a bad taste in our mouth. I hope it doesn't in his. We wish him the best."[70]

Dunbar would have nothing more to do with Journey though in May 1980 he instructed lawyers to sue Nightmare, Herbie Herbert's company, for a reported $43.2 million. Since there are no reports of the case ever having come to court, it can probably be assumed that a confidential out-of-court settlement was agreed.

A Massachusetts native, Steve Smith, born August 21, 1951, was persuaded to leave the Californian-based rock band Montrose in late '78 and join Journey. Dunbar moved on to Jefferson Starship and later worked with Whitesnake, UFO and Jake E. Lee. Smith said: "I never subscribed to the idea that the way to be successful in the music business is as a member of a band, although I did have the opportunity to do that with Journey. I took advantage of that opportunity when the offer came my way..."[71]

Herbert Herbert has nothing but praise for the jazz-trained ex-Montrose drummer: "He was a monster and remains one of the top drummers in the world."[72]

With a new drummer on board Journey lost no time in making plans for a new album and went into Cherokee Studios in Los Angeles in late '78, again with Roy Thomas Baker in the producer's chair. Herbie Herbert: "I really didn't wanna make the next record with him but I was able to leverage an improvement on Journey's contract with CBS if I agreed to use Baker again, so I wound up using him, but I must say I don't have a lot of respect [for him]."[73]

Evolution, as the title makes clear, saw the band were evolving their sound in much the same way that *Infinity* had moved on from the groups first three albums. Steve Perry was at pains to point out that there was nothing wrong with making music that is commercial by its nature: "Commercial is a misused word. I don't see how you can use that word pertaining to music that catches on because people like it. If you've got to tie it to monetary value, I'd say successful would be the word to use. And what's wrong with being successful?"[74]

For the band's new drummer, making the album was a vastly different experience from playing in Montrose and his previous collaborations with Phillip Catherine, Focus and Jean-Luc Ponty. Steve Smith: "When I joined the band, I knew I'd need to learn a lot. I want to know how to play everything. I've slowed down a lot, made my style more open, and concentrated on a good, steady rock-solid feel – a real energy everyone could walk off."[75]

Indeed, looking back, Steve Perry felt that the band had most certainly made the right choice in replacing Dunbar with Smith. "Aynsley has one style really down, he's excellent in the free-form majestic progressive stuff," said Perry. "But when it comes to doing other things, he really can't. He's so stylised that he's locked and that's because of his background. Steve is not locked and this band plans on going everywhere. To be truthful, I don't think Aynsley could have done the *Evolution* album for us."[76]

However, working with Roy Thomas Baker again was not an easy ride for some of the band. Steve Perry admitted after the album's release: "He [RTB] was more involved on *Infinity*. I can't really say what it was – the guy gets the ball going and then sits back and says, 'OK, next'. I personally don't want to work with him again. I may work with him again, we may do it with him again, but I don't think he provides a positive feedback through the control room glass that you need from a producer."[77]

The band finished 1978 with a hometown gig on New Year's Eve with the new line-up of Perry, Schon, Rolie, Valory and Smith. It had been a whirlwind year, their most successful to date, with major performances at Soldier's Field in Chicago with the Rolling Stones, the World Series Of Rock Festival in Ohio with ELP and Foreigner, and Oakland Stadium in California with Ted Nugent and AC/DC, among other shows. With a new album about to be released the following year, things would just get bigger and better. Gregg Rolie attested: "I'm totally into a group effort because I think it's the best way. When you get a bunch of good musicians together whose ideas coincide and who understand that it's not one man's show, it's really terrific."[78]

It may have seemed like a team effort from the perspective of those on the outside looking in, but was it really? Rolie and Schon had always asserted themselves; after all it was basically their band. As soon as Perry came into the equation, he made an immediate impact and voiced his ideas, and Smith would do the same in time, but what about the band's long time bassist, Ross Valory? Was he the so-called quiet member of the band, similar to Queen's bassist John Deacon? "Ross and I were childhood friends," says Herbie Herbert. "I'll always love Ross but Ross is a bit player in this. [He] never was a power. Never asserted himself. And at times [he] didn't have a whole lot of vertebrae. When things happened he would just be a pacifist..."[79]

Evolution was released in April 1979 and would go on to sell over three million copies in the US alone. It peaked at number 20 in *Billboard* and charted in Norway, the UK, Japan and Canada. "*Evolution* was a continuation of where *Infinity* was," says Steve Smith. "We wanted to just try and further grow on that *Infinity* concept a bit more. The concept was good songs and a lot of vocals. Before, the band wasn't really song-orientated, it was playing-orientated more than anything."[80]

Evolution was also a milestone album for the band in that it featured their first hit single in the US, 'Lovin', Touchin', Squeezin', which peaked at number 16 and gave Journey significant airplay. "Single success has a lot to do with the success of a band, and we are in business – it takes money to run it," said Rolie.[81]

"Journey have honed and refined their newly found top forty chart capabilities and constructed an album that in my estimation is simply stunning," enthused Geoff Barton in a review of *Evolution* in *Sounds*. "No potholes in the road, just a gentle and scenic ride through the realm of drive-time American adult-oriented rock, designed to rake in the dollars for sure, deep and meaningless most of the time certainly, but busy on the ears and brain…"

Manager Herbie Herbert disputes the notion that the band sold albums on the back of the stream of hit singles which commenced with 'Lovin', Touchin', Squeezin''. Instead, he points out, he organised a subtler form of promotion wherein Journey's songs were played in shopping malls and workplaces, thus instilling the belief that Journey's songs were hits even though they never made the charts.

"Although people want to swear up and down that 'Lights', 'Feelin' That Way' and 'Wheel In The Sky' and all these familiar songs, you know, 'Lovin', Touchin', Squeezin'', 'Anyway You Want It', and songs that got so goddamned much airplay you got pounded by them [were hits] but they really were never hits," he says. "A lot of that airplay was subliminal. And a lot of it was not really subliminal… it's called foreground music. [There were] these companies up in Seattle, Washington at the time, [such as] AEI Audio Environments Inc., and their lobby's loaded with all of Journey's platinum and gold because they played up nationwide like you can't believe on their in-house proprietary music systems. We did big promotions with all their people – access to Journey tickets and merchandise and meet and greets and things like that – and, oh my God, the airplay we got from that was incredible. So every shoe store, shopping mall, restaurant from the Rusty Scuppers to Houston's, you know, there it is. Getting all that airplay, those are all gross impressions and they came up to a level of recognition and familiarity that makes people really believe that those songs were hit songs. They were heard so much it just wasn't on normal, it certainly wasn't on contemporary hit radio which is how you get a hit single."[82]

Evolution opens with the short instrumental (though there are some backing vocals) 'Majestic' before 'Too Late', a ballad comes into play. Perry's vocals are perfect and there's even a central guitar solo from Schon which adds appeal. 'Lovin', Touchin', Squeezin'', their seductive, mid-paced, blues-tinged song with an infectious melody, has became a staple song in Journey's back catalogue. 'City Of The Angels' also has a distinctive chorus with production effects on the band's backing vocals but overall, it is not a standout track. 'When You're Alone (It Ain't Easy)' is more upbeat and rock based, the toe-tapping melody helped along by Smith's consistent drum beat. 'Sweet And Simple', a piano-led ballad that is perhaps even too slushy for Journey's most forgiving fans, is followed by 'Lovin' You Is Easy', a mid-paced rocker with a catchy riff, some distinctive keys and an immaculate vocal performance. 'Just The Same' begins with a piano riff, but what marks this song out from the rest of the album is Rolie and Perry's shared lead vocals – though it is largely down to Rolie – and there's yet another excellent guitar solo leading to the song's climax. 'Do You Recall', perhaps the album's weakest song, has a repetitive beat that grates a little and the musicianship fails to impress: by Journey's standards it is fairly lightweight. The intro to 'Day Dream' would not have sounded out of place on Journey's albums before *Infinity*, its spacey ambience surprisingly progressive. Perry gives a fairly restrained performance at first but then some aggression kicks in, adding depth to the album. The final track, 'Lady Luck', sounds like the band were jamming Deep Purple-style in the studio with some excellent joint guitar and organ work, a fine climax to the record.

Evolution had showed the world that Journey had evolved; and though the album does have its faults, the band sounds strong, confident and totally committed to their new sound. It still sounds like smooth, polished American melodic rock.

"Boston released one album," said Perry, commenting on how Journey's sound had evolved, "their first album [and it] was a mammoth thing, a mammoth sound, a different sound. Everyone was going, 'Wow, these guys are going to turn it around'. What ended up happening was, that album got so saturated, they came out with a second one, and that one [did] just nothing. It turned out that they are just another band. They are fantastic, but they are just another really successful band. We are in that group too. We are just another really successful band. But we are trying to make statements at all times."[83]

To promote *Evolution*, the band committed themselves to more touring. Having made a considerable dent in the Japanese music scene for some time now, Journey began 1979's touring schedule with a trip to Japan, playing Nagoya, Osaka and Tokyo. They flew back to the US to begin touring their homeland in Medford, Oregon on May 2. It was a lengthy road jaunt but ticket sales were at their highest ever, and both *Infinity* and *Evolution* just kept on selling. A big date for the band was July 28 when they played at the World Series Of Rock festival in Cleveland, Ohio with headliners Aerosmith and Ted Nugent, Thin Lizzy, AC/DC and The Scorpions.

The heavy touring schedule had by now turned Journey into a superbly drilled live band, often note- and chord-perfect. They were fixated about getting the songs to sound exactly like they did on record, especially the vocals, which certainly made it tough on Perry night after night. "What makes us different is Neal plays guitar like nobody I know," said Perry. "He has a style of his own. I sing, in my opinion, very different than most singers. I'm into making a different vocal style – aggression with feeling... Everybody in the band is unique in their own way and the combination of all that really makes something."[84]

Tales of rock star hedonism – the drugs and groupie scene associated with Led Zeppelin and US bands like Mötley Crüe – are rife, but Journey have never had a reputation for backstage or hotel-room indulgence. Much of this was due to the influence of manager Herbie Herbert, a thorough professional who ran a tight ship, discouraging distractions and focusing completely on turning Journey's potential into a lucrative business operation.

But they didn't behave like choir boys all the time. Steve Perry: "Ross and Gregg might project that very laid-back image, because that's what they're like. If you're wondering if we've destroyed a Holiday Inn, well, sometimes it happens. One time, Gregg and I went out and bought 25 extension chords. We figured that the extension chords were just long enough to reach from our room to the first floor. And we took a colour television, we plugged it in and tossed it in the pool. It was a wonderful sight… I'm telling you man, it goes up in a beautiful colour. It explodes. It's great!"[85]

And behind the scenes Neal Schon had developed a taste for vodka. He admitted some years later: "I believe I was a functioning alcoholic. And the reason I didn't realise that I was an alcoholic is that I didn't have to wake up in the morning and pound down a six-pack. I could go out and I could have eight, nine, ten vodkas, and then I wouldn't drink for another three or four days. When I did drink, it was in excess. And I think I made a lot of really bad decisions over the years, because I was messed up like that."[86]

The *Evolution* tour finished on September 2 in Oakland, California, and the band took a brief rest before making their next move. Despite a massive rise in both album and ticket sales coast to coast, Journey were hardly darlings of the rock press, and were far better received by British critics than their American counterparts. Journey were – and still are – lumped into the genre of rock music called AOR, album-orientated rock, melodic rock designed for American FM radio, and in some quarters – especially the offices where rock magazines are produced – this is deeply unfashionable.

Herbie Herbert: "I never gave a flying fuck in a rolling doughnut what a critic thought. They don't know how, can't do it, how to play music onstage, have no fricking idea whatsoever. They're trying to find some angle and the angle that was most popular with Journey was to call them 'the fathers of corporate rock', which was funny because in that genre – Styx, Foreigner, Boston and so forth – well, those bands have virtually all come and gone. Journey opened up shows to Boston. They were ahead of us, yet we came in at the very, very end even after the train had left, and some how became fathers of the genre! I always found that to be kind of funny, how that works. They were critical of Journey being corporate and the money orientation and so forth, shit, try that nowadays. Nowadays, if you're not making money you're just not hip."[87]

Steve Perry: "The band's biggest critic is itself. That's why we don't give a damn what anybody writes. We know in our hearts how we've got to live up to our own expectations. And nine times out of ten we don't. It's not that we don't think we didn't play well; it's just that we always think we could've done better. We're the ones who keep us on our toes."[88]

On November 5, 1979, Journey entered Automatt Studios in San Francisco to record their sixth album. Opting not to work again with Roy Thomas Baker, they choose Geoff Workman, the first engineer on *Infinity* and *Evolution*, and Kevin Elson, their live engineer, who had also engineered Lynyrd Skynryd 1977 album *Street Survivors* and worked with .38 Special and Molly Hatchet. Certainly hooking up with Elson – who had never produced an album before – gave the record a "live in the studio vibe" in contrast to the two previous albums.

Geoff Workman: "I'd worked with Journey on two previous albums, so we all know each other well and there is a particular kind of trust. They know I'll record them well, I know they won't come up with a bunch of band songs, and Kevin [Elson] can keep an overall eye on everything."[89]

Kevin Elson: "My background is more as a straight-ahead rocker. In past Journey albums, I've felt the bass and drums didn't stand out well enough and were not properly heard in the mix. This album also represents more facets of the band, because they enjoy playing lots of different music. There's real good rock, some ballads, a little blues, some jazz... this album is a departure in the sense that there's more variety of material. A lot of solos, and even some vocals, have been done live so there's more of a feel… All the musicians are happy with the results of this approach."[90]

No fewer than 19 songs were written and demoed for the album but only 12 made the final cut. While the band were on the road promoting *Evolution* they worked on ideas for songs and lyrics, rehearsed them during soundchecks and crafted them at Neal Schon's home studio on an eight-track system.

"Our rehearsal schedule was 10am to 3pm," said Elson, "although we go a little longer in the studio. Journey is comprised, pretty much, of early people; they're not real blazers, where they go to three or four in the morning. They like to use the daytime, when there's the most energy, and have the night off to do whatever they want to do. If you've got business to do during the day and then go into the studio, you'll be worn out. We felt a daytime schedule would give the most productivity."[91]

Steve Smith said at the time: "We rented the studio for 24 hours a day so we can use it as long, or as little, as we want. On the last record we worked eight hours a day, seven days a week, real steady, and this time we'll try to do something like that, maybe even more, because we don't have just eight hours. We can go in for five hours and take two hours off and then go in for five or six more hours."[92]

Since the release of *Infinity*, the band had become increasingly fond of backing vocals and vocal harmonies. Herbie Herbert: "When Journey first started, they couldn't even sing. Neal Schon did not sing, and he [actually] said, 'I will not sing'. Somewhere along the line, somebody's mind must have changed, because the band began taking voice training lessons, and by the time Perry joined, they could sing like canaries."[93]

How had the rigorous touring and recording sessions impacted on Perry's voice? He was never the typical rock singer like Steve Tyler, Mick Jagger or – heaven forbid - Iggy Pop, all singers with a flexible attitude towards pitch perfection. "I have a little preparation I make that works very well for me," he admitted. "It is glycerine, like you buy at the drugstore, half glycerine and half fresh lemon juice. What I do is gargle with it, and aerate to get some moisture to the cords. Then I do not talk. Between the lemon making me salivate, and the air sending it back, hopefully I will get some extra lubricant on these cords. Which is what they need. If they do dry, you start to get into nodules."[94]

Opting to call the new album *Departure* – the third consecutive album with a single-word title - it was released in March 1980. It peaked at number eight in *Billboard*, also charting in New Zealand and Canada, and it spawned a classic Journey song in 'Any Way You Want It', a top 30 single in the US which has since been used excessively in TV commercials and remains a regular feature in their setlists.

John Orme's review in *Melody Maker* read: "The emphasis [is] on glossy, stacked harmonies and song-structures that boost the singer rather than the band's erstwhile swirling instrumental prowess, and in particular the distinctive guitar talent of Neal Schon... All of which means a modern rock package of one dimension..."

'Any Way You Want It' opens *Departure* and is followed by 'Walks Like A Lady', a blues-tinged, mid-paced track. 'Someday Soon' is among Journey's most underrated songs though some have called it nothing more than filler material; it has a wonderful melody, some strong guitar work, dulcet harmonies and lead vocals shared between Rolie and Perry. 'People And Places' has a progressive edge with another shared vocal, this time between Perry and Schon. 'Precious Time' is a bluesy song with some harmonica, acoustic guitars and a toe-tapping melody, and 'Where Were You', a strong rock track, would soon become the opening song in concert. 'I'm Cryin'', a slow sentimental ballad, is followed by 'Line Of Fire', another stand-out rocker filled to the brim with energy and vigour. The title-track is similar to 'Majestic' in that it's a brief instrumental with some minor vocals. 'Good Morning Girl' is a beautifully crafted ballad in the Journey tradition, as is 'Stay Awhile' with its fine vocal performance by Perry. Unfortunately the closing track, 'Homemade Love' is disappointing, a fairly average attempt at boogie-woogie, never Journey's strong point. On the whole, though, *Departure* is a strong, focused album which suffers from the inclusion of more ballads than necessary. With more variation than *Infinity*, *Evolution* and the albums that followed, it is a still a worthy addition to the band's catalogue.

Journey kicked off another lengthy road jaunt on March 26, 1980 in San Francisco and continued to tour right through to mid-October.

Reviewing the band's gig in Chicago in May, Bill Paige wrote in *Billboard*: "Journey, especially the energy-bound Perry, delivers 17 crafted yet still exciting songs, leaving no stone in its relatively short career unturned. Smiles, rather than complaints, punctuate the remarks of exiting fans."

The Babys, a melodic rock band which at that point featured singer John Waite, keyboard player Jonathan Cain, bassist Ricky Phillips, guitarist Wally Stocker and drummer Tony Brock, hit the road on some dates as support to Journey. Phillips remembers opening for Journey on that tour: "Well, I thought they were amazing and we got on well with them. On the two bands' first flight together, Steve Perry told me I reminded him of his old bass player… They were amazing to watch. I've never watched another band as much. They were tough on us though. They barely gave us enough room to do our show each night… which turned out good actually, because it pushed us right to the front of the stage, and we rocked our asses off. They gave us about half the sound system at first but started adding as they grew to like us. It was always unsettling opening to empty seats [but] that made us rock hard from the start. We would sell records in every city we played so the pairing was great for us."[95]

"I used to jam with Neal and Steve [Smith] after shows," Phillips recalls, "and days off in clubs or wherever we could. They were playing some very outside non-Journey stuff and I mentioned that Jonathan had some chops of his own and he should sit in some time. I remember Jonathan jamming with us a few times and thinking it sounded great. One night Steve Perry and I went into a club that was attached to the hotel. We were just killing time while luggage was being loaded onto the busses after a show in Illinois. The band in the little club took a break and he said: 'You know "Mustang Sally" don't you?… every bass player knows "Mustang Sally!"' And we jumped up on stage without asking. Steve picked up the drum sticks and I grabbed the bass and started the opening riff. He came in with that amazing voice while slamming down some pretty funky drums. The house band was looking on from across the room at the bar. No one could really believe what was going on. At about that time, Neal Schon came in and grabbed a guitar. John Waite and Anne Marie LeClair, our back-up singer, came in and jumped up to add some harmony… I don't remember if it was Jonathan or Gregg Rolie who jumped on the organ but Perry called out, 'Midnight Hour' and we segued straight into it. After about 15 minutes of soul tunes one of the tour managers came up to the stage shouting, 'Come on guys we have a long drive tonight… let's go!,' and that was the end of that. I'll never know the conversation that followed in that little club that night."[96]

Journey also played dates in Germany, Switzerland, England and Japan. "It's a lot of hard work being on the road as much as this band is," Perry commented. "It can make you very crazy."[97]

On the other side of the coin, Smith enthused: "I find that I look forward to going on the road still because it's a chance to play a lot and I love that."[98]

However, the drummer did admit that the first few years in the band required a lot of hard work: "When you practise, practise with dynamics… For my first three years in Journey, I did that intense practising as much as I could. I practised not only the slow tempos, but all different tempos. I practised a lot with the drum machine to make myself very aware of my time, my tempo, and the spacing of the notes – the subdivision of the beats. Those were things that were brought to my attention, especially by Steve Perry, who is a good drummer himself and has great time as a musician. He made me very aware of those things, because he needs them in order to do what he has to do. He really demanded that of me. Then he helped me find out how to develop that, too."[99]

For the singer, being on tour so much can be very rough on the vocal cords. "A guitarist can be sick with the flu and go out and play," Perry said. "The singer can't go out and buy a new voice or strings. You have to have the voice you came with and that is all you are going to get. Of course, there are kinds of surgery these days; you will never be the same, though. You are better off keeping what you have, and making sure you have it for a while. That takes discipline and it is frustrating. I enjoy going out and partying with the guys as much as anybody. There are times I just have to go out and have a good time."[100]

Did Perry ever struggle through some shows during their relentless touring schedule?

Herbie Herbert: "No. There was one time we had a four-night run at the Reunion Arena in Dallas and his voice got really rough and we had a doctor come and he gave him something. He got us through and so what I'm saying is: that's why I have such respect for Perry as a performer. He was very consistent. He was spot on. He rarely had anything approaching a bad show. I used to say, 'For the whole band the disparity between the best and the worst Journey show is almost indistinguishable to anything but the most trained ear.' They were so consistent and so good; and Perry hardly ever postponed or cancelled a show… maybe one time and it was not a tremendous inconvenience, and a few days later we played it or whatever… [We] didn't have to circle back or go through any major [inconveniences]. That is such a relief to a manager to be able to have that kind of consistent, solid performance level. I'd love to tell you he had a lot of bad shows. He didn't. So to that I will always have great respect."[101]

Gregg Rolie: "Technically, you can find very little fault in what Perry did. He sang background and lead vocals… six to eight months out of the year, and did not falter. That's incredible. Because that singing is at the top of anybody's range. That's pretty good."[102]

As if the touring wasn't enough to keep them busy, between October 13 and 22 they found time to compose the soundtrack to a Japanese animated film titled *Dream, After Dream*. Produced by Kevin Elson and the band, it was released in December and has been little heard of since. Neal Schon's father, Matthew, provided the album's orchestrations. Steve Perry said of the film's premise, and the recording experience: "It's about this young guy who comes upon a castle in the desert and finds these two beautiful girls and an old soothsayer living there. The fortune teller tells him that the girls are really birds who'll be returned to their natural state if they don't kill this guy… it was pretty easy because the film dictated what we had to write. We did some really good sound effects on it too. Neal does a fluttering sound on his guitar for a sequence about an owl, and I do an *Exorcist*-type voice in one of the heavier scenes in the picture."[103]

What is noticeable about the soundtrack is that Perry sings in a deeper register than previous Journey records. "Steve is singing in a lower register with a different tonality. He did that on this album intentionally. He wanted to move on," said Ross Valory.[104]

The release of *Departure* and the subsequent tour – one of the first rock tours to feature a dazzling array of pyrotechnics – proved to be the end of an era for the band in that their original and founding member Gregg Rolie decided to quit. It was a significant blow to them, especially to their manager who continues to have nothing but praise for the organist/keyboardist/singer.

Herbie Herbert: "[It] was 1980 and I can remember going out to lunch in Frankfurt [Germany]. We're on a round the world tour and he [Rolie] told me at the end of the Japanese tour that he's going to leave. *Captured* – the live album that was recorded on that tour – was his last. He wanted to have a family and all that. In Santana, he was the band leader; he was our boss. He was the guy who probably had 40 IQ points on Carlos [Santana]… I was just fucked up."

Rolie suggested to Herbert that the Babys' keyboard player Jonathan Cain might be a suitable replacement but Herbert was profoundly affected by Rolie's decision. "It was really the last thing I wanted, so I was deeply, personally affected by that. It was a losing battle for me because Gregg was my total supporter. He knew that I was locked on and focused on exactly what to do to continue this career and supported me one hundred per cent every step of the way and all the negative stuff came from other quarters, mostly Steve Perry. [Perry] was just a classic shit stirrer and perhaps had some resentment about how long and close I was with Neal and Gregg. We'd been working professionally together for years and years… we were really close. Not that I wouldn't want to be that close with him, but he's just not that kind of person. He was just wanting to be destructive."[105]

Born on February 26 in Chicago, Jonathan Cain was a multi-instrumentalist and songwriter who'd released his first album *Windy City Breakdown* in 1976 as the Jonathan Cain Band. Though not quite as seasoned as Schon or Rolie, he joined The Babys in 1979 he had plenty of input on their two 1980 albums *Union Jacks* and *On The Edge*.

As it happened, The Babys were falling apart anyway. "John [Waite, singer] decided that he wanted to go solo," said Cain, "and I called him in New York and told him I had an offer from Journey. I told him that I didn't want to pass it, that I felt I could relate to the guys in the band, and that I wanted to go with them. But I wanted his blessing. He said: 'You got it!' and that is where it ended. I told everybody that I was leaving after Christmas... The difference between Journey and The Babys was management. Herbie is a genius and we owe a lot to our manager and our crew. By the time The Babys had a decent manager, the ship was sinking and it was over."[106]

Gregg Rolie: "I just had enough of travelling and I wanted to start a family. I saw a lot of kids on the road that I just wanted to go hang on a tree somewhere. And it's not their fault, nor their parents, they just needed stability. It was probably the most mature thing I did in my immature life... So anyway, that was my major reason. Perry made that an easy decision to make. He was always saying, 'We've got to have a band meeting about this, about that, about this, about that,' where you didn't have to have one at all. The band was being run by manager Herbie Herbert, who did a great job, and it was unnecessary. I was pretty much through with it anyway. I just did not like touring anymore. You know, the funny thing about travel, or anything that you do, is that you do it because it's fun and when it's not, it's over. You recognise it or you don't. I just didn't like doing it anymore..."[107]

Ricky Phillips, formally of The Babys and now in Styx, looks back and recalls, "He [Cain] called me and told me what was going on. Also, I was friends with Gregg Rolie and I knew he had sort of chosen Jonathan as his successor to the keyboard throne in Journey. This all ties in to the after show jams. I had gotten to know Gregg and Lori, his girlfriend and now wife of many years, on the road and they told me they wanted to start a family and he was going to leave the band. I couldn't imagine leaving a band at their peak since it was everything I had ever wanted. Jonathan wanted to know what I thought. And did I think Waite would come around? He told me he had talked to Waite and he had said to 'go for it'. Meaning take the opportunity, because he wasn't coming back. I thought it was a great opportunity for Jonathan so I said: 'With everything taken into consideration mate, you'd be crazy not to go up to San Francisco and give it a go.' In retrospect I'm sure he'd already made up his mind but it was nice of him to call and confide in me."[108]

On the subject of Steve Perry, Rolie remarked: "Steve... no-one got along too well with Steve. I don't like to be pinpointed quite that way. But yeah, he made it an easier choice, that's for sure. It was time to go. For both our sakes..."[109]

Herbert Herbert: "Gregg pointed him [Cain] out to me. I just said: 'Gregg, how the fuck will I ever replace you? I want to shut this thing [Journey] down. He says, 'This kid that's in the opening band.' I said: 'The fucking Babys stink!' He's like, 'No, man, watch him again, watch him again.' That keyboard player's got some talent."[110]

Captured – released in February of the following year – proved to be the last Journey release to feature Gregg Rolie. Produced by Kevin Elson and dedicated to the late AC/DC singer Bon Scott, *Captured* sold over two million copies on its initial release and peaked at number nine in the *Billboard* album charts. A fitting way to end Rolie's career in the band, it features well-known Journey songs - 'Lights', 'Any Way You Want It', 'Wheel In The Sky' and 'Lovin', Touchin', Squeezin'' - alongside an unreleased track called 'Dixie Highway'.

Speaking on the difference between the band's studio recordings and their first live album, Ross Valory said: "I would tend to think, on average, the stage performances are better than performances on the albums, sound wise and otherwise. Anyone who writes a song and attempts to literally freeze it in time on record will find that later in time, the song continues to grow and tends to become more unified and better performed. Our performing end of things is a moving picture and a recording is a still taken at a certain moment. As far as Journey goes, I'd say the performances are generally better and more exciting than the recordings. The performance is a better representation of Journey than songs on an album."[111]

Rolie went on to start a family and undertake various solo projects. Later he would reunite with bassist Ross Valory and drummer Steve Smith in the nineties Bay Area rock band The Storm, managed by Herbie Herbert. Looking back on those Journey years, Rolie admits being in the band was a massive, life-changing learning curve: "I learned a ton off of Journey in the first place. But mainly, what I got out of Journey was songwriting skills that I did not have in Santana. I had feel and the ability to jam and, I don't know, grab a hold of jazz things and make them your own, along with any music you just kind of make it your own. But the real skills, the technical skills of writing songs, with courses, beats sections and bridges, and breaks and things like that, I learned a lot from Journey."[112]

With the addition of Jonathan Cain – who later admitted "I was in shock for a week after I joined the band. I thought it was a mistake at first"[113] – Journey would go on to create their most important and successful album in their entire history.

CHAPTER 3

Don't Stop Believin':
Journey's Glory Years
(1981–1983)

"We're probably the only band in rock that's not being ripped off. I like money, I like to have it. I like to be able to buy a new guitar when I want one, but that's about it. This band is in it for the music, anything else is secondary."

Neal Schon[114]

The recording of Journey's follow-up to *Departure, Escape* – the first album to feature Jonathan Cain – took place in late 1980 and carried on into the New Year at Fantasy Studios in Berkeley, California. The album was produced by Kevin Elson and Mike Stone who was well-known for having engineered Queen's albums from their self-titled debut in 1973 through to *News Of The World* in 1977, which he also co-produced. Stone had also worked on albums by Peter Criss and Paul Stanley of Kiss, so he was a familiar name to rock fans. Jonathan Cain seemed to fit right in with the band, and his piano riffs and melodies gave the new album much of its pathos. He also co-wrote every song on the album. "For our end of it," Ross Valory stated, "it was fairly smooth in acquiring Jonathan Cain… he's even more versatile than Gregg and he sounds like he's been with us for a while, at least that's the way it seems to me. So it wasn't such a traumatic experience as it could have been."[115]

From the band's point of view hiring a new member was a positive thing, as singer Steve Perry said: "He's brought some very fresh ideas into the band, and his ability to play keyboards, guitar and sing has given us a flexibility which we really haven't enjoyed in the past. I think it's really good for a band to get some new blood in its veins every once in a while, and Jonathan came along and re-energised our whole musical outlook."[116]

Herbie Herbert had nothing but praise for Cain as a musician but, as with Perry, he had mixed feelings about his personality: "There is absolutely nothing to say or do to take away from Jon Cain's talent as a keyboardist and as a songwriter… certainly at this particular point, when he came to the band, I believe I had Steve Perry established as the foremost contemporary vocal stylist in the world, so on that professional level I have nothing but the upmost respect for Steve Perry's talent and Jon Cain's talent… where the grey area comes in is because it's imbued with your personal feelings for these people as people. That's a whole other thing. You might be a tremendous talent but that doesn't mean you're not a consummate asshole. I would say Jon Cain is a fallen angel with visible halo compared to Steve Perry as a person, but he's still an asshole. I wouldn't want to cross the street to see him [Cain] or Perry or to say hello."[117]

Escape featured some striking artwork by artist Stanley Mouse, who was much respected for his Grateful Dead album art and his concert posters in the Sixties. Mouse was a familiar name with Journey fans, having been employed by the band since 1977.

Stanley Mouse: "I was working with [Alton] Kelley for many years and that came to an end just before *Escape*. We did a few Journey covers together. I did the *Escape* art by myself and, now that I think about it, the album was well named for my escape. I had escaped many things at that time when I look back at it. I had an agent that also was Journey's marketing agent, Jim Welch. My lady was pregnant with my daughter at the time (might be something to read into that). My influence was from a German artist who did a similar bursting, breaking out smashing explosion. I don't recall his name, but it left a big impression on my mind. I was really into messing with lettering at the time. I liked the lettering a lot. I was worried about someone in the Journey organisation saying that it was not legible but they didn't. You might say *Captured* and *Escape* was some 'breakthrough' art for me."[118]

Escape turned out not only to be Journey's most successful album but also their most widely reviewed when it was released in July 1981. It was their first and only number one in the US and also charted in the UK, New Zealand, Japan and Canada. At one point it was selling a reported 462,000 a week. The album also had a clutch of hit singles, including the iconic 'Don't Stop Believin'' and the classic ballads 'Who's Crying Now', 'Still They Ride' and 'Open Arms'. The latter appeared on the soundtrack to the film *Heavy Metal*. *Escape* went on to sell over a million copies by the end of 1981. It also generated sales for the group's previous records.

Herbie Herbert: "It was huge. It went to number one and at some point there was *Escape* and then *Infinity, Evolution, Departure, Captured* and *In The Beginning*, which was a compilation of the first three albums, all in the top fifty in [the] *Billboard* charts at the same time while *Escape* was number one. I think [we had] five albums in the top fifty!"[119]

Critics remained unimpressed. *Melody Maker's* Michael Oldfield wrote: "The theme of this collection of tired old high-energy (i.e. low inspiration) riffs is, surprise, surprise, escape: a bunch of mediocre songs about people running away from things – perhaps this album?"

Nevertheless, *Escape* was such a phenomenon that a computer game for the Atari 2600 called *Journey Escape* was developed and released in 1982. "Jim Welch, our promotion man in merchandising, came up with the idea and Herbie took it from there," said Ross Valory. "It's a game that was developed around real-life situations. The player has to leave the gig as soon as he gets done."[120]

Jonathan Cain: "We were involved in the project from the very beginning. It wasn't a situation where some company came up to us and offered us a bundle of cash in order to use our name. We had virtually complete control over the project from start to finish. The concept was ours, and the finished result had to meet with our approval. We're not about to take advantage of our fans by letting our names be put on inferior products. The *Escape* game is a great deal of fun, and we hope that our fans enjoy it."[121]

While in the 21st century merchandising on all sorts of levels has become the norm in rock, in 1982 the idea of a game based around an album was construed in some quarters as selling out, as indeed was the melodic content on *Escape*. The band denied this.

Neal Schon: "There's a brand new audience out there, a totally new generation. A lot of kids who've never heard of Cream or Jimi Hendrix, they don't hear Led Zeppelin any more, and they don't want to hear something like that, something out of the same era but new. I don't think what we're doing now is a cop-out. I don't care what they say about you. You know who you are."[122]

Steve Perry: "A band like ours knows that it needs to please people in order to remain successful. We're not The Clash or a band like that which can survive by appealing to a relatively small band of dedicated followers. We want everybody to like what we do. We know that's impossible, but it's an ambition I hope we always keep… Any time anyone wants to insult us by calling us a success, well, that's one thing I think we can learn to live with."[123]

Escape opens with the classic piano riff to 'Don't Stop Believin'', now one of the most popular power ballads ever recorded, and a showcase for Perry's immaculate vocals during his peak years. 'Stone In Love', a guitar-based rocker, has strong, slightly aggressive vocals from Perry, a sturdy bass line and steady drumming. 'Who's Crying Now', another Jonathan Cain piano-led track, has since become a fixture in the band's live setlist; it is perhaps too soppy for some, but is cherished by Journey fans the world over. 'Keep On Runnin'' is the album's standout rocker: fast, aggressive and groove-laden with an anthemic chorus that's great for the live stage. 'Still They Ride' is an elegant ballad with a wonderfully melodic chorus. The title-track is a fast and furious rocker with some excellent backing vocals and a memorable lead riff. 'Lay It Down', another rocker, has the same traits as 'Escape' with equal amounts of confidence and energy. 'Dead Or Alive', perhaps the album's least known track, boasts a boogie-woogie style melody with a nifty guitar solo mid-way through. 'Mother, Father' is a powerful ballad, perhaps one of Journey's most profound songs. Finally, 'Open Arms' is another Jonathan Cain track with some haunting keys and a majestic vocal performance from Perry.

Escape was another big step in the right direction, containing Journey's most distinctive and anthemic rockers. There was no weak track on *Escape*, no filler, and each track succeeded on its own merits. With Jonathan Cain and Neal Schon's stamp all over it, the departure of Gregg Rolie and the arrival of Cain seemed to have benefited the group. "Well, on the likes of 'Any Way You Want It' or 'Lights' it was just me and Neal, but Jonathan came in and had a huge impact on the band. Let's face it, he co-wrote the whole album!" said Steve Perry.[124]

Jonathan Cain himself enthused: "It feels good to be part of Journey, an American institution, but I did cut my teeth – pardon the pun – on some very great music. I think The Babys have probably been the most misunderstood band, and some day people are going to realise that we did make some good and serious attempts at making statements and musical concepts. I'm proud that we went out on a high note... I'd say The Babys are the reason I'm here today."[125]

Journey hit the road on June 12 for yet another lengthy tour, gearing up for the release of what turned out to be their biggest selling album of all time. Opening with three nights at Angels Camp in California, they continued their trek right through to December 22 when they finished in Honolulu. They were supported by Billy Squier, Greg Kihn Band, Point Blank and Loverboy on selected dates.

Ken Keenen wrote in *Night Rock* magazine: "Both Poplar Creek [September 3 and 4] were astonishing. Each Journey member is a dedicated pro and an expert in his respective ability... Perry is unquestionably the visual, confident leader that critics claim Journey lacked before his arrival."

Regardless of the extraordinary success of *Escape*, Journey were happy to support The Rolling Stones at JFK Stadium in Philadelphia on September 25. Jonathan Cain: "It was quite an experience. But I think it may have been something of a mistake for us. We had the best-selling album in the country at that moment, yet we were there showing 90,000 people that we were still willing to be an opening act. We were only given 45 minutes to play, and, let's face it, a Stones crowd really isn't a Journey crowd… It was the thrill of a lifetime in one respect. I couldn't believe some of the assholes who were at that show. They were yelling that Steve Perry couldn't sing like Jagger. I should hope not: Steve Perry's a trained vocalist. I'm not sure what Jagger is."[126]

Unlike, say, certain members of The Rolling Stones, Journey disdained drugs. Having witnessed the downfall of the original Santana band through unquantifiable consumption of cocaine, Herbie Herbert saw to it that Journey steered clear of this particular vice. "I fired a whole crew bus of people for getting high on cocaine," he said. "It's not because I'm a goody two-shoes or anything, or that I never did cocaine myself or anything else, it's just that I've got a business here to run… I tried my best to keep cocaine out of it. I didn't care if people had a beer or smoked a joint but the cocaine thing can really cause you to cancel a tour or something radical."[127]

For Journey, it was all about the music, though they did enjoy living the lifestyle that comes with platinum albums. More to the band's advantage, the November 6 gig in Houston, Texas, was recorded for MTV and eventually released on DVD and CD in 2005.

The setlist for the concert ran as follows: 'Escape', 'Line Of Fire', 'Lights', 'Stay Awhile', 'Open Arms', 'Mother, Father', ' Who's Crying Now', 'Where Were You', 'Dead Or Alive', 'Don't Stop Believin'', 'Stone In Love', 'Keep On Runnin'', 'Wheel In The Sky', 'Lovin', Touchin',' Squeezin'', 'Any Way You Want It' and 'The Party's Over (Hopelessly In Love)'. Aside from some dates in Japan they stuck to North America with no further dates abroad.

By the end of 1981, with the release of the mammoth-selling *Escape* album and the subsequent tour, Journey were fully established as a corporation. Herbie Herbert's company Nightmare was making millions of dollars a year with everything at Nightmare done in-house. Herbie Herbert: "I am not trying to create the military-industrial complex rock group here, but I have acquired autonomy over the years and we completely create everything we do under one roof. We produce our music, record it, master it; we create parts, and we ship those parts direct to the manufacturing plant around the world. We create our art, come up with the image, the layout – we do everything from spine information [on the album sleeve] to the bar-code. We know how to magnetically strip in a bar-code so that when it is run over a computer, the cash register will go, 'ding – $7.98'..."[128]

In this respect Journey seemed to be the epitome of "corporate rock", whatever that meant. Was it simply rock music that was successfully marketed? Perhaps it was rock music that is catered specifically for a target audience with the aim of selling millions? At one point or another, lots of successful rock bands have been dubbed "corporate rock", from Kiss to Def Leppard, from Journey to Foreigner. The one thing they have in common is that they have sold millions of albums. "What that really means is that we ran our business much better than most bands of any standing did," Ross Valory commented. "This corporate rock image – good, bad or indifferent, whatever it was – was the result of the organisational skills and, in some cases, the new approaches to running a band as a business by our founding manager/partner and general creator of the concept of Journey, who is Herbie Herbert. And he set some standards in the industry that quickly became recognised by the people in the industry as an advantage and not a gift..."[129]

Gene Simmons probably learned a thing or two from Journey when it came to creating Kiss' multi-million dollar empire, and possibly Ron Smallwood – Iron Maiden's manager – learned some tricks as well. Lesser known rock bands such as Thunder eventually created their own little empires and did everything in-house. It has since become more widespread for bands to have full control. Mick Jagger, who studied economics, was intrigued by the empire that Herbie Herbert had created with Journey and wanted to take a peak inside Journey's world for inspiration.

Ross Valory: "He brought his staff to our corporate offices in San Francisco in the early Eighties and spent several days visiting with Herbie Herbert to learn from him how one runs a rock band smoothly. The idea is that Herbie simply made money for the band, without owing a lot of money, while owning most of what it took for the band to put on a show, including a trucking company, a lighting company, a sound company, and production company, which also provided for other organisations at the times when we were not using our staff and crews and equipment. And Mick came over to learn how it all worked, and Mick went home with some very good operating principles to apply to his own band…"[130]

Another route the band's manager took was to found a fan club, which he called Journey Force. Herbie Herbert: "They were pretty established, but *Escape* certainly cemented the deal. Unlike the rest of the band members – they thought I was crazy – I was always a 'Deadhead,' and now the Grateful Dead are getting acknowledged for their business acumen and for really having started the earliest of the social networking. I always felt I should be the manager of the Grateful Dead. Of course, I was such an unabashed capitalist that it probably wouldn't have worked out. I felt I was always more of a hippy than anybody. I just had a different philosophy: I believed that if you're anti-establishment the best thing to do with these corporations is to get them by the money. That's the only thing that they understood, and so I was into that style. I understood how effective the Grateful Dead's mailing list and fan-club activities were, and so I just wanted [to] emulate that and do it, but make it hipper and more professional, modernise it and computerise it and so forth.

"The Journey Force fan club was a very powerful entity… I don't believe I ever was able to describe it in a way that [made] the band members… understand its importance, so they always treated it like a pain in the ass, something to run. It costs money to run… [but] it makes money, and it did make a lot of money, but they always looked on it as a liability, as opposed to, 'This is your direct contact with your fans'. This is you in control: [there is] no record company or anybody between you and your fans. This is you going direct, and this is what really has the power. But they never treated it with respect, so the fan club was subsequently sold off to Tim McQuaid, the guy I had hired to run it. He started signing up other bands because everybody was envious of their fan club, and all of a sudden they had Aerosmith and all kinds of major bands. He changed the name from Journey Force to Fan Asylum so he could represent lots of other groups. It was very successful."[131]

While 1981 was hectic, 1982 was fairly relaxed by comparison. *Escape* continued to sell by the bucketload. Steve Perry passed comment on the album's success: "I think one of the reasons why it was such a successful album is because there was a certain type of acoustic texture… I think that had a lot to do with the palatability of the album. The way it went down. The way people liked it."[132]

The band were simply worn out and wanted to enjoy the fruits of their success. The fact is they were so damned popular in the US even the Disney empire wanted a piece of the pie: the band were asked to contribute songs ('Only Solutions' and '1990s Theme') to the 1982 science-fiction movie *Tron*, featuring Jeff Bridges and future *Babylon 5* actor Bruce Boxleitner. Neal Schon even found time during 1981-2 schedule to work with Jan Hammer on a couple of albums under the moniker Schon/Hammer.

Herbie Herbert: "1981 was a huge touring year and '82 was the first year ever we were not going to release an album in January, but I thought we should tour. The band was just the biggest band in America at that moment. I put this stadium tour together for '82 and the band came back and said: 'No, we don't want to do it. We've worked all these years, so hard; we want to sit by the pool and enjoy our success.' I said: 'You've got the rest of your lives to do that.' No matter what I did – and I was a pretty good speaker and very influential – I couldn't turn them around so I cancelled the whole tour, including many stadiums that had already gone on sale, so it was a pain in the ass. I went to my dear friend [concert promoter] Bill Graham. Bill Graham says, 'I won't hear of it, they can't do that.' I go, 'Yeah, they can Bill. They can do whatever the fuck they want.' He said: 'I demand an audience with the band.' No-one else would I even consider that for, but since it was Bill, I said: 'OK Bill, I've got a meeting with them at their rehearsal hall tomorrow, you come on down.' And he did and… I said: 'Bill would like to speak with you guys… give him your undivided attention for a few minutes; and so he came in and explained how important these two stadium shows of his were: he had the open stadium Day On The Green and the Rose Bowl in LA, which is a hundred thousand seater. He said: 'This is the centre piece of my summer.' They said: 'Well, we're tired. We just want to relax.'

Bill goes, 'You're taking the food out of my children's mouths... won't you please reconsider?' Steve Perry said no. And then Bill drops to his knees, clutching his hands in front of his chest and said: 'Steve, I beg you, at which point Steve Perry cracked like an ice cube and said: 'Well, OK, if Herbie can figure out how to make a stadium intimate then I'll do it, but if he can't, I won't.' Bill said thank you and ran with this little victory and left me with the task of trying to make a stadium intimate.

"In the next two weeks I came up with the idea of the large screen video, if it could be full colour and really high resolution and high quality. I didn't know a thing about video. I set out to study and learn as much as I could. In '82, it hadn't been thought of [yet] and researching things like this was very difficult... I figured it all out, figured I could do it, set about to do it. Nocturne, our video production company that I still own today, is the pre-eminent video production company in the music business."[133]

Journey – or rather Herbie Herbert and his staff – created the huge video screens that are common place these days with major touring acts of any musical genre. Indeed, thanks to their manager, Journey were at the forefront of many aspects of touring which are taken for granted today. Herbie Herbert: "We pioneered this technology. That's my thing, production, so they had somebody right there. I'm managing, but I'm right from the back of the truck and I want to be on the leading edge. Just like Steve Miller was the first national tour to have in-ear monitors and it created a whole revolution. No monitors on stage, no equipment on stage. Everything off stage, just drums and keyboards and that's it. No speakers on stage, nothing, clean, clean, clean stages, and I was certainly all about that in the Journey stage design. We carried our own stage and we were so oriented in sound, lights and production. We owned all that stuff, and you know, I'll tell you, it's somewhat of a phenomenon that, as egocentric as the music business is, other bands would unabashedly approach us for production services. They would swallow their pride and come to us and ask us to do it for them. Whether it was The Who on their farewell tour wanting their set designed and video on their '82 farewell tour, or Loverboy wanting us to do the lights for them and just various production services, we must have had 20 concert halls pay us to build barricades like ours for them for their venues. Our stage and our barricades and the design and they were portable and they were put together and they were bullet-proof. You could not bend or break these barricades and so you know, just good stuff like that."[134]

This advance in technology, which continued through the decade and beyond, led not just to Journey becoming one of the major stadium live acts of the early Eighties, but also paved the way for bands such as Queen, Kiss, Aerosmith and AC/DC. Bands that sold thousands upon thousands of tickets could recoup the enormous production costs that such a live show would entail not only through ticket sales but, more importantly, through sales of merchandise. However, while some bands used stage distractions - video screens, pyro, lighting - to overshadow the music, Journey managed to successfully balance the stage's visual grandeur with excellent playing and well-paced setlists. The term "stadium rock" then came into use in the Eighties, and reflected how Journey became a brand name and a vast money-making machine: five musicians and their management on tour, with around ten trucks filled with stage equipment and merchandise. They had close to 100 people to feed on a daily basis from the grippers to the road managers. Herbie Herbert was the mastermind behind the Journey machine and, for the most part, everything was ultra-professional and ran like clockwork.

In 1982 the band continued touring and did indeed play Day One of the Day On The Green in Oakland on June 26. They kicked off the year's schedule in Japan on April 9, flying to Canada for shows, with US tour dates beginning on May 11. They finished where they started, in Japan on July 10. Journey were more popular in Japan than any other country outside of the US before Perry joined the band; and just as Japanese rock fans had been loyal to Journey, Journey stayed loyal to them by regularly visiting the East Asian country. Other parts of the world, however, proved to be a tougher nut to crack.

Jonathan Cain: "I'd really like to see us break the Continent and Australia… [These] are about the only places in the world where we're not very successful. The last album really broke things open for us in Canada and Japan, so now we've set our sights elsewhere. I don't see why we shouldn't be just as popular in Europe as we are here [in the

United States]. But it's healthy for us to have places where we still aren't successful. With Journey, we'll always be looking for new worlds to conquer."[135]

With millions of records sold, hundreds of thousands of tickets sold, and a clutch of hit singles, Journey didn't really have to worry about where their next pay cheque was coming from. They didn't even have to rush into the studio for another album, but they did.

Neal Schon admitted: "This has all been great. I love money. I want to make as much money as I can. I have expensive tastes, and the only way to keep them happy is by making as much money as I can and then spending it. I just bought my third sports car – a Lamborghini that can do 210 miles per hour. That's one of the benefits of our success. People in the press and in other bands sometimes put Journey down, but I think a lot of them are jealous."[136]

The cycle of album-tour, album-tour remained as the band headed to Fantasy Studios in Berkeley, California in the middle of 1982 to record their next album with producers Mike Stone and Keith Elson. Following up *Escape* was always going to be a difficult task and perhaps there were some fans – most certainly critics – that were dubious about whether the band could pull off another success story like *Escape*. For some bands, success comes early, but after a couple of albums creativity tails off. For others – such as Journey, AC/DC and Kiss – there are many years of hard work and a string of albums before success eventually arrives. Of course, the hardest part about getting to the top, as the cliché has it, is staying there. Journey were at the top of their game in 1981–2. They were just about the biggest band in the United States so they had their work cut out for them on the next album.

During the making of what was to be called *Frontiers*, the band cooked up 17 songs, ten of which made the final cut. "I'd say that maybe a quarter of the material is written on the road. We are actually playing or rehearsing only about two hours a day. There is some time," commented Ross Valory.[137]

It took about two months to write and record the material for *Frontiers*. There are two ballads on the album which went on to become two of Journey's most beloved recordings: 'Send Her My Love' and the piano-led 'Faithfully', the latter most definitely a Jonathan Cain track. Producer Keith Olsen, who worked with The Babys, remembers the genesis of that song. "While we were cutting Tane's [Jonathan's then wife] album he said that ['Faithfully'] would be great for John [Waite]. I said: 'Well, do you have a demo of it?' And he said no, so I said: 'Let's cut a demo if it'. We sat down on an electric piano and a mic, and he just played and sang one pass through it. And he sang this song. I presented it to John Waite: 'Here John, this is from Jay (we called him Jay or Jon) for your solo record.' And so he listened to it. The song was 'Faithfully'. Now, that song was not recorded by John Waite. John Waite said to me: 'I'm not going to sing any song about any circus.' You remember the second verse 'circus life?' And I kept trying to say, 'It's not about a circus John, it's about the rock 'n' roll way.' And he didn't quite get it."[138]

Jonathan Cain: "It was a road song I wrote in Saratoga Springs, New York. That one began on the tour bus on a napkin. I took it to the hotel room and finished it up the next morning. I had this cheap Casio keyboard in the room and plunked around on it. I took it to soundcheck and thought it was a pretty good song. We – the crew and everybody, there was something like 70 of us on tour – we were all missing our families and I wrote it for everybody. I recorded a demo and played it for Steve and he wanted it for his solo record. I told him the song was about me and Journey, not about his solo record. Later, when we were recording *Frontiers*, the producer asked me if I had a ballad and I pulled out this song. And Steve was like, 'Oh, that song'. Steve put his brand of special magic on it. We did three takes. We never even rehearsed the darn thing. It took about forty minutes to write, honest to God. Not many of them came that easily. It's funny. You got to live your life and feel the feelings and identify them. If you can do that, it just flows."[139]

For guitarist Neal Schon, recording *Frontiers* was an emotional experience: "Some of it was really difficult for me to do. I had just finished going through a very difficult time with the lady I was living with, and when I was doing songs like 'Send Her My Love', I was really hurting inside. I had to wear sunglasses in the studio when we were listening to the playbacks because I was sitting there crying. It was a very emotional time for me, and I think that emotion is something that everyone who hears the album can relate to. Pain is a very universal thing."[140]

Frontiers would continue *Escape*'s balance between ballads and rockers, but in a typical Journey style, though they did want to offer fewer ballads than on previous releases. Jonathan Cain enthused: "I think the album is Journey's most daring and that the change is something we've all shared in. The sound is recognisably Journey, but with more fire than we've ever captured on tape before. It sounds real live, like a concert. Steve Perry did a lot of the vocals live, in an isolation booth, to help get that sound."[141]

Of course, there were some sides of Journey's fan base that felt Jonathan Cain had too much influence on the rest of the band and had made Journey's sound too commercial, too lightweight and too glossy, and they yearned for the Gregg Rolie days and the progressive elements he brought to the band in the *Infinity* to *Departure* years. What did Cain have to say about those comments?

Jonathan Cain said: "I've heard people say I've changed Journey. Some people don't like it, and some people do. I've had a lot of input, but so has Steve Perry and everyone else in the band. We all contribute to create the best album and show. On stage, the focus is on Steve Perry and Neal Schon, but we all have different colours that create an aura on that stage. Each night it's different. We're like actors in a play and we enjoy what we do."[142]

Perhaps *Frontiers'* standout track would be the magnetic 'Separate Ways (Worlds Apart)'. The song's co-writer, Jonathan Cain said of the song: "Steve [Perry] and I both wrote it. We wanted to write something rhythmic and still have a strong and haunting melody. We needed a main rhythm to run through the synthesizer and Steve Smith designed that kind of drum beat to let everything breathe. It's really a throwback to all of our roots and the Motown sound. Steve has always listened to a lot of Motown records, songs with a strong chorus approach, songs that were real urgent-sounding, but still had rhythm and melody."[143]

One song Jonathan Cain did write for *Frontiers* was 'Allies,' which the melodic rock band Heart ended up recording in 1983 for their *Passionworks* album. Cain remarked in 2001: "I just found an old copy of 'Allies', my original version, you know, and it's so funny because I did it on my little four-track so it's all hissy and stuff but I must've scared somebody because I wrote it for the *Frontiers* album, and it never saw the light of day. Steve Perry just refused to let me have a shot at it. We tried to do it as a duet, and it just wasn't his song, and it just sort of went down the wayside."[144]

Cain also admitted that he wrote a song with Eric Bazilian which Cain sang on but did not make the final cut because it did not sound like a typical Journey song.

Steve Smith remembered his influence over the direction of the album: "Steve Perry and I went in a lot and listened to the mix. If we liked it, we left it. If we didn't, we'd suggest changes, and they'd make them, and we'd finish the mix right there. We'd leave, and they'd go on to the next tune. We'd come in in the morning with a fresh perspective, and that's how we finished the mixes."[145]

For the drummer, working closely with the singer was an integral aspect behind the making of a successful rock album. He said: "When Steve [Perry] was singing, I was focusing everything through him to make him feel comfortable, to stay out of his way, and to support what he was doing. I was listening very closely to what he was singing and to his phrasing. I made sure that what I was giving him felt good for him. I could usually tell how he was singing and if the tempo was right. One of the more important things in working with a singer is that the tempo has to be right, so you can hear the words. With an instrumental thing, a lot of the times you can play tunes a little faster than the record, and it will still be OK. But with lyrics, the words can get squashed together, and you have to make sure the tempos didn't get too fast."[146]

Perhaps bassist Ross Valory summed up the new album's sound most accurately. He concluded: "*Frontiers* is a bigger step away from *Escape* that *Escape* was from *Departure*. It was more of an attempt to modernise the band's sound."[147]

And drummer Steve Smith commented: "I guess you would say that the first side of this album is for fans and the second side is for us. We wanted to test ourselves and see what we could do to build upon the music we've done before. We didn't want to make another *Escape*. That wouldn't have been fair. The fans would have probably gotten sick of it and said: 'Hey I didn't need to buy this. I already own the last one.' We didn't want that. That's why on *Frontiers* we really tried to pull out all the stops."[148]

Frontiers was unleashed in February 1983 and peaked at number two in the *Billboard* charts. It remains the band's highest charting album in the UK (number six) and it also charted in Norway, Sweden, Japan and Canada. Frontiers spawned the hit singles 'After The Fall' (number 23 in the *Billboard* Hot 100), 'Send Her My Love' (number 23), 'Faithfully' (number 12) and 'Separate Ways (Worlds Apart)' (number eight). "We've never gone out of our way to write hit singles," singer Steve Perry stated. "We all have a natural feeling for writing songs with strong melodies, so our music naturally goes in that direction. But we're not trapped by any particular sound. No one can say that songs like 'Back Talk' or 'Edge Of The Blade' are reminiscent of things that appeared on *Escape*. We've got to keep challenging ourselves to keep things interesting. That's what this album represented – a project that would be entertaining for us, yet enjoyed by our fans."[149]

Interestingly, the album's tracklisting was altered by Michael Dilbeck, the band's A&R man, who took out 'Ask The Lonely' and 'Only The Young' and replaced them with 'Back Talk' and 'Troubled Child'. Perhaps it was a twist of irony that both the omitted 'Ask The Lonely' and 'Only The Young' – which was released as a single in January 1985, charting at number nine in the US and used on the soundtrack to the film *Vision Quest* – became two of the band's most enduring songs. *Frontiers* became the band's second biggest selling album after *Escape* and went on to sell over six millions copies, a staggering amount by any band's standards.

"Nothing in this group happens by accident," said Herbie Herbert. "Journey trains for platinum albums the way athletes train to win gold medals at the Olympics. We even went so far as to go through a sensitivity training together so we could relate to one another and play together better."[150]

"It has a certain originality which occasionally takes it above the usual metalloid yawns produced by the legions of coliseum plod rocks, like REO Speedwagon, Foreigner, Nutzinger, etc," wrote Joe Fernbacher in *Creem*. "But it ain't metal like so many people like to believe it to be, and I just wanted to get that straight out front. Metal has more purity of essence, more power and less slickness. Journey is a band that relies more on intensity of production and lyric than on the leatherette unconsciousness of most nouveau bands. Thought I should point out that a few trad-metal bands, like Def Leppard, are beginning to cross over into Journey's turf to explore the possibilities of that next big thing: pop metal."

As referenced on his website, famed American rock critic Robert Christgau wrote in one of his *Consumer Guide* reviews: "Just a reminder, for all who believe the jig is really up this time, of how much worse things might be: this top ten album could be outselling *Pyromania*, or *Flashdance*, or even *Thriller*. Worse still, Steve Perry could run for the Senate as a moderate Republican from, say, Nebraska, where his oratory would garner excellent press – and then, having shed his video-game interests, ram the tape tax through. D+"

Frontiers opens with the alluring 'Separate Ways (Worlds Apart)' which has some distinctive keys, an incredible chorus and majestic melody. It remains one of the band's most iconic and widely played tunes. 'Send Her My Love' is a haunting ballad with an unforgettable melody, with Steve Perry at his most passionate. 'Chain Reaction' begins with a surprisingly progressive electric riff, and is certainly a departure for the band in that Perry's vocals are surprisingly aggressive. 'After The Fall' is memorable, though not one of their best ballads, with Perry singing in a slightly higher register than on other songs on the album. 'Faithfully' is beautifully crafted tune led by Jonathan Cain's controlled piano keys, and Perry sounds utterly entrancing. 'Edge Of The Blade' is an excellent rock ballad with a sturdy riff, a prominent bass line, an energetic vocal performance and some unforgettable keys. 'Troubled Child' is one of the least interesting songs on the album, while 'Back Talk' has an unmistakable groove and some excellent drumming. 'Frontiers' is a slightly experimental track compared to other songs on the album and it does have a certain charm, even though it sounds somewhat dated now. Finally, 'Rubicon' is an excellent track with some great guitar work, impressive use of the synthesizer and a catchy melody.

Frontiers falls short of *Escape* but remains a superlative melodic rock album with some of Journey's most perfectly conceived songs; it is undoubtedly an accurate representation of high-standard American melodic rock.

The band began a major tour of Japan on February 22, 1983, playing in Nagoya, Osaka, Fukuoka, Kyoto, Tokyo and Yokohama. A tour of the US and Canada commenced in Seattle on May 28 and finished on September 6 in Honolulu. They were supported by Bryan Adams throughout much of the tour.

Reviewing a show at the Reunion Arena in Dallas, one journalist wrote in the local *Fort Worth Star-Telegram*: "Drawing card that he is, Perry isn't the group's only talent. Neal Schon, lead guitarist and a hard-driving singer in his own right... and keyboardist Jonathan Cain's instrumental talents were displayed in a spectacular solo intro to 'Rubicon'. Drummer Steve Smith and bass guitarist Ross Valory also had their moments to shine."

Squeezed in between the opening and closing dates was a performance on June 4 at Philly's JFK Stadium with Bryan Adams, The Tubes and Sammy Hagar. The setlist for the tour read: 'Chain Reaction', 'Wheel In The Sky', 'Line Of Fire', 'Send Her My Love', 'Still They Ride', 'Open Arms', 'No More Lies', 'Back Talk', 'Edge Of The Blade', Jonathan Cain solo/'Rubicon', Steve Smith solo/'Escape', 'Faithfully', 'Who's Crying Now', 'Don't Stop Believin'', 'Stone In Love', 'Keep On Runnin'', 'Lights', 'Any Way You Want It' and 'Separate Ways (Worlds Apart)'.

The band continued to use the best in modern technology to make their shows as eventful as possible. "We've been using the screens throughout this American tour," Schon said. "They're great because now even people in the back can really feel intimate with us. If I start to blow on my guitar strings, they can all see that – not just the people in the first row. We're really into the video screens – in fact The Who rented ours during the last tour. We helped them set them up, and we think we can do that for all the major bands as well. It's another little side project that we're getting more involved with. You know the old saying, 'Busy bands are happy bands'."[151]

In the US the roar of the huge crowds at some of the nation's biggest venues was deafening, and Perry could not hear himself sing, yet the five members of Journey remained mystified by their lack of success in other territories, which is probably why they kept their touring schedule within the confines of North America and Japan. Neal Schon: "We've never been that big in England. It's hard for us to understand, but it's not something that bothers us. We'll go out and tour there and see what happens. I'm sure we'll have our share of fans. But even if we don't sell out the places we play that'll be alright. It's fun to still have a challenge like that. Those are the things that will keep Journey going for a long time to come."[152]

Meanwhile, during the *Frontiers* tour, there was growing tension in the Journey camp as egos clashed and power struggles over the future came into play. "During that tour," Herbie Herbert admitted, "he [Steve Perry] was really upset for the most part with this ongoing success, and me continually being right about all of these things. I had this grand plan that I presented before the *Infinity* album. I said: 'Here's the title of all of our albums – *Infinity, Evolution, Departure, Captured, Escape, Frontiers* and *Freedom*. And here's our artwork, fresh from Kelley/Mouse' and everything else. When we got to *Frontiers*, Steve really wanted to interrupt that. And he fought like hell to change the art and the imagery... I prevailed on the name, and he prevailed on changing the art. Which was still a merchandisable, space-alien kind of thing, but it was a real compromise from the quality of what our packaging had been. And it was our signature style. It was instantly recognisable. We had achieved that with *Escape*. *Escape*, the basic album package, shows up in stores, and you can't read Journey, or the name Journey anywhere, but there wasn't a soul that walked into a retail outlet that didn't know immediately that that was Journey... that's what should've continued with *Frontiers*. That's where he [Perry] really started to do that. At which point the meetings disintegrated into a pissing act between myself and Steve Perry and his attorney, with all of the other members of the band watching, like a tennis match. This is where I lost enormous amounts of respect for Neal Schon, Ross Valory, Jon Cain..."[153]

Despite what was going on behind the scenes, the *Frontiers* tour was a big success. Though Neal Schon and Ross Valory in particular were veterans of the live music scene, with careers that went back well over a decade, Steve Perry was little more than a novice when he joined Journey and the impact of their success was therefore much greater.

Herbie Herbert: "When he joined the group he was a fine vocalist and a decent composer, but not much of an entertainer. Now he's grown and really earned his place at the forefront of this band. And as far as the other guys are concerned, it shows how secure veteran stars like Neal Schon and Gregg Rolie are that they would let this new guy have the spotlight."[154]

As much as Schon enjoyed being on the road, Perry found it tiresome; singing each day required a high level of energy, while the vocal strength needed to sing Journey's growing back catalogue was evidently tiring on the frontman. Those songs, and the band's insistence on playing them in their original keys and vocal registers was becoming too demanding, as it would be with any singer. The increasing tension within the Journey camp came from Perry's desire to take over the band, to make the big decisions and perhaps change their sound. In order to affect this type of change Perry would have to be manipulative, playing the musicians and manager against each other for his own ends. Whatever his plans, they certainly clashed with Herbie Herbert's plan for Journey's future…

By the end of '83 the band had sold around 25 million albums, and along with fame came the consequence of celebrity, not least a malicious rumour that Steve Perry had cancer. Fans had already questioned why he had lowered his vocal register for the soundtrack release *Dream, After Dream* and it was noticeable that his vocal range was also obviously lower on *Frontiers*. Fans came to wonder about his health. A spokesperson for the band's management told the press: "Steve came down with laryngitis one night and had to cancel a concert. Maybe that's how the rumour started. People figured that because he had to cancel a concert it was something more than what was announced."[155]

However, for Herbie Herbert, the dawning of a new year was truly the end of an era. He says, "After Gregg left I knew it was only a matter of time, but I was able to get the *Escape* album out and get the *Frontiers* album out… By the end of '83 it was pretty much over."[156]

Perhaps more to the point, during the *Frontiers* tour the band even made a rockumentary called *Frontiers And Beyond*, which goes behind the scenes and offers exclusive interviews and live performances. "Now that *Frontiers And Beyond* video has an interesting legacy to it and I'm not sure if this is what you want to hear," Steve Perry told AOR enthusiast Rob Evans at *Powerplay* magazine, "but that video was put together by our manager, and at the time the group wasn't that pleased with it. He was sort of on a self-promotion of himself. You'll notice that there is very little to do with the band, he's talking about the crew and himself and his accomplishments. There wasn't a lot to do with the music. So maybe it has a tendency to paint a picture that is not necessarily true."[157]

Indeed Perry appears excluded from the rest on the band on the video, a lonely, isolated figure on his own. He explained: "There were definitely times where, on the road, I was a melancholy individual. I would keep to myself and would always be evaluating my life from moment to moment… I think that is was much more intensive, at that time, for sure."[158]

It's a fascinating slice of rock music history and offers an interesting slant on what it was like to be a major rock band in the early Eighties. Maybe the documentary should have been renamed *Frontiers And The End*?

Herbie Herbert: "At the end was Holleder Stadium, with everybody on stage waving and singing whatever… and Bryan Adams and Jim Vallance – and many many people in the industry were up there on that stage at the end. And that's where the movie ended I guess in a freeze frame of some sort. That was the end of that fucking band, right then and there, that very day."[159]

CHAPTER 4

The *Raised On Radio* Era
(1984–1987)

"Steve Perry, the tail kind of wagged the dog, and he really didn't give a shit about these guys and he still doesn't. He acts like somebody did something to him, in particular, me. I made him forty million bucks and he's gonna get even if it's the last thing he does."

Herbie Herbert[160]

When 1984 arrived, many of Journey's melodic rock peers had passed their peak. REO Speedwagon's career was coasting; their most commercially successful and well-known album remains 1980's *Hi Infidelity*, and though subsequent albums *Good Trouble* (1982) and *Wheels Are Turnin'* (1984) would do well, their career seemed to slide thereafter. Styx had folded by the release of their first live album *Caught In The Act* in 1984. Survivor were lucky when they hired new lead singer Jimi Jamison and scored a big comeback in 1984 with the fantastic *Vital Signs*, which produced the hit singles 'I Can't Hold Back', 'High On You' and 'The Search Is Over' before the 1985 hit 'Burning Heart' for the *Rocky IV* soundtrack. Britain's very own Def Leppard had achieved a massive hit with 1983's *Pyromania*, but it would be four years before they released a follow-up album, by which time Bon Jovi had stolen their thunder with 1986's *Slippery When Wet*.

Punk and progressive rock were the antithesis of each other, but both genres belonged to the past. In the mid-Eighties there appeared a slew of young, energetic and thirsty bands like Mötley Crüe, Quiet Riot and Ratt, and though not exactly expert musicians they nevertheless appealed to a younger generation of fans and seemed relevant at the time. Many of these bands fell under the banner of 'glam metal', which would peak by the late Eighties.

So what was Journey up to?

Steve Perry went off and recorded a debut solo album, *Street Talk*, which, with the help of Herbie Herbert, was a big success and made him even wealthier. For the rest of the band, however, it was tough. Having relied on Journey to make the kind of money that gave them luxurious lifestyles, they discovered that side projects and solo work failed to provide in the same way. Herbie Herbert: "They were not prepared … [for the lack of] work in '84 and '85 and so they had significant financial difficulties. I was able to escape but it was not easy on me either."[161]

Neal Schon contributed the song 'I Can't Stop The Fire' to the soundtrack for the film *Teachers*, with vocals by Eric Martin, who went on to co-found the melodic rock band Mr. Big, managed by Sandy Einstein who also worked for Journey at the time. Schon also toured briefly with his short-lived band HSAS (Sammy Hagar, Neal Schon, Kenny Aaronson, Michael Shrieve), who released their only album *Through The Fire* on the Geffen label in '84. Ex-Journey singer Robert Fleischman was busy with his latest project Channel, who released their self-titled debut album. A couple of years later Fleischman would go on to work with ex-Kiss axeman Vinnie Vincent.

During 1984, Herbie Herbert – at the request of the band because they needed the cash – liquidated certain assets, including Nocturne, the successful video production company which Herbie Herbert bought himself, knowing a good investment when he saw one. Neal Schon also invested in Nocturne.

Indeed, Nocturne is still owned by Herbert and Schon and remains a multi-million dollar company that deals with sound, lighting and video screens for major global tours by high-calibre artists, including legendary thrash metal band Metallica.

Herbie Herbert: "After the '83 tour, which was very, very successful, these guys just walked away, without any honesty. I would try to call Ross every now and then, and he wouldn't even call me back. I was like, 'What's the problem, man? What was happening? What are you doing? You don't come round, you don't show you're face?' And it turns out that Ross had made investments that were dependant on touring. He and Jon both [made investments] in '84 and '85, when there was no tour, and Steve Perry just wouldn't respond, and didn't want to work. We were having band meetings, and he was just like, 'You're making me feel like I have to work.' We're like, 'Well, we expected you to work. We expect you to do work. Is it so wrong to depend and rely upon each other?'... So, by the end of '84, he says, 'We feel like we're slaves. All these properties, and these production companies and everything else, I don't want to work anymore.'"[162]

Having sold off those properties, by the end of 1984 it seemed that Journey had effectively been shut down. Since the foundation of Nightmare – which was formed to service the needs of the band – in March 1973, it had taken 11 years to build up the band's name, image, brand and business and then it was mostly all for sale. But the band did not let slip to their fans what was really going on behind the scenes.

Neal Schon: "No way Journey's ending. We're all too committed to this band to ever let that happen. In fact, one of the reasons we decided to go off in separate directions for a while was to keep the band as strong as ever. You can get sick and tired of one another after a while. That's only human nature. We lived with one another for nearly nine months last year between recording *Frontiers* and touring the world. You can get really fed up with anyone after that much time. Actually, it's rather amazing that we still feel as close as we all do."[163]

However, Steve Perry did admit that the band did not always see eye to eye: "There are definitely run-ins with Journey, but that's what a band's all about. And the tension is good sometimes. It creates good music. We are a very strong-minded band, and I'm speaking of myself too. Collectively and individually, we're a bull-headed group."[164]

Moving into 1985 and Steve Perry had got his solo ambitions out of his system. Other members of the band had worked on their own projects too, including Jonathan Cain, who penned a couple of tracks ('Working Class Man' and 'American Heartbeat') for the Aussie AOR singer Jimmy Barnes on his album *For The Working Class Man*. It was time for Journey to reconvene, but would things be the same? Sometimes a break or a separation can be a good thing: it makes you realise what you had and gives you perspective; but at other times it makes you think that life offers more, and the chemistry is just not as strong as it once was. At least Journey fans managed to get their hands on a copy of 'Only The Young' in early 1985, the band's first single since 'Chain Reaction' the previous year, making it to number nine in the *Billboard* Hot 100. Ironically, the New York band Scandal had beaten Journey at their own game by releasing a cover of 'Only The Young', a track from their sole album *The Warrior*, the previous year.

Steve Perry: "To be perfectly honest, I think the band is ready to get excited about itself again. It needed something to rejuvenate itself, and I believe the hiatus was what we all needed. It's been healthy, very healthy, and the projects in between have been good for us all."[165]

The prospect of a new album from Journey was not something that had been on the cards, as Jonathan Cain explained in November 1986: "Three years ago this summer, there was no Journey. There wasn't going to be an album. There wasn't going to be another tour. The band was basically defunct."[166]

But, what exactly was the reason the band regrouped for a new album?

Steve Perry: "Well, Jon [Cain] called me on the phone, and said there were unfinished songs that weren't written. And it can't be over yet, because there seems to be too much of a creative drive, and, basically, that was some of the reasoning; but mainly, my mother was very ill… and she could barely speak at all, and I posed it to her, I said: 'I'm dumb-founded which way to go; what would you do?' And she said she'd do another Journey album, basically, and so that's why we got together…"[167]

By the time the band reconvened at Fantasy Studios in Berkeley during the latter half of '85, Steve Perry was in the producer's chair for what was to be called *Raised On Radio* (not *Freedom*, as Herbie Herbert initially planned) and, ultimately, he took control of the outfit.

Steve Perry explained: "It wasn't like some people thought, 'Steve's coming back into Journey to change things.' We were concerned that other producers might try and change the band's sound and I was for making it sound like Journey. I think the album reflects that. The group itself has changed a lot... but I'm extremely happy that it turned out sounding like Journey. I mean, it really does, even with the change, I feel really good about it."[168]

Perry admitted that it was not solely his idea for him to produce the new album: "We had a meeting, and everybody was really pushing for me to do it because they liked what I did with my solo album, so I went ahead and produced it. It really was a group decision, and it really more or less protected the value of letting everybody else have their production ideas involved too."

Songwriter and producer Randy Goodrum: "I co-produced Steve's vocals... I only worked with Steve and the engineer, Jim [Gaines]. Neal and Jon came by once, maybe twice. It was very clear to me from day one that my involvement was entirely Steve's idea. For me this was an entirely different experience than *Street Talk* as the tracks were already done. Also, it was a Journey record which is quite different in so many ways from the vibe of *Street Talk*; not better or worse, just different. Steve worked hard and ended up with great vocals."[169]

It was evident that Perry, the band, and Herbert were drifting apart during the early stages of *Raised On Radio*. Herbie Herbert admits: "When the record was half done, all the basic tracks were recorded, that's when they called me to say they wanted meet with me and say they wanted to change the bass player, the rhythm section. They wanted to get rid of Ross Valory and Steve Smith. That was Steve Perry driving that. Of course, that was the stupidest fucking thing in the world."[170]

What was Perry like to work with as a producer on *Raised On Radio*?

Herbie Herbert: "Bad attitude. If Steve Smith didn't play drums correctly, he was just on his high horse. I don't know that he gives interviews, or talks to anybody, or has anything to say, but how he would fucking justify his behaviour in '84 and '85 now? How he would explain... why is it Steve Perry wanted Ross Valory out of the band and Steve Smith out of the band? I think Steve Smith has been voted best 'All-Around Drummer' in the world four years running in *Modern Drummer*... I know what a brilliant talent he is. To kick somebody of the pedigree of Steve Smith out of your band, I think it's fucking hard to justify that now. Giving him the benefit of hindsight, what could have been [his] thinking?"[171]

Steve Smith admitted that his dismissal from the band was both confusing and deeply emotional and that the reasons were not clearly defined. "He [Perry] quit the band, and to get him to do another record, we agreed to his producing the record and that he could bring in anyone he wanted to play on it," said Smith. "Most of the material for this new record was written by Jonathan and Steve together or Neal, Jonathan and Steve together. The band ceased being a band..."[172]

However, months before the making of the album Steve Perry said: "Independently, I believe that everybody is as strong as the Journey thing. But independently there's an opportunity to just go and do something, or maybe it's easier for Neal to hook up with somebody else. But when you put us in the same room together there are times when we have to compromise and collaborate. This is what a group is all about."[173]

Jonathan Cain reflected on Perry's role as producer and the band's amended line-up: "I don't think it had that much ego involved, I think the responsibility did get to Steve [Perry] eventually, and he even threw his hands up in the air a couple of times, and it was hard. We all had to adjust and learn the roles that we had to play, as supporter, and pipe-in with your things... It [Journey] has its problems now. I don't think there is any utopian situation. A band's always going to be a band, and even if it's only three of us, it's still a band, and it still has its sticky moments."[174]

Nevertheless, Journey's manager still took care of the bassist – who was dismissed during the second week in the studio – and the drummer, who was forced to leave after a couple of months into the making of *Raised On Radio*. Herbie Herbert: "I forced him [Steve Perry] to pay them as if they were there on the tour and everything... that's what I

Journey circa 1978. Steve Perry surrounded by his new cohorts the year *Infinity* was released.

A young Neal Schon in Santana, circa 1969. (EDDIE KRAMER)

Santana (Neal Schon is slouched on the right). (PHOTOFEST)

The multi-talented Gregg Rolie in 1969. (BARRY Z LEVINE/GETTY IMAGES)

A close-up of bassist Ross Valory on stage. (ROBERT KNIGHT ARCHIVE/REDFERNS)

Journey on stage in LA: Ross Valory (bass), Neal Schon (guitar), Steve Perry (vocals) and Gregg Rolie (organ/keyboards). (DEAN MESSINA/FRANK WHITE PHOTO AGENCY)

On stage in 1977: drummer Aynsley Dunbar and guitarist Neal Schon. (RICHARD E. AARON/REDFERNS)

Neal Schon in the early days - despite Journey's future success Schon would rarely be recognised as a truly great guitarist by the mainstream press. (MOGANE/DALLE/RETNA PICTURES)

Steve Perry looking relaxed for the camera.
(BARRY SCHULTZ / SUNSHINE / RETNA PICTURES)

Manager and Journey mastermind Herbie Herbert.

Steve Perry doing what he does best – singing his heart out. (CHRIS WALTER/PHOTOFEATURES)

Bassist Ross Valory
(BARRY SCHULTZ/SUNSHINE/RETNA PICTURES)

Gregg Rolie – a somewhat unsung hero in Journey's legacy. (SUNSHINE/RETNA PICTURES)

Guitar wizard Neal Schon. (BARRY SCHULTZ/SUNSHINE/RETNA PICTURES)

Liverpool-born drummer Aynsley Dunbar. (BARRY SCHULTZ/SUNSHINE/RETNA PICTURES)

Journey in 1979: Steve Smith, Ross Valory, Neal Schon, Steve Perry and Gregg Rolie.

think you do for your people. There's very little chance that Ross Valory or Steve Smith would remember it let alone reciprocate, but that is the honest to God truth. I made sure they were taken care of."[175]

Though Steve Smith is credited in the album album's sleeve as having played drums on 'Positive Touch', 'The Eyes Of A Woman' and 'Why Can't This Night Go On Forever', Ross Valory had no input at all. However, according to Valory, he left the band on his own accord. He explained: "At that point the band was hugely successful and egos swell: there were struggles for power and control of the band's direction. In that setting, Steve Smith and I left. We'd had enough and I think it was probably a good time to do so."[176]

The band brought in additional studio players. Bassist Bob Glaub gave a helping hand and then Randy Jackson (who had previously made bass contributions to two tracks on *Frontiers*) came into the equation a few weeks into the making of the album. After a couple of months, drummer Larrie Londin, who had worked on Steve Perry's solo album *Street Talk*, joined the sessions and spent a couple of weeks tracking and redoing some of the parts Steve Smith had already laid down.

"Steve [Perry] just felt that what had been recorded didn't live up to the demos," admitted Smith. "On one hand, I wasn't completely surprised, because it wasn't fun going to work every day. There was so much tension. I felt a bit relieved to be out of that pressured situation... When they got Larrie, they wanted him to play everything again. When I heard Larrie was there for two weeks tracking, it was a terrible time for me. Nobody called me to talk to me about what was going on. It became very impersonal. I ended up calling the other members... It got so uncomfortable that my attorney was informed that they wanted me to retire from the band... I felt really hurt, personally betrayed, and really unappreciated. During the whole thing, it was, 'You're not happening.' I was constantly made to feel that I wasn't a good musician, and that hit me where I live."[177]

Larrie Londin explained: "I just got a call from Steve Perry one day to come and play drums. I've heard some of the stories that surrounded that album, but I think the whole thing was kinda blown out of proportion. The whole thing boiled down to the fact that Perry wanted to use a click track. I never knew whether Steve Smith refused to play with a click track because he felt it insulted him, or if he just couldn't handle it. I've heard both stories – but that's why they called me. I laid down the drum tracks and got my paycheck and that was the extent of my involvement."[178]

Certainly the drums on *Raised On Radio* turned out to be significantly inferior and less distinctive than on previous Journey albums. Steve Smith explained his contributions to the album: "They did very extensive demos of the songs at Jonathan's studio, complete with drum machine beats and bass parts that they specifically wanted. So I felt a lot less involved, and there was much less leeway in what I could contribute. They also felt that the parts they had come up with were integral to the tunes. First they said: 'Let's record the whole album with the drum machine and have you maybe put some parts on later.' They felt that the drum machine itself was part of the compositions. I started feeling that it wasn't a band, and it certainly didn't have the same band approach as when we wrote collectively."[179]

Looking back on his complete back catalogue with Journey pre-*Raised On Radio*, Steve Smith, who went on to have a successful career in the jazz field with Vital Information, said: "I really like what I played on 'After The Fall' from *Frontiers*. What I played on *Frontiers* is what actually started that tune. I came up with this drum feel, and we wrote the tune from that. That's not to say I don't like the other tunes, I do, but I think those tunes are very special. On the *Escape* record, I like what I played on 'Mother, Father', 'Don't Stop Believin'', and 'Dead Or Alive'. Those are my favourite performances. I can't remember very much before then. 'Walks Like A Lady' on *Departure* was something I really liked. I played brushes on that one tune, and that was pretty neat. I like a lot of the stuff on the live record *Captured*, and there's a Japanese album called *Dream, After Dream*, on which there are some really great performances."[180]

Jonathan Cain expressed his own thoughts on the album: "It's a blend of all the different things that have influenced us over the years. It's probably the closet thing to a roots album for us, although we're exploring some new territories and sounds."[181]

Raised On Radio, Journey's ninth album, was released in May 1986 and scored a batch of hit singles in the US over the course of the following twelve months: 'Be Good To Yourself' (number nine in the *Billboard* Hot 100), 'Suzanne' (number 17), 'Girl Can't Help It' (number 17), 'I'll Be Alright Without You' (number 14) and 'Why Can't This Night Go On Forever' (number 60). However, even the choice of singles caused some contention. Herbie Herbert: "I remember one time he [Perry] phoned me at my house and just went nuts about 'Be Good To Yourself' having been the first choice of a single off of *Raised On Radio*. And I said, 'It's a great song, it's a great production, it's great sound, it's Journey.' That was the problem. It sounds too much like Journey. Well too many of the other songs sound too much like a glorified Steve Perry solo record."

Raised On Radio was the band's lowest charting album in the US since *Departure*, peaking at number four in the *Billboard* 200 albums. In the UK it peaked at number 22 and charted in Sweden, Switzerland, Japan and Canada.

Rich Sutton wrote in *Song Hits*: "*Raised On Radio* is a fully fledged Journey record for better or for worse… Does it work? As I write this, *Raised On Radio* sits firmly entrenched in the top five. I guess so."

Howard Johnson wrote in *Kerrang!*: "This is a good album, proof positive of what a bloody fine act Journey are, have been and will be until the day sugar-sweet daddy in the sky gives 'em the final nod!… Indeed, *ROR* is much more akin to solo Perry than earlier Journey outings, an interesting mélange of styles all a-comin' home to roost in the AOR genre."

Raised On Radio opens with the unmistakably Journey-esque 'Girl Can't Help It', an intoxicating ballad with a wonderful melody. 'Positive Touch' is an upbeat Motown style track with a good guitar solo in the middle, and there's even a brief sax solo courtesy of studio musician Dan Hull. 'Suzanne' has a strong R&B flavour with a funky bass; again, it doesn't sound like classic Journey but it does have a memorable chorus. 'Be Good To Yourself' is a fantastic Journey-style rocker with some excellent keys, a strong melody, sing-along chorus and great guitar work; it's one of their best ever rock songs. 'Once You Love Somebody' soaks up yet more R&B/soul ingredients with a prominent bass line with plenty of groove and the chorus is quite catchy. By Journey's past standards, 'Happy To Give' is a distinctly average ballad, while the title-track offers a bluesy harmonica intro and a surprisingly sturdy electric lead riff; Perry's voice sounds a little tied on the higher notes but it's a good song. 'I'll Be Alright Without You' is a moving ballad with a haunting melody and passionate vocals. 'It Could Have Been You' goes back to the R&B and soul sound, but this time the guitar has just as much groove as the bass line; a curiously likeable track. 'The Eyes Of A Woman' is a below par ballad which furthers the R&B sound. The final song, 'Why Can't This Night Go On Forever', offers a surprising Jonathan Cain-led piano intro and, though it's not up there with the best Journey ballads, it's a good attempt. Perry is in fine form on vocals and the melody is tranquil.

Raised On Radio has some excellent songs and a slick production but it doesn't sound like Journey. Influenced more by Steve Perry than Jonathan Cain, it somehow lacks Neal Schon's distinctive touch on guitar, and needs a stronger rock sound to match Journey's usual standards. Some argued at the time that it was the weakest of the albums that feature Perry, and it remains a point of debate amongst Journey die-hards. Over 20 years later and with the benefit of hindsight, the general consensus of opinion seems to be that *Raised On Radio* is not the best album they released, but it's also not the weakest.

By the time of *Raised On Radio's* release Journey were beginning to sound somewhat dated. The latest breed of rock and metal bands, taking their cue from the hedonism displayed by Guns N' Roses, were hungry for controversy and thirsty to wreak havoc wherever they roamed. Some bands move with the times and soak up new influences, but between *Infinity* and *Frontiers*, Journey stayed within the boundaries of their trademark sound. *Raised On Radio* broke that tradition for them, but in the meantime thrash acts like Metallica, Megadeth and Anthrax had become far more appealing to young fans. Even Alice Cooper made a comeback in 1986 with the thoroughly enjoyable *Constrictor* album. Aerosmith made a major comeback in 1987 with *Permanent Vacation*, which spawned three massively successful singles: 'Dude (Looks Like A Lady)', 'Rag Doll' and 'Angel'. Ozzy Osbourne released the successful

The Ultimate Sin album in 1987 and Kiss scored a hit with 1987's *Crazy Nights*; and there was good business from Def Leppard and Bon Jovi with *Hysteria* and *Bad Medicine*, respectively. Rock and metal often cross fanbases so it wasn't uncommon to read about a heavy band like Metallica in the same music magazine that would cover Journey.

Though not as popular as they were when Valory and Smith were in the band, Journey retained a dedicated fan base, mostly on the younger side. Jonathan Cain explained: "We've always stayed with the kind of music we play best. We haven't tried to fool anybody, including ourselves. We were raised on radio – Motown, Bob Seger, the Four Tops, those kinds of things. They're parts of our lives, so that's all the way we sound… young people are our future, and if our music reaches them, if they like you or even know who you are, it's an honour. That's why we wrote 'Only The Young' – it was a homage to the youth. They're positive, they're fresh, they're unjaded. They just want to rock. We're not trying to be teenagers or teen idols."[182]

What naysayers at the time needed to understand was just how excellent the band were as individual musicians. Certainly Neal Schon was never given due praise during the band's peak years. Had they succeeded as a progressive jazz-fusion rock band, things would have turned out differently, and Schon would possibly have been cited as one of the top guitarists of the Eighties. But as it stood – and still stands – he gets little recognition when guitarists from well-known rock bands such as Queen or Aerosmith are regularly name checked. Herbie Herbert: "He's the most underrated guitarist to ever strap on a [guitar]. His touch could be the subtle nuance of everything he does when he plays. I mean, the guitarists know, and I think that his influence has been just pervasive… It's never been cool to say, 'My biggest influence has been Neal Schon'. I think that everybody that ever saw him is competing with him, and you can't. He's just so extraordinary. I mean there's a few guys, Steve Vai and Joe Satriani and Eddie Van Halen, but each one of them would probably tell you the guy [Schon] is a melody [wizard]."[183]

Nevertheless they still sold out venues all over the US when they kicked off the *Raised On Radio* tour. Joining Steve Perry, Neal Schon and Jonathan Cain on tour were two session musicians. Herbie Herbert:

"Randy Jackson, now the judge on *American Idol*, is who they chose [on bass], and Mike Baird, the drummer. I never watch *American Idol* but I hear he talks about Journey all the time. He was not right in Journey at all. It wasn't Journey; it was a Steve Perry solo [project]. After that, that was pretty much it…"[184]

Prior to joining Journey, Randy Jackson had worked with Jean-Luc Ponty, Taxxi and Keith Richards, while Mike Baird was a renowned drummer who had played in Ironhorse, Airborne, Airplay and Animotion.

The tour opened at Angels Camp in California on August 23, 1986, and closed with two shows on January 21 and 22, 1987, in Anchorage, Alaska. Speaking about the band's first show in Angels Camp after three years away from the stage, and given the drama that enfolded during the making of *Raised On Radio*, Jonathan Cain said: "Once we played and saw the reaction of the people and how much the band were really missed, that's when we saw that all the struggle was really worth something, because people still like this band. Our fans know that when we come to town, we'll give a total, professional act. When we get caught up in all this negative stuff, we have to realize, 'Hey, this is what it's all about. This is why we do what we do. This is why we go through all the trouble to get everything just so'."[185]

Perry had found touring exhausting as early as 1982, when Journey's schedule was very hectic and the band were among the biggest rock outfits in the US. It's no wonder he took time off in between *Frontiers* and *Raised On Radio*. "People made threats to him, and other things were happening that were very painful," Jonathan Cain said in 1993. "Physically being a singer is very demanding, and Steve isn't like Mick Jagger, just prancing around. He'd bleed a little every time he sang. I think he was tired of bleeding."[186]

Perhaps what surprised some fans of the band, certainly in hindsight given the apparent division between Perry and the rest, was that Journey played 'Oh, Sherrie' and 'Strung Out' from his 1984 solo effort *Street Talk*. "You know what," Neal Schon said, "to be quite honest about it, I did it because we had played one of my songs off of the record I did with Jan Hammer; we were playing 'No More Lies'. So I couldn't very well say, 'No I don't want to play something from your solo record,' because I had already done the same thing."[187]

They were supported by Honeymoon Suite, The Outfield and Glass Tiger on selected dates. Journey even allowed MTV to record the tour for a music documentary called simply *Raised On Radio* that included interviews and live footage. They had to cancel shows in Virginia on November 9 and 11 because Jonathan Cain was too ill to play.

The setlist for the tour looked like this: 'Only The Young', 'Stone In Love', 'Any Way You Want It', 'Girl Can't Help It', 'Send Her My Love', 'Open Arms', 'Still They Ride', 'Strung Out', 'Suzanne,' 'Lights', 'Wheel In The Sky', 'Raised On Radio', 'Ask The Lonely', 'Who's Crying Now', 'Oh Sherrie', 'Lovin', Touchin', Squeezin'', 'Jailhouse Rock' and 'Separate Ways (Worlds Apart)' with 'Be Good To Yourself', 'Don't Stop Believin'' and 'Faithfully' as encores.

The band – in particular bassist Randy Jackson – changed their look to one that seems horrendously dated now and which some fans, even back then, found difficult to take seriously. The smart jackets in primary colours and striped shirts seemed at odds with the attire of other rock bands at the time. Herbie Herbert: "It's pretty rough and they've actually showed videos of him [Jackson] wearing those clothes on *American Idol*. Hey dude, your lack of humility knows no bounds. I mean wow, that could be embarrassing. But I guess it's so dated that he, you know, and it's his link to credibility really. Everything else, well he was just a hired side guy there too."[188]

Randy Jackson was awe-struck by the power of Steve Perry's voice as he commented two decades later: "No one will ever be Steve Perry. He's one of the greatest singers to ever grace the microphone."[189]

They did not play any dates in Japan, Canada or elsewhere outside of the US, which suggests the road did not have the appeal it once had. Herbie Herbert: "I didn't go on the entire tour. My father died during that tour and just before that tour [Steve Perry's] mother died, so we all went out to the funeral for his mother."[190]

At the time of the *Raised On Radio* tour Herbert was busy with other projects. "They [Journey] just don't understand that there's something more to it than just writing songs and singing and playing, that business component of it, and… I was pretty much solely focused on that. All the other activities were done in the vacuum of their absence. They said, 'Well we're not going to, even after *Raised On Radio* in '86, I said, 'Fuck it then, I'm going to do this band Europe from Sweden.' I got the job for Kevin Elson to produce it, I'm going to break it, they released it, they failed, I'm going to rerelease it and make it a home run. I was playing it on the back of a band bus outside of the Rosemont Horizon on Journey's *Raised On Radio* tour, and Steve and Neal came into the back of the bus and said: 'Oh man that's tired and in the weeds. That'll never happen.' That was 'The Final Countdown'. It went fucking number one all over the world… then I did the Roxette project and that was very successful, almost dominated the charts there for several years."[191]

Asked if there was going to be another album, Steve Perry explained during the planning stages for the tour: "Probably so. I mean, at this point, we're just trying to be what we are, and stand by it, and go on the road and enjoy ourselves. I mean, this pre-time, making the album, rehearsing the show, getting it ready, building the stage, getting our crew designed: getting it done has been time-consuming, and a very, very emotional strain. The fun part now is just to go on the road and play, but that's where everything comes from first. So that's what we were looking forward to first before we think of anything else."[192]

Some have said the split – though it was never officially confirmed as a split, just a hiatus – was down to Perry. Steve Smith said: "I would have to say that it started with Perry's solo record, and how that experience really changed his approach as a musician/songwriter. In my opinion, he became more interested in being a solo artist and enjoyed the feeling of writing songs with maybe one or two other people, rather than a whole group situation."[193]

On the flip side of the coin, Steve Perry said: "No. I think the beginning of the end was when Neal started his solo career. Neal did a solo album, way before I was thinking about it, with Jan Hammer. And I said to Herbie, the manager, 'I think this is a bad idea' – that it would fracture the band on some level. And he said: 'No, he's got to do what he's got to do. I've tried to talk him out of it, but he wants to do it.' And then he did his second one, and I said: 'OK, look, if he does a second one, I'm probably going to end up doing one.' Then [drummer] Steve Smith wanted to do a jazz record. And the theory coming from Steve, and I kind of understood it, was that everybody'll go out and be able to express themselves musically in some other areas, and then when we reconvene, perhaps we will have discovered or found things that we can bring to the group to help the group evolve. And so I thought that was OK. So after Neal did his second solo album, I went to LA, and in about three weeks, I wrote *Street Talk*..."[194]

Relationships between Schon, Cain, Perry and Herbert at the time of *Raised On Radio* had sunk to an all-time low. There were both creative and professional differences. Perry, apparently, did not like Journey's music being used for commercials and other commercial endeavours, and he was plain tired of touring, which was affecting his health and, more importantly, his iconic voice. Enough was enough, he thought.

"I called Jon and Neal together," Perry explained. "We met in San Rafael, we sat on the edge of the marina, and I just told them, 'I can't do this anymore. I've go to get out for a while.' And they said: 'Well, what do you mean?' And I said: 'That's exactly what I mean, is what I'm saying. I just don't want to be in the band any more. I want to get out, I want to stop.' And I think Jon said: 'Well, just take some time off, and we'll think,' and I said: 'OK, fine.' And I just sort of fell back into my life. I looked around and realised that my whole life had become everything I'd worked so hard to be, and when I came back to have a regular life, I had to go find one."[195]

After the release of *Raised On Radio* and the subsequent tour, Journey fans did not expect to wait ten years for the next album from their favourite band...

CHAPTER 5

Separate Ways:
Steve Perry's Escape
(1988–1994)

"I said never again, never. I had burned out. I couldn't sing or listen to music for a year. I was oblivious."

Steve Perry[196]

After the release of *Raised On Radio* and the tour of the US to support the album Journey went into an indefinite hiatus. However, to keep fans happy Columbia released the sublime *Greatest Hits* collection in November 1988. It remains one of the most perfect collections of hit songs ever assembled, with a mouth-watering track listing for fans: 'Only The Young', 'Don't Stop Believin'', 'Wheel In The Sky', 'Faithfully', 'I'll Be Alright Without You', 'Any Way You Want It', 'Ask The Lonely', 'Who's Crying Now', 'Separate Ways (Worlds Apart)', 'Lights', 'Lovin', Touchin', Squeezin'', 'Open Arms', 'Girl Can't Help It', 'Send Her My Love' and 'Be Good To Yourself'.

Journey's Greatest Hits went on to become one of the biggest selling albums of its ilk, shifting over 15 million copies since its release and spending 750 weeks in the *Billboard* album charts up to 2008. It continues to sell between half a million and a million copies per year, and as of 2010 was in the top ten biggest selling greatest hits collections in the US. Of course, the success of *Journey's Greatest Hits* gave rise to criticism from skeptics who said that Journey – like Queen – are a singles band that never made a great album, only select songs. They are wrong, of course. Journey – like Queen – recorded some wonderful albums that continue to strike an emotional chord with the listener; *Escape* and *Frontiers* spring immediately to mind. For Journey's *Greatest Hits* collection, the compilers were astute and hand-picked the band's most immaculate recordings. One error Journey could still make is to release a sequel just as Queen did; *Queen's Greatest Hits II* is a strong set, but they really milked it with the third lackluster collection. Journey have stuck with one volume so far, and rightly so. Although there have been other collections featuring the band's songs in selected territories around the world, the original 1988 collection remains the most finely crafted. The collection kept the band in the limelight when nothing was happening and the members were off doing their own thing.

Steve Perry seemed to go into hiding for a while, but Neal Schon and Jonathan Cain kept busy. Speaking about the chemistry between the pair, Herbie Herbert said: "To me it's always been a situation where I felt from way back that they should just move on from Steve Perry."[197]

Moving on from Perry is exactly what they did after the *Raised On Radio* tour. Schon and Cain hooked up with Jimmy Barnes for his *Freight Train Heart* album in 1987, not only playing on the album but the co-writing a whole bunch of tracks for the Australian singer, with some help from Randy Jackson. In 1988, Schon and Cain – with singer John Waite and bassist Ricky Phillips, both formerly of The Babys, and powerhouse drummer Deen Castronovo – created the melodic rock supergroup Bad English and released their excellent self-titled debut album 1989, followed by a disappointing second and final album *Backlash* in 1991.

Herbie Herbert had been busy getting Swedish duo Roxette a deal in the States and they went to number one in the *Billboard* album charts with 1988's *Look Sharp!*. He had also been hired by Mr. Big and in 1989 got them a deal with Atlantic. Though their self-titled 1989 debut album was not a massive hit, their follow up, *Lean Into It*, was their breakthrough album, getting to number 15 in *Billboard*. Their first album also features a songwriting credit for Jonathan Cain on the track 'How Can You Do What You Do'.

Herbie Herbert: "The first single was 'Addicted To That Rush' [from *Mr. Big*]. I was bold. I wanted to have the real thing. I didn't want to homogenise those guys, but eventually if you want to have broad-based appeal you've got to go with something that gets you that hit. And you know, 'To Be With You' [from *Lean Into It*]... boom. All of a sudden they sell ten million records around the world. So how do you argue with that?"[198]

Meanwhile, in 1990, Gregg Rolie, Steve Smith and Ross Valory created a new band called The Storm, fronted by former 7070 singer Kevin Chalfant, who has always claimed Journey to be a major influence on his voice and career. Managed by Herbie Herbert and Scott Boorey, the band was – and remains so, despite their obscurity – popular with long-standing fans of Journey and melodic rock/AOR in general.

On forming in the Bay Area, the band signed to Interscope under the umbrella of Atlantic Records in 1990 and released their self-titled debut album in 1991. Produced by the celebrated Beau Hill, the album was not a commercial success, peaking at number 133 in the *Billboard* 200, but did give birth to a couple of rock radio hits: 'I've Got A Lot To Learn About Love' and 'Show Me The Way'. But before they even went on tour, Steve Smith quit and was replaced by Ron Wikso.

Ron Wikso: "I was in Cher's band at the time and I had been referred to Herbie Herbert by four other drummers, including Deen [Castronovo] which was really nice of him. The others who recommended me were Steve Smith (who was leaving The Storm), Pat Torpey (who was in Mr. Big at the time) and Mickey Curry, who was playing with Bryan Adams and who asked their manager, Bruce Cohen, to call Herbie about me. I wound up having to audition for the band, along with about 30 or 40 other guys, and I hit it off with Gregg, in particular, right away. There was an initial audition and then a call back, where they listened to me and one other guy – Bobby Borg – and I was asked to join the band.

"At the time, I wasn't entirely sure if it was the right thing to do because I was making good money playing with Cher but I thought that joining a band with people like Gregg and Ross, with managers like Herbie Herbert and Scott Boorey, was an opportunity I shouldn't pass up. If the band took off, I would do a lot better than I ever could as a sideman with Cher. We had actually just started rehearsals with Cher for a European tour and I had to tell her that I was leaving right in the middle of that, but she was pretty cool about it. I actually wound up playing with her again only a few months later because she didn't like the drummer who replaced me for some reason. It so happened that they fell right in the time periods where The Storm wasn't working so I wound up doing both tours that year!"[199]

The band began touring the United States in March 1992 as support for Bryan Adams as well as supporting dates with Peter Frampton, Eddie Money and Tom Cochrane.

In 1993, The Storm recorded their second – and final – album *Eye Of The Storm*. Ron Wikso remembers: "Well, I co-wrote two of the songs, which was great fun and one of them – 'Waiting For The World To Change' – was actually chosen to be the first single so I was really excited about that. Unfortunately, Interscope decided not to release the album so that was a big disappointment. I still think that record has a lot of great stuff on it and just never got the attention it deserved. We did pre-production rehearsals at our rehearsal facility in Petaluma, California, and then recorded all the basic tracks at Fantasy Studios in Berkeley. Nigel Green co-produced it with us and Bob Marlette and Nigel engineered it as well, which was great... he was Mutt Lange's engineer and worked with Mutt on Def Leppard, Bryan Adams and whole lot of other big records. The record was mixed at Battery Studios in New York City."

Drummer Wikso recalls a couple of anecdotes from the *Eye Of The Storm* recording sessions: "I remember meeting BB King and Robert Cray, who were recording in another studio at Fantasy. I also remember Gregg telling me, after I had recorded all my drum tracks in about three or four days, that Kevin had tried to get them to hire Mickey Curry (Bryan Adams' drummer) to play on our record instead of having me play on it.

He told me that his response to Kevin was something along the lines of: 'Were you on the same stage I was last year?' I really appreciated Gregg sticking up for me, plus he viewed it as a band and he wasn't interested in having a session guy come in. He also told me that Kevin later admitted he'd been wrong about it, which was nice to hear as well."[200]

So, why wasn't *Eye Of The Storm* released in the year it was recorded?

Ron Wikso: "The industry was changing direction, musically, and they were changing with it. This was around the time that the focus was moving towards grunge and rap. We were a whole other kind of music that didn't fit that, so they just didn't want to release it or support it, despite having spent over $250,000 on it."[201]

After the band had folded, *Eye Of The Storm* was eventually released in the UK in 1996 through Music For Nations. Avex/Bareknuckle released it in Japan in 1997 and Miramar released it in the United States in 1998.

Back in the world of Journey, Steve Perry reunited with the band (well, Neal Schon and Jonathan Cain) on November 3, 1991, to perform 'Faithfully' and 'Lights' at concert promoter Bill Graham's wake, following his death in a helicopter accident. The free concert, held at Golden Gate Park, was dubbed 'Laughter, Love & Music' and saw performances by Santana, Grateful Dead, John Fogerty, Crosby, Stills, Nash & Young and others.

Herbie Herbert remembers that day: "He [Steve Perry] was a complete jerk to everybody and what was really stunning is he was late and I remember… he says, 'OK, what songs?' And I said: 'Well, we were thinking about these songs, 'Don't Stop Believin''…' He said: 'Okay, well tell Jon and Neal to transpose them down two whole steps… So you have them drop the keys and you write out the lyrics for me.' This is 1991 and he didn't remember 'Lights' or 'Don't Stop Believin''. I don't know these songs so I had to figure out the lyrics, write 'em down within an hour before they're supposed to go on and perform in front of how ever many people were in Golden Gate Park. What I said once in an interview – and I don't do these interviews very often – is, 'You know, all you people that think it is just sour grapes that I say these ugly things about your beloved Steve Perry, well, surely, if there's a couple hundred thousand people in the park, somebody [would have] recorded Journey's performance that day? Get a hold of it and you will hear a horrible, wretched performance.' If you go to your piano and put the CD on and determine the original key and the key in what he was singing that day. It's two steps down and he still can't sing, he still can't sing the notes."[202]

After that performance, the band again went their separate ways. The music that was popular during Journey's peak was a world away from what was popular after Bill Graham's wake. Rock and metal music for the most part became a trend of the past, replaced in the early Nineties by grunge from immensely popular bands, many from the Seattle area, like Pearl Jam, Alice In Chains, Soundgarden, Temple Of The Dog, Mudhoney, Mother Love Bone and, most especially, Nirvana. Their music was the antithesis of what bands like Journey had to offer: introspective, brooding, angry and angst-ridden, with distorted guitars creating a wall of aggressive backdrops. Canadian singer-songwriter Neil Young was so enraptured by it that he made a major comeback with 1990's *Ragged Glory* recorded with Crazy Horse. Grunge bands often spoke about their loathing of Eighties rock and metal bands, especially those from the Sunset Strip that came under the banner of hair/glam metal. However, it was startlingly obvious that some of those grunge bands – in particular Alice In Chains and Soundgarden – owed a huge favour to rock and metal bands of the 1970s. "During my break," Neal Schon commented, "I watched the whole music scene radically change. But grunge – to me, it just never entered my soul. I saw rock 'n' roll greats – the early Who, Jeff Beck, Jimi Hendrix, Cream – and to me the whole grunge thing didn't come anywhere close to that. It was pointed in a dark, ugly direction. I didn't see the musicality in it."[203]

Schon, meanwhile, continued to keep busy during the long lull in Journey's career, hooking up with the melodic rock band Hardline (also featuring Deen Castronovo) for their debut album *Double Eclipse*, released in 1992. That same year Journey fans were treated to the box-set *Time3*, which takes the listener on a chronological journey through the band's history from 1975 to 1992. It peaked at number 90 in the *Billboard* charts, and features several unreleased tracks and alternative versions. Following his collaboration with Hardline, Schon (with Castronovo and bassist Todd Jensen) hooked up with former Free and Bad Company singer Paul Rodgers in 1993 for some live shows and released the live five-track CD *The Hendrix Set*, which was recorded at Bayfront Park in Miami on July 4. Castronovo, who was discovered by Journey's former lightning director Ken Mednick, manager of the Oregon metal band Wild Dogs, which Castronovo wound up playing drums for, would later play a significant role in Journey.

Herbie Herbert recalls being impressed by the drummer's eclectic talents when Rodgers' band went on tour with Steve Miller, who was then also managed by Herbert. "Watching and working with Deen every day on that tour was just a joy. The guy's not just a monster drummer, he's a monster singer and he's a monster everything. One day I was in the production office and he walks in and he gives me this funny look and there's several guitars on stands. He pulls up an electric guitar, taps me on the shoulder and says, 'Watch this!' goes down on one knee and plays 'Eruption' by Eddie Van Halen note perfect, [then] puts the guitar down. It's the first and last and only time I ever saw him with a guitar in his hands. But you don't just pick up a guitar cold and play 'Eruption'. I think Deen is just awesome. I remember standing on the side of the stage one time with Sammy Hagar and we were both watching Deen play and he was grabbing me going, 'Herbie, the guy is just stupid good'. He really is. I love him."[204]

A big surprise came in October 1993 when Neal Schon and Jonathan Cain, along with singer Kevin Chalfant, performed at a private dinner for Herbie Herbert at Bimbo's in San Francisco. It was then suggested that the trio, along with Steve Smith, Ross Valory and Gregg Rolie, would reform as a new line-up of Journey. "Journey is probably the most talented collection of musicians that I have ever seen or had the wonderful opportunity of working with," Chalfant enthused. "I love them and consider them all a part of my family. I am not looking back with bitterness. They have opened many doors for me and I will only hold them in the highest regard. They make choices as we all do. They made theirs and must live with it, so must I."[205]

"Kevin was very good," says Herbie Herbert, "and Kevin was probably a better choice than [future singers] Steve Augeri or Jeff Scott Soto but is not as good as Arnel Pineda."[206]

Skipping to 1994 and Steve Perry released his underwhelming second solo album *For The Love Of Strange Medicine,* and commenced a North American solo tour that ran in to 1995. However, it was obvious to many that his voice was not as strong as it once was. "And you know, it just goes away. It's a muscle, it's something that has to be exercised and trained and to get to that level of conditioning its hard work," commented Herbie Herbert. "And you know I think Steve Perry's really tried. When he had a solo career and his solo tour he tried to do it. I've heard that he's gone to the greatest vocal teachers and got the best help that you can get and it's just not there anymore."[207]

CHAPTER 6

Can't Tame The Lion: Steve Perry And The Return Of Journey (1995–1997)

"We've all done our own separate projects. But when you put a band together, there's a different kind of energy that happens. And that energy was there."

Steve Perry[208]

The year 1995 turned out to be a busy one for Journey and their fans. While Mariah Carey released a cover of 'Open Arms', a massive hit for her, which kept Journey in the press, and Neal Schon released his second solo album *Beyond The Thunder*, bigger things were afoot.

"We were kind of at the top of our game when we split," said Steve Perry. "It's not like some bands that break up at the valley of their careers. I'll take responsibility for the break-up. The merry-go-round was going real fast. Musically, we'd said everything we were going to, and bands interacting the way we do, we needed a break – maybe for forever."[209]

It turned out otherwise. In 1995, Perry himself made the surprising decision to rejoin Journey on the condition that Herbie Herbert would no longer be their manager.

Herbert Herbert told the author:"They came back and said:'We want to reform now.' At which point it had been five years almost since I'd seen Steve Perry at Bill Graham's wake and he was an arsehole then, and almost ten years since we had worked and toured together. I looked at Jon Cain right in the eyes and Neal Schon right in the eyes, I said: 'Look, if you guys want to go forward and reform Journey I'll help you. You'll have to make that offer to Steve Perry…' I'll always describe their relationship to Steve Perry as this: they could be drowning in the middle of the ocean and Steve Perry would come along in his luxury liner and offer them a life raft. If they had any self-respect at all they would have to decline the life raft. Any event that Perry accepts and says, 'OK, I'll tour again' then I'll set it all up, but 'Gentleman, I'll [bail] out. I'm not going to work with him again.' I've had nearly ten years of bliss not having to deal with that guy…"[210]

With Herbie Herbert out of the picture, in October '95 the band hired the managerial services of Irving Azoff, who at the time of writing in 2010 is chairman of Live Nation Entertainment. He represents, or has represented, such artists as The Eagles, Steely Dan, REO Speewagon, Van Halen, Bush, Alter Bridge and Guns 'N Roses. He is one of the most powerful men in the music business.

The most famous and successful line-up of Journey – singer Steve Perry, guitarist Neal Schon, bassist Ross Valory, keyboardist Jonathan Cain and drummer Steve Smith – began work on Journey's tenth studio album, the first that particular line-up had recorded together since 1983's *Frontiers*. Rehearsals commenced in October.

"That's the quintessential line-up," commented Perry, "although, I don't want to take any credibility away from the line-up that existed with Gregg Rolie and Aynsley Dunbar. That was the earlier line-up that I joined and had its own musical direction that was valid. It was a different kind of a band, then it changed when we got Steve Smith in there and Gregg Rolie stayed. Then we got Jonathan Cain and I think the band turned a bigger corner. That became the *Escape* line-up that launched itself to another series of albums, songwriting and performing that was bigger. By bigger I mean it had a bigger pronounced sound to it... a mightier unity of the players than the previous one."[211]

As always in the music industry, there were some politics involved, as Ross Valory explained: "The reuniting of the band in 1996 consisted of the members that made the band the most famous. That was the agreement with the management team and the record company. That's what was asked for. There were some complications."[212]

Drummer Steve Smith admitted he was apprehensive about joining the band after his dismissal during the making of *Raised On Radio* back in the mid-Eighties. He explained: "As far as I can tell, how we got back together started with Columbia first working towards reuniting Steve with Jonathan and Neal, and then including Ross and me in the mix. It was difficult to get it off the ground initially. Steve was happy doing a solo project, as were the other guys. Eventually Steve got interested, and he really was the crucial piece. The rest of us had had some dialogue about whether we'd be interested in doing something like this if the opportunity arose. The other members were into it. When he consented to get together with everybody, we went into a rehearsal hall in LA and just played."[213]

He continued: "Actually, the story there was that we were supposed to play on a particular day in September of '95, though we were going to get into town the night before and set up the instruments on the rehearsal stage. But you can't get people to just set up their stuff and not start playing. So it ended up that the four of us set up and started jamming right away. We had a list of some of the old Journey tunes we were going to play, which none of us had played for all those years. We were having a lot of fun, and then Steve Perry called to find out what was going on, and we said: 'Come on over'. So it actually started a day early. He came over, we ran through a bunch of the songs, and it felt really good. The next day we got together again and played, and the chemistry was instantaneous."[214]

However, Steve Perry tells it somewhat differently. It was A&R guru John Kalodner who reportedly enticed Cain, Schon and Perry into reforming. Kalodner, a noted Journey fan who has often said Steve Perry is his favourite singer (along with Robert Plant and Steve Tyler) came up with the notion of getting the band to talk to each other again when he was remastering their albums for Columbia. "I was excited... [Jonathan Cain's] number hadn't changed. I hadn't talked to him in years and I said: 'Just listen man, before it's too late. For reasons God only knows, there's a lot of people out there who love us, and I saw some of them not too long ago. Maybe it's time to try again.'"[215]

After Perry met Cain in a coffee shop to discuss reforming, Schon was brought into the picture and they began the process of writing. "That was the first thing we had to do – see if we had the spark to write again," said Perry. "If that was there, perhaps instead of putting together a touring campaign, which is not what this is, we could come back as a real band. That's exactly what we've done."[216]

It was then a matter of rekindling their friendships, letting bygones be bygones and sorting out the legal side of the reunion and all the necessary paperwork. Each of them had got their solo yearnings out of their systems though Perry did admit: "Individually, none of us made the magic as magically as we collectively make it together."[217]

Trial By Fire – as the album was named – was recorded in early '96 at The Site and Wildhorse Studio in Marin County, and Ocean Way Recorders in Los Angeles. The band hooked up with the celebrated South-African born producer/recorder Kevin Shirley who, before he moved to the United States, produced Silverchair's debut album *Frogstomp* in Australia where he had lived since 1987. His first production credit, however, was in 1983 for Robin Auld, the South African singer. Now based in Malibu, Shirley was not the band's first choice however but was brought to Journey's attention at the request of Columbia. Initially, Journey had other producers in mind: Mike Clink, whose credits include Guns N' Roses, Glen Ballard who has worked with No Doubt and Alanis Morissette, and Ritchie Zito, famous for his work with Heart and Poison. Perhaps it made sense for the label to use Shirley because he was not particularly a fan of the band and thus had no preconceptions towards them and their back catalogue. This would also be the first time Journey had worked with a producer who was also a musician, so Shirley had much to bring to the table; he was interested in bringing a different musical aspect to the songs as well as the personalities of the members of the band.

However, because of how the band had worked in the past and the nature of Shirley's work ethic, there was some tension, as there often is in band situations. Journey always worked hard on pre-production, working on demos, trying out ideas, and rehearsing songs that were near completion. At one point they had around 30 songs near completion, which they then cut down to 18 and then down to 16 that were ready to be recorded, which in the end took four months. They were so well prepared they knew how to play the songs live before any recording was actually done.

Neal Schon explained the way Journey had made albums in the past: "With the exception of a few songs, Journey has never really gone into the studio and cut rhythm tracks, or laid down the drums and a bass and a rhythm guitar and then go back and overdub. We always just go in and play live, and I play live solos and then I go back and put rhythm guitars on later. Or if I need to clean up the rhythm guitars, I'll do that later... I know for myself it's better to catch me live as far as soloing and stuff like that and actually jamming with the band."[218]

However, when they were actually ready to record those tracks with Shirley, the producer wanted to try a different approach. Steve Smith: "He [Shirley] wanted us to rehearse the stuff like we were a young band," said Steve Smith, "and get the music to the point where we had it just about memorised and could perform all the songs like a set. That is something we used to do way back when, but we didn't want to do it this time. So there was a lot of grumbling, but we did it. We spent three weeks rehearsing the songs that had already been written."[219]

The disagreements that Smith hinted at were echoed by Steve Perry: "We didn't know if we'd get in the studio and chew each other's faces off or be grateful to be back together. There were some clashes. Democracy is a nice concept, but it doesn't work easily in rock bands... It's amazing how many changes happen in the process toward the final CD. It makes the journey worthwhile."[220]

Kevin Shirley explained: "I tell you what, that band is fantastic. I'd be sitting in that room in San Francisco, and Journey would play this album for me every day for six weeks. It was a lot of work, but it was such a treat at the same time. They were magnificent musicians. The cool thing was when we got into the studio, they just played the songs. There was a lot less for me to do at that point than just wait for magic to happen. The song that was the biggest hit on there was all one take, including the guitar solo. You'll hear the guitar starts when the solo kicks in – that's Neal [Schon]. He stops playing rhythm, plays his solo, then goes back to playing rhythm. That's the band playing. We later overdubbed an orchestra on it."[221]

Jonathan Cain commented on the making of the album: "He [Kevin Shirley] was stunning. He had a lot to do with the arrangements, and we worked hard with him. We were done with the basics in about two and a half weeks. It was pretty amazing. It was all live, we played live at the site. We had these isolation rooms for the drums, and guitars and keyboards even. But we could see each other and played live. Most of the record you hear is live. The overdubs are just little things here and there. You know, like backing vocals and a lot of the vocals. Steve [Perry] kept some of the things we did live."[222]

For drummer Steve Smith, regrouping with his former bandmates required some research. He read a biography of Sam Cooke, probably Steve Perry's biggest musical influence, and listened to a lot of early American blues, which had a profound affect on Neal Schon, as well as Schon's heroes like Eric Clapton and Jimi Hendrix. Smith said: "When I realised this reunion was inevitable, I decided to really do my homework on rock 'n' roll. When I first joined the band in '78, I was coming from more of a jazz background, with pretty limited rock 'n' roll knowledge. I knew of the groups of the sixties, like Hendrix, Cream, and Led Zeppelin, but I had never done any major research on rock 'n' roll history. I had done that with jazz. In the last few years, I really traced the roots of the instrument, the music, and the different players. When I first joined Journey, I played the music intuitively I was sort of a toned-down fusion drummer at the time. But for this reunion, I decided to approach the music from a completely different perspective, more from the roots of rock 'n' roll."[223]

Steve Perry himself said of the songs: "We figured that if the songs came together and were as honest as the early ones, then we'd have a reason to make an album. We didn't want to resurrect a dream just to put it on life support."[224]

For Journey, the idea of getting together was only going to happen with the intention of producing a new CD. "Some of the other bands that have reunited in the past," said bassist Ross Valory, "have more relied on a few new studio cuts and a live recording. I think Journey took a bigger step, in recording material that was completely new and didn't rely so much on our past popularity. And I think we're better off with that, too."[225]

Neal Schon passed comment on what it was like working with Steve Perry after many years apart: "It was great, working with Steve again. Really. You know, he's definitely the voice of Journey. And it was great to get creative with him again. It had been a long time since we really hung out and played together. We used to have a lot of things going on between him and me on stage, a lot of exchange. Because my guitar playing, I think, in Journey, is an extension of his vocals."[226]

Kevin Shirley explained the chemistry between the band members in the studio during the recording of the album: "One of the amazing things is that you'll often find that the best creative teams generally get out of the studio and diss each other terribly."[227]

"We became very close just friend-wise as well as musically," said Schon on the relationship between the producer and the band, "and he became a good friend of the band…"[228]

Also, as the band and Columbia were gearing up for the release of the so-called reunion opus, the label reissued eight of Journey's best-selling albums, along with Perry's *Street Talk* album, to drum up support for *Trial By Fire*. Special stands were made that held all eight albums, including the *Time3* box-set, which were erected in retail stores all over the US. Journey was still one of the country's most loved rock bands. The label was really keen to milk the Journey reunion for all its worth.

There was a state of heightened anticipation for a planned tour, as Perry said: "We're still clearing up some of our past legal ties. Some were in the way of the re-formation and have gotten cleared, and some have yet to be cleared. But my [hope] is that we will tour in the early part of 1997."[229] However, it was not meant to be.

What certainly did not help sales of the album was the fact that the band did not – could not – actually go on tour to support it. Speaking about what turned out to be his last proper gig with Journey in Anchorage, Alaska at the end of the *Raised On Radio* tour on January 22, 1987, Perry said: "I remember signing autographs… I knew that was the last autograph I'd sign in a while, so I stayed up 'til 3 am signing everybody's everything just because it was the end of the road. I was depressed for weeks after that."[230]

Journey fans, too, would be depressed for years after that.

Much to the frustration of fans the world over, and indeed members of the band, after having announced that the album had been completed, in August of 1996 Steve Perry injured his hip whilst hiking in Hawaii on a ten-day break. The timing could not have been more unfortunate. "I got to the top of this hill, and I was in trouble. I could hardly walk. I don't know what had happened, but the pain was like an ice pick. I'd had some pain in my left hip area before, but I didn't think nothing about it because it would come and go. I just thought it was part of the aging process."[231]

The accident caused a delay of the album's release date, a massive bombshell for the band and their label, Columbia. Ross Valory: "And at that point, here we had the band back together and we were just like… stopped suddenly, and the record company, on hearing that we weren't going to tour, pulled the plug on the promotion for the album. We had a second hit on the turntable, so to speak, called 'If He Should Break Your Heart' so the careful success of *Trial By Fire* was cut short."[232]

It was also been suggested that Perry was already suffering from back problems due to arthritis and a degenerative bone condition. The band, and obviously Columbia, were so desperate to go on the road it was even proposed that Perry sit on a stool to sing throughout each concert.

There were others who believed it was all smoke and mirrors, and that Perry used it as an excuse not to go on the road because his voice was not as strong as it used to be, that he could no longer hit those famous high octaves and his once iconic voice had simply changed too much since Journey's peak years. It was thought that physicians had recommended he undergo a hip replacement but he was not sure what to do and so did nothing, not immediately anyway. Perry himself said some years later: "I put a lot of effort in trying to put Journey back together for the *Trial By Fire* era and I worked hard with those guys so that we would keep our original integrity and write some good music and we did. Then I had that hip problem and it crashed on me. I had to go have surgery."[233]

The singer continued to comment on the actual nature of his health: "It's [the hip] completely replaced. It's very good. It's beyond better... Well, I have some other physical issues. I'm not a teenager anymore."[234]

In the event, Steve Perry and Journey would never perform live again, making Bill Graham's wake the last time Perry played live onstage with the group. Speaking about his role in their reunion and Perry's reluctance to tour, John Kalodner said in 2002: "I've never seen such craziness as what goes on with Journey fans. The greatest thing to me would be a tour with the original band, with Steve Perry. God knows I've tried everything I know for the last six or seven years and I don't know what else I could do. I'm sick of people writing to me about this because there's nobody who wants Steve Perry to sing with Journey more than me. So I don't know what else to do... He's not interested in touring. Maybe one day he will be. Probably one of the greatest singers in history. So I talk to him a lot and there's nothing I've said that motivates him. I don't know what else to do about it. I'm sick of these people writing to me... Well Kevin Shirley had to change his AOL account because he got so much hate mail from those people."[235]

What annoyed many fans was that Perry did not initially disclose to the press or his fans what the problem was and why the band did not go on tour. Jonathan Cain admitted: "You know, we tried to get him to come forward with some television and talk about the problem and what he is going through. Just share it with everybody, tell the fans what's up and come out and sing a little bit. Sit on a stool or something, and tell people what's going on. We had an opportunity to all these television programs and he passed on all of them, the American Music Awards and everything. It was really sad. We all wanted to do these things, but we couldn't. That's the end of that, and I don't know what we are going to do now."[236]

Herbie Herbert looks back at the Steve Perry-Journey *Trial By Fire* reunion, of which he had no part, and says, "They gladly threw me under the [bus] at the bad time for the potential to make a record and tour with Steve Perry. I said 'Okay, fine' like I said I have no interest in working with Steve Perry again so that's fine by me but I will tell you this: 'As your friend Neal, as your friend Jon, if he ever fucking sets foot onstage with you I will shit and bark at the moon. You can designate the time and place that I will take turds of your choice, consume them. I promise.' Of course he never performed with them ever again and I assured them that that would be the case: 'He will never set foot with you onstage again... He doesn't like you. He doesn't want to help you. He just wanted to get you to find new agreements, reaffirm his control of the name and likeness and things like that...' and that's exactly what he did."[237]

Asked at the time of writing (early 2010) if he would ever speak to Journey's most famous vocalist again, Herbie Herbert comments: "Through the fan-club girls, they wanted to know if I was going to be at the [San Francisco] Giants game with him and I go, 'Why? No, I've moved up on the coast. I'm not going.' I was a season ticket holder for the Giants and the Niners for 35 years. 'No, I'm going to give up my tickets. I'm not going to be there.' 'Oh, that's too bad.' I go, 'Why?' 'Well, Steve Perry was hoping to maybe see you there and have a conversation.' A conversation about what? What is there that I would want to talk to him about? [He] fucked up all the lives of all the people that I cared about... [He] was just a prick... there's nothing he's got to say that I want to hear that would change my life one iota. There's nothing I have to say to him."[238]

Unfortunately for all concerned, when it was finally released *Trial By Fire* turned out to be Journey's worst selling album featuring Steve Perry, although it did go platinum in due course. "Did they sell any records with that thing?" asked Herbert. "Their live greatest hits was put out [in 1998] because they didn't earn back their advance, I know that. They had to have the live greatest hits to pay money back and the *Greatest Hits Live* was a live record where the audience had been extracted. That was awful. That was soundly rejected by the consumers. I know that didn't work."

After *Trial By Fire*, it would be quite some time before Journey would receive another platinum record for a new studio album. In the United States, *Trial Of Fire*, released in October 1996, hit number three the following month in the *Billboard* album charts; elsewhere it charted in Sweden, Netherlands, Germany, Japan and Canada. However, the album did give birth to the single 'When You Love A Woman' which peaked at number 12 in the *Billboard* Hot 100 and was nominated for a Grammy in 1997 under the category of Best Pop Performance By A Duo Or Group. Such was the changing state of popular music trends, even though the single sold approximately half a million copies, the promotional video was never played on MTV much to the frustration of the band. The kind of rock Journey played was not seen as "cool" anymore, simply not in vogue with younger generations of music fans. 'When You Love A Woman' was also included as a bonus track on later reissues of Journey's mega-selling *Greatest Hits* collection and it fitted in neatly. Other songs from *Trial By Fire* released as singles were 'Message Of Love', 'Can't Tame The Lion' and 'If He Should Break Your Heart'.

"Rarely have a re-formed rock band whipped up new material and then gone to such jaw-dropping lengths to make it sound exactly the way it would have during their commercial peak (circa 1983)," wrote one journalist in *Entertainment Weekly*.

"This is one fine album, chock full of exactly what one would expect Journey to sound like…" Andrew McNiece wrote on Melodicrock.com, "But for an album of eighty-minutes length, and with each member of the band getting their moment in the spotlight and sounding smoother than ever, it gets my vote for album of the year."

Trial By Fire opens with 'Message Of Love', a decent start but lacking the band's trademark harmonies and a distinctive melody, and sounds a little messy, though Perry's voice seems in good shape. 'One More' is too contrived and fails to make an immediate connection, although Valory's bass is thankfully turned up. Schon's guitar work is pedestrian at best and the backing vocals sound quite poor. 'When You Love A Woman' is the album's standout track, as close to the classic Journey sound as this album gets, with Perry's voice in good shape, dulcet backing vocals, beautifully crafted piano and a memorable chorus. 'If He Should Break

Your Heart' is a pleasant ballad with some fine tuning on the backing vocals and an indelible melody, though it falls short of Journey's best songs in this style. 'Forever In Blue' is a bit too fluffy compared with some of Journey's more upbeat tracks; even Schon's guitar is a little too repetitive. 'Castle Burning' opens up with a surprisingly gritty electric riff and though it sounds out of place on this album, it is a pretty good song with an angry, toe-taping chorus. 'Don't Be Down On Me Baby' is only memorable for Perry's passionate vocal performance and some effective piano but it doesn't quite lift off the way it should. 'She Still Cries' is a bland love song, while 'Colours Of The Spirit' opens with some tribal beats but fails to go anywhere interesting. 'When I Think Of You' continues the album's reliance on distinctly dull ballads that are certainly not a patch on Journey's best work of the past. 'Easy To Fall' is a curiously effective power ballad with some nifty guitar work, a sturdy vocal performance and a catchy chorus. 'Can't Tame The Lion' is a neatly infectious song with an interesting arrangement, though it fails to sound like a typical Journey song; still, it offers a good central guitar solo, steady and effective drums and a consistent sound. 'It's Just The Rain' is a mellow and somewhat heart-warming slow-tempo song that has a passionate vocal performance from Perry. 'Trial By Fire' is an uneventful, hollow track and finally, 'Baby I'm Leavin' You' is an uncharacteristic reggae-influenced song.

All told, *Trial By Fire* is an inconsistent, disappointing album that fails to match up to Journey's past work. Much of it is uninspired, lacking the charm of their better albums and, ultimately, failing to sound like Journey. That is not what Steve Perry would have you believe: "One of the things we've always known is that there are certain musical directions that fit what [our] chemistry is about. We're going to sink or swim being what we are and not by trying to reinvent ourselves and not by trying to be the flavour of the month."[239]

Bands rarely criticise their own work. Ross Valory said of *Trial By Fire*: "I think it's a fine album, there may not have been enough rock 'n' roll in there for some people but it was an accomplishment."[240]

However, Neal Schon later admitted that perhaps the album had too many ballads and Journey fans just wanted to hear the band rock: "Even on our last record, the *Trial By Fire* record, a lot of the rock stuff just got shelved and ended up being like 20 ballads, I don't know how many ballads."[241]

To keep busy after the release of Journey's tenth album and waiting on Steve Perry to make up his mind about whether or not he could go on tour, most of the band members moved on to solo projects. Neal Schon released his *Electric World* solo album in 1997 and created Abraxas Pool with his former Santana buddies, including Gregg Rolie and drummer Michael Shrieve. Meanwhile, Jonathan Cain released a solo album called *Body Language*, which was quickly followed by *For A Lifetime* in early 1998.

The band appeared to be stuck in limbo between the release of *Trial By Fire* and a proposed tour, but things would start slowly picking up again for Journey...

CHAPTER 7

We'll Be Alright Without You: The Arrival Of A New Singer (1998–2004)

"We are in limbo really. That's all I can tell you. We are all doing solo projects, and you know, everyone is just moving on with their life."

Jonathan Cain[242]

"I get the idea of 'How can you miss me if I don't go away', you know, but they went away for 15 years. And to live through a couple generations like that, and a wholesale change in the way music is bought, sold, distributed, listened to and everything, I mean you know it's pretty amazing that they have such depth of popularity," explains Journey's former manager Herbie Herbert. "And you know they are a definitive evergreen. And a definitive evergreen is an artist that sells far more in death than they did in life. Journey in 1986 had sold 22 million records and when they resumed business in '98 they were somewhere around 70 million records. And they hadn't played a song or a show or done an interview or done a video or done a damned thing in 15 years. And without any benefit of their presence or involvement or any exposure in the media they more than tripled their total lifetime sales. So that's an evergreen for you."[243]

Indeed during those inactive days in the 1990s, Journey were still popular, and though they may have lost their household appeal and their towering success was certainly way behind them, they were still beloved by millions around the world. In the US, Journey remained one of the country's most cherished rock bands. Their music stood the test of time while the group retain their popularity amongst a particular generation of rock fans who will always save a place in their hearts for Journey.

Kevin Shirley explained Journey's appeal accurately: "Journey are one of the biggest of America's supergroups. They are part of the fabric of life here. People have met their sweethearts and lost their virginity to Journey songs, been married to them, been buried to these anthems, and they deserve to be heralded as such and not disposed of by any shallow MTV-flavour-of-the-month shoulder-shrug."[244]

So, even though *Trial By Fire* was not the mammoth success the band or Columbia had hoped for, the remastered back catalogue was well received and proved that few rock bands can write about universal themes the way Journey can. Songs about a yearning for love, the demise of a relationship, the concept of love or lust and a desire to be in a relationship, are emotions that every human being experiences at some point in their life. Perry said: "I can't tell you how many times I get a tap on the shoulder and somebody says, 'I really love your voice and you guys were the greatest band.' Or, 'This was my prom song.'"[245]

Journey's Greatest Hits continued to sell several hundred thousand copies a year during the Nineties and it kept the band's music in the limelight. But what the band really needed – and wanted – to do was to go on the road for the first time together since 1987.

"Steve [Perry] hasn't really signed off yet," explained Jonathan Cain after the release of *Trial By Fire* and as the band thought about hiring another singer for the road. "So until he really decides that he doesn't want to. We still want Steve number one, and we are just giving him a little bit of space here to see what he wants to do. So that's really the truth, in the interim that's what we are doing. We owe it to him and ourselves to give him a little space and check it out, and [see] if he's into it, and really wants to come back. And if he doesn't, we will face those consequences... Everybody has worked hard to make this band a success and we feel the music is powerful and has a lot of life left to it. I feel that, the band still feels that. If the band sounded old and tired, it wouldn't even be a consideration, but the band sounds so darn good. It would be a shame to let it go to waste. We'll see. Ultimately, it will be Steve's choice to carry on or not with the band. We are hoping that's what he decides to do. But it is something you don't want to rush."[246]

Perry was said to have had a hip replacement back in October 1997, but because of the nature of the surgery he could not simply rush out and tour with the band right away. Of course, the surgery came a year after the release of the album and Perry quite rightly felt that his health, and such a major decision as having surgery, was not a band decision but his alone and one that should not be taken lightly but with serious thought. "My intention was not to not tour," he explained, "it was not to not continue. My vision was to turn Journey into the cyclic version of the Rolling Stones who tour their hearts out and then they stop for a year. I wanted to have a life and do something that I loved to do, that's what I wanted to see happy. They agreed to it and that was my intention until that [hiking accident] happened."[247]

As the weeks and months went by and the New Year had passed following the release of the reunion album, the band got restless. They tried out some new singers in January, informing Perry and stressing how keen they were to tour again. Perry's was said to be furious that the band had gone behind his back; after all it was he who had called Jonathan Cain about getting Journey back together for *Trial By Fire*.

He explained: "In January [1998], Jon told me on the phone, 'I just want to know.' And I said: 'Don't call it Journey. Because if you do, you will fracture the stone. And I don't think I'll be able to come back to it if you crack it. If you crack it – it's got so much integrity. We've worked so hard. Can't you just, you know, not do that?' And, he asked me again: 'We want to know when you're going to surgery. Because we want to get out there.' That particular set of words. I said: 'OK, you do what you got to do, and I'll do what I got to do.' And I hung up the phone, and when the dial tone came back, I called my attorney, and I said: 'Start the divorce.' And he said: 'What divorce?' And I said: 'The *divorce*.' And I told him what happened. When somebody says, 'We've checked out a few singers,' it's like your wife's saying, 'Look, while you were gone – I know a few guys, and I just wanna know what you've decided to do, because I need to know.' My feeling at that point is very simple: 'What am I going back to now? If you go back to that, what are you going back to now?' So that's why I said: 'Maybe we really are done.' I'd left to find my life, once before, gone back to it, to try to reclaim something we once had, and then we kind of fell into that same place again. You know? So I thought, 'Well, maybe I'm not supposed to be there.'"[248]

Such a sticky situation effectively put the final nail in the coffin and the end to the Steve Perry-led line-up of Journey. On May 8, 1998, Perry was freed from his ties to the band and all his contracts with them and Sony/Columbia. That was it – the end – though, interestingly, that same month he recorded two tracks ('I Stand Alone' and 'United We Stand') for the *Quest For Camelot* soundtrack. It was ironic that he ended his relationship with Journey only weeks after the release of *Greatest Hits Live*, which certainly did not accurately represent the band's best live work and peaked at number 79 in the *Billboard* album charts in the US.

Herbie Herbert: "Well, the *Greatest Hits Live* album… that was John Kalodner, the A&R guy at CBS. He said: 'Let's do a *Greatest Hits Live*' and then no audience on it. Take all the air and the excitement and volume out of the record and zero audience on a live *Greatest Hits*. The guy's a fucking genius, isn't he? That was a management deficit right there. That's where they really needed management…. I like Irving [Azoff] a lot and I think he's done as good a job as you can do with these guys, but I think one place where he was wrong was to let Kalodner put that live *Greatest Hits* [record out]."[249]

"Culled from 1981-83 concert tapes, *Greatest Hits Live* showcases Journey at the height of its creative powers… after the drag of 'Who's Crying Now', Journey rushes through 'Any Way You Want It' too fast to unleash its power properly or to allow the audience to quickly sing back…" wrote one journalist from *Associated Press*.

Andrew McNiece wrote on Melodicrock.com: "I have only a small wish for the record – that the crowd gets a little more recognition and was bumped up in the mix a little more. Also, most of the rapping from Perry to the audience is removed. I have a couple of soundboard live recordings and a radio show, and he does talk more in those. The crowd gets a little chance to sing in 'Any Way You Want It', and hear from Perry in 'Who's Crying Now', but not much elsewhere… A great-sounding live record, and a fantastic collection of pure AOR brilliance, and I dare say a better pick up than Journey's regular *Greatest Hits*."

Perhaps ending his association with Journey was a liberating experience for the singer, but after time he may have felt some regret about how it closed. Though it had been topsy-turvy since it began way back in 1977, it was prosperous, unique and creative. "When I was in Journey," Perry reflected, "there was a camaraderie. It had a purpose, it had a mission. We scrapped and had difficult times with each other and battles over musical differences, but that never stopped us from being the best we could be."[250]

Following his official departure from Journey, Perry worked hard at maintaining an aura of mystery around him, disappearing from view and popping out of hibernation only every once in a while. No doubt the songwriting royalties from Journey's back catalogue and his own solo work left him comfortably off without the need to work again. "I don't have management," he admitted years later. "I have completely shut down the store. The store has been shut down forever. I own Steveperry.com, but I haven't flown it. I've really had to let go because emotionally… to be perfectly honest with you, if I do decide to sing again and record again, I'm going to do it for the right reasons."[251]

While Perry chose to semi-retire from the music business and cut all ties with Journey, there was no way Neal Schon, Jonathan Cain and Ross Valory were going to let the band rest. Perry left big shoes to fill but that was not going to stop them from hunting down a new singer/frontman, and they also needed a new drummer. Steve Smith felt that Journey would not be Journey without Perry, and so went back to his career in jazz and his project Vital Information.

To replace Smith the band looked no further than Neal Schon's buddy Deen Castronovo, who since playing in Bad English with Schon had worked with Ozzy Osbourne, Steve Vai, Geezer Butler's band G/Z/R and Social Distortion. Not only is Castronovo a brilliant sticksman but he can also sing well. His hiring was a no brainer for the band.

As for a vocalist, Kevin Chalfant was mentioned in dispatches but the band ultimately went with ex-Tall Stories vocalist Steve Augeri, who as well as sharing a first name as the band's former singer, also sounded and looked rather similar. Others discussed included bassist/singer Glenn Hughes ('The Voice Of Rock') and Geoff Tate of the progressive metal band Queensrÿche, who wasn't right for Journey. "Yeah, he was a really great guy, a super nice guy, we got along really well," Neal Schon said. "We ended up writing a song, but it sounded nothing like Journey."[252]

"He [Augeri] wanted to get access to Journey," says Herbert, "and he'd approached me then about that so I thought it was pretty wild that they wound up finding him. I think he's a good guy and he looked good onstage..."[253]

"There were only really two [singers] that we had checked out," Neal Schon admitted. "We had played with Kevin Chalfant a long, long time ago, and we kind of felt that since Kevin had done The Storm thing, that it wasn't the right thing to do. We felt that The Storm was a mini Journey band."[254]

Steve Augeri's background was completely different from the other members of Journey. For one thing, he was raised on the East Coast of the US; of Italian descent, he was born on January 30, 1959 in Brooklyn, New York. Raised on sounds as diverse as R&B, early rock 'n' roll, country, soul and crooners like Sinatra and Dean Martin, he studied music at the High School of Music & Art in New York City, which deepened his passion for classical music. He even taught at the French Woods Festival for the Performing Arts one summer before getting his first break as a backing singer for Michael Schenker, the famously difficult former guitarist of German hard rockers Scorpions and classic British rockers UFO. Augeri would then go on to co-form the melodic rock band Tall

Stories with guitarist Jack Morer; they were joined by Kevin Totoian on bass and Tom De Faria on drums.

Tall Stories had some success in the melodic rock field, but unfortunately for them, their timing was bad as record labels, radio stations and music channels were switching their attention to grunge and hip-hop. Still, Tall Stories released their self-titled debut album via Epic Records in 1991 and they were nominated for 'Best Debut Album' and 'Best Debut Male Vocalist' at the 1992 New York Music Awards. The band broke up in 1995, their show in Paris on New Year's Eve being their last. Augeri then went on to front the acclaimed melodic rock band Tyketto and sang on their 1995 album *Shine*, but their 1996 live album *Take Out And Served Up Live* was effectively their swansong. With a wife, Lydia, and a new born son, Adam, to support Augeri effectively retired from the music scene.

Augeri was brought to the attention of Neal Schon and Jonathan Cain through a mutual friend and fellow Brooklynite, guitarist Joe Cefalu. Augeri had sang on some of his demos not long after the release of Tall Stories, just before Cefalu moved to San Francisco. Augeri explained: "To put it as simply as possible, I had a great deal more success in my career than a great deal of other musicians, especially people that I know. I was able to release a couple of records. I toured some of the world. I made a lot of friends along the way. I was able to perform my music in front of thousands of people and I felt myself very fortunate. But at the time, success hadn't come my way. And the fact is, I have a family, I had a child. I guess I was doubting myself perhaps. I guess that's reality."

To support his family Augeri took a job at The Gap. "I was a maintenance manager for thirty stores in Manhattan. So when they would fall apart, I'd have to fix them. Everything from broken plumbing to electrical and painting, you name it. So a year goes by and Joe Cefalu, this wonderful guitarist gives me a call. He says, 'Listen, Steve, I'm friendly with Neal and I was speaking with Neal the other day and he tells me that Steve Perry is no longer with the band and they're starting to look for vocalists. They are wanting to reform Journey and go on with another singer.' It had been a year since I began working at The Gap and it was two years since I even sang a note in public. So I was like, that's really great but, regardless of whether I was singing or not, I thought it was just crazy.

Out of my reach. It was a wonderful, flattering thing but I thought he was just bonkers."[255]

Augeri was reluctant at first to even contemplate singing in one of America's most successful rock bands. It was like moving from a non-league team to the premier division in soccer. Cefalu asked Augeri for the Tall Stories album, which had become rare, to send to Schon and Cain so they could hear his voice. A week went by and Augeri failed to send a copy of the album. Then, after taking a phone call from Cefalu, who had handed Neal Schon a tape containing three songs with Augeri's vocals on them, it turned out that Augeri was already on the band's mind as they'd heard of Tall Stories from Schon and Cain's Bad English days. They liked his voice, his style and his stage presence and were keen to have him audition as Perry's replacement.

"The only thing I needed to do was... I begged Neal and Jon to give me a couple of weeks to prepare. Because after two years of not singing, I was basically like... nothing was really there," said Augeri.[256]

Augeri took time off work from his job at The Gap so he could fly to San Francisco from New York and prepare to audition for the band. The audition itself took a whole week with the last day focusing on songwriting and getting to know the band members. It was a tense experience at first for Augeri but once his vocal cords had warmed up he gave it his best shot, singing 'Don't Stop Believin'', 'Faithfully' and 'Separate Ways (Worlds Apart)'. Those songs were recorded and sent to John Kalodner at Columbia who gave Augeri the thumbs up. Cain and Schon were happy. After his stay in San Francisco, Augeri flew to Los Angeles to visit a vocal coach.

Augeri explained: "And this guy got me on-track real fast. And then I saw a couple of people here in New York. And quite frankly, I truly needed one. I hadn't sung for two years and I kind of grew up singing just the way I wanted to and never had any true guidance. Going out on the road for months at a time you've got to be in amazing... you've got to be an animal to be able to last five shows, two hours a night during the week and go a few months at a time. When I was younger, when you're younger, period, you have the muscle stamina, you have the muscle tone."[257]

Behind the scenes, legal issues were dealt with for a new Journey line-up of singer Steve Augeri, guitarist Neal Schon, keyboardist Jonathan Cain, bassist Ross Valory and drummer Deen Castronovo. However, a few more ideas were flung in the air, as Ross Valory explained: "When we put the band back together without Steve Perry, Gregg Rolie was certainly in mind. But then again, the record company and the management voted against including him. I think it would have been fine to have both players and it's something Jonathan was up for as well. I think it would have been a great idea, but it was something that was not agreed by the record company."[258]

The new line-up set about writing and recording some new material, the first project a contribution to the *Armageddon* soundtrack, a massive sci-fi summer blockbuster movie directed by Michael Bay and starring Bruce Willis and Ben Affleck. The song 'Remember Me' may be relatively obscure, but it showed Journey fans that the band had, at the time, made the right choice in hiring Steve Augeri. Inevitably, perhaps, there those who thought it was cynical to hire a singer so similar to Perry. "I wasn't aware of it so much until people kept approaching me and I kept on hearing it more and more and more," said Augeri, commenting on the vocal similarity. "Obviously there are similarities in timbre and even style. But honestly, it was a subconscious thing initially. Then when we did the Tall Stories record, as much as Jack Morrow, the guitarist would deny it, he was the first one to keep telling me Steve, you got to lay off of the Perryism. That was the word he used... the Perryism."[259]

While Journey were thinking up new projects, by 1998 the popular music landscape had changed yet again. Grunge had been and gone, and rock was still hovering around the fringes of what was considered mainstream and popular. While established bands continued doing what they did best, rock in the Journey's style was still not as popular as it had been in the Eighties. Filling up the charts were hip-hop and pop crossover artists, and a new sound called nu-metal, which merged rap with metal, though this was not universally popular with metal traditionalists.

AOR and melodic rock continued to be popular with a relatively small but dedicated band of global followers, though only some of the more mainstream acts would find a place in the charts. The rest mostly struggled to get by on independent labels, self-releasing their own products. Foreigner had released *Mr Moonlight* in 1994 after singer Lou Gramm returned to the band, but it was far from their biggest success both critically and commercially. Gramm had surgery in 1997 to remove a brain tumour which affected his vocals and weight, and he left the band in 2003 to be replaced by Kelly Hansen. Survivor struggled with a number of line-up changes throughout the Nineties and didn't release a new studio album between 1988's *Too Hot To Sleep* and 2006's disappointing *Reach* (which reunited Jimi Jamison with the band). Meanwhile, REO Speedwagon also hit hard times in the Nineties after losing their record deal with Epic. They were forced to release 1996's *Building The Bridge* on a small label called Castle, but it received mostly negative reviews. Thankfully, the band underwent a revival of sorts following 1999's *Ballads* as they began to capitalise on past hits and release several compilations thereafter. Styx reunited in 1995 and released the underwhelming *Brave New World* in 1999, their first studio album since 1990's *Edge Of The Century*. Formed back in 1973, Heart – led by sisters Ann and Nancy Wilson – released only two albums in the Nineties, 1990's *Brigade* and 1993's *Desire Walks On*. The band suffered from a number of line-up changes, and in 1998 Ann went on tour without her sister, calling the band Ann Wilson & Heart (though they would reunite in 2002 with a new line-up).

After a rehearsing with new members Steve Augeri and Deen Castronovo in Marin County, the new line-up of Journey flew to Japan, always a stronghold for the band, to play four gigs beginning on June 20 and finishing on the 25th in Nagoya. "It's a little like we are reborn again," Neal Schon said on the subject of the band's first tour in over a decade. "The guy that we got, we couldn't have got a better replacement. We have so much old material that we need to play, that the fans want to hear, otherwise I don't see the purpose of going out and doing Journey. Our *Greatest Hits* is probably the biggest record we ever had. And it continues to sell and be played on the radio. That's what fans want to hear, so it was very important to find someone that could cover the older stuff and do it very well, and Steve Augeri definitely is that. He is able to take us some new places that we weren't able to go before, which is a fresh outlook on where the band can go. He is more of a rocker I think."[260]

Discounting instrumentals and solo spots, the setlist looked like this: 'Separate Ways (Worlds Apart)', 'Can't Tame The Lion', 'Only The Young', 'Stone In Love', 'Castles Burning', 'Send Her My Love', 'Lights', 'Who's Crying Now', 'I'll Be Alright Without You', 'Open Arms', 'Just The Same Way', 'Anytime', 'Remember Me', 'One More', 'Escape', 'Wheel In The Sky', 'Be Good To Yourself', 'Anyway You Want It' and 'Lovin' Touchin' Squeezin'' with encores of 'Faithfully', 'Don't Stop Believin'' and 'Ask The Lonely'.

After launching their online webpage (www.journeytheband.com) Journey began the Vacation's Over tour of the US on October 10, winding up on December 31 in Reno. They found time to play some outdoor festivals that year too. "Right now we have a pretty cool set that we come out rocking," said Neal Schon, "and rock for four or five songs, and then we do a ballad thing in the centre, then we rock out all the way through the end. So it is pretty cool. And when we can mix in more of this new stuff it is going to be exactly what we need."[261]

Following the comeback tour with new singer Augeri and drummer Castronovo, they went back on the road in 1999 for a string of dates in the US beginning in Minnesota on June 2 and finishing up in Michigan on September 6. The band could not have been happier with how easily Augeri fitted into Journey. "He's the guy that goes to the next plane," said Jonathan Cain. "He's an ambassador that represents the legacy of what Journey's about. He's a great guy to have at the helm, you know. He's got the moxie. He's tough, and he's humble, and he's talented. And he's funny too. He's always joking and doing his Marx Brothers thing. He's just one of those guys that are very passionate and dedicated to his craft."[262]

Of course, plans were already afoot for a brand new studio album featuring Steve Augeri, the band's first album not to feature Steve Perry since *Infinity* way back in 1978. They hooked up again with Kevin Shirley who had produced *Trial By Fire* and went in to Avatar Studios in New York in March 2000, finishing in August. There was plenty of material to pick from, some of it written by Neal Schon and Jack Blades of Night Ranger. "I first heard a batch of songs," Augeri said. "That was, I think, three that Neal had sent me that he had written with Jack. And each and every one of them was better than the last. One after the other knocked my socks off. In fact, there were a handful of others that I couldn't believe didn't make the record. I personally think you would have absolutely flipped out because they were really melodic, really in the vein of classic melodic rock."[263]

Much of the songwriting on the final album was obviously completed by Neal Schon and Jonathan Cain, but Steve Augeri also had some lyrical input. He was involved in the writing of 'All The Way', 'Live And Breathe', 'Nothin' Comes Close', 'To Be Alive Again', 'Kiss Me Softly' and 'We Will Meet Again'.

Asked what the ingredients of a classic Journey track are, producer Kevin Shirley said: "It's in the melody. It's the song between the piano and the guitar, and then the voice tells a story that floats above the music and there's triumph. Journey is also unabated energy and passion, and a boatload of emotion. I think it's rare to find that without the cheese factor, but the musicianship is so real that it achieves it."[264]

Neal Schon noted the difference between the two Steves: "I think Steve Perry is more prone to sing ballads than rock 'n' roll, more the R&B influence in there. So a lot of the rock stuff that I had written [for *Trial By Fire*] was a lot harder, and he's never been able to rock into that as well as some of the other people I have worked with. So it wasn't a natural thing, and the stuff is still sitting there on the shelf. I have been throwing them at Steve Augeri, and he just jumps right on it!"[265]

Following the completion of the new album, the band finished off the year by hitting the road again for a series of shows in Latin America and the US, beginning on September 22 in San Juan, Puerto Rico. Prior to finishing 2000 with a show in Phoenix, Arizona on December 31, their performance in Las Vegas on December 30 was filmed for a DVD – the band's first official live DVD – to be released under the moniker *Journey 2001* and to coincide with the new album the following year. The setlist was filled mostly with staple Journey songs but also included some fresh material. Excluding the intro and solo spots, the setlist looked like this: 'Separate Ways (Worlds Apart)', 'Ask The Lonely', 'Stone In

Love', 'Higher Place', 'Send Her My Love', 'Lights', 'Who's Crying Now', 'Open Arms.' 'Fillmore Boogie', 'All The Way', 'Escape', 'La Raza Del Sol', 'Wheel In The Sky', 'Be Good To Yourself', 'Any Way You Want It', 'Don't Stop Believin'', 'Lovin', Touchin', Squeezin'', and 'Faithfully'.

Journey kicked off 2001 in style with a tour of Japan which commenced in Tokyo on January 30 and finished in Sendi on February 7. "It's not easy for any one person to fill and he's done a great job at that," Ross Valory remarked about Steve Augeri as a live performer. "Perry has a commanding aura about him. He would demand that you listen to him. He would be right in your face. Augeri is sort of the other end of the spectrum. Not to say Perry wasn't humble with his audience, but Steve Augeri approaches it differently. 'May I sing for you?' You know, he plays it that way. He takes it from the other approach in terms of stage presence and he's quite a good dancer. He moves well."[266]

The band would have a busy year in 2001. The previous year Journey fans had already been treated to a special triple-pack that featured *Infinity*, *Escape* and *Frontiers*, but this year Japanese fans were treated to the compilation *The Journey Continues* in March, while *The Essential Journey* compilation was released in the US and the UK in October. A comprehensive set of more than 30 songs, it ignored songs from the Augeri album and focused on the band's past. However, the big news for the year was, of course, the release of a brand new studio album.

Arrival was actually released in Japan in late 2000 but with heavy imports and internet downloads, copies of the album quickly infiltrated the market in the US and foreign territories. The version of *Arrival* which was unleashed in the US and the UK in April 2001 was different from the Japanese release. "They've really stuck with us through thick and thin," Jonathan Cain said of Journey fans, "and it's a shame that a lot of them knew about the album, or were waiting for it. If you really wanted it, you'd get it from Japan and so many people did, which was great. And so that's why we decided to come out with some new art work and put a couple of new songs on it. We actually paid for it out of our own pocket."[267]

Indeed, the American version was noted for having fewer ballads and being more rock-orientated than the Japanese version. Evidently fans who had heard the initial Japanese cut were not keen on its reliance on ballads so the band recorded two new rock tracks ('World Gone Wild' and 'Nothin' Comes Close') for the delayed American release. Even after the release of *Trial By Fire*, Journey fans just wanted to hear the band rock again.

Neal Schon explained: "I went on our website and I started talking about [how] everybody was asking whatever happened to 'World Gone Wild' and this other song 'Good Times' that we were playing live and then all of a sudden we weren't playing it… [and] then it wasn't on the record because John Kalodner didn't OK it and Kevin had never heard it and so everybody was asking about the song, 'Why is this not on the record, I can't believe it didn't go on the record'. So I started a fire on the website and I said, 'How many people would like to hear this and how many people would like to hear this sort of a song and what do you think if we added it to the record', and everybody came back almost like 100%, yeah do it. And so once I got the fire started then I got on the phone with management, then I talked to everybody in the band and basically twisted arms real good and then we went back in the studio and did it."[268]

The Japanese release looked like this: 'Higher Place', 'All The Way', 'Signs Of Life', 'All The Things', 'Loved By You', 'Livin' To Do', 'I Got A Reason', 'With Your Love', 'Lifetime Of Dreams', 'Live And Breathe', 'Kiss Me Softly', 'I'm Not That Way', 'We Will Meet Again' and 'To Be Alive Again', while the American release added 'World Gone Wild' and 'Live And Breathe' but omitted 'I'm Not That Way'.

The gap between the release of the original Japanese version and the American version meant that sales suffered enormously and the label was less than happy with the disappointing sales.

Arrival peaked at a disappointing number 56 on the American *Billboard* album charts and even the friendly radio hit 'All The Way' failed to boost struggling sales. "The band and CBS/Sony had sort of a mutual dissolution after the lack of success of the *Arrival* album," said Ross Valory, "we mutually agreed to call it quits."[269]

"It'll be interesting to see what happens," retired A&R maestro John Kalodner said after the release of *Arrival* and Journey's departure from Columbia. "I can't imagine that they would be brought back with Steve

Augeri. That's just a guess. The Steve Perry thing… that might be another story. I just don't know."[270]

Columbia had released every Journey album since their 1975 self-titled debut. It must have been a frustrating episode for the band, especially as Jonathan Cain, who around the time of the American release of the album had praised Columbia for their handling of the launch of a new phase of their career with a new relatively unknown front man. "The label has been very generous," he had enthused. "This latest commitment to the Direct TV special was really awesome. They came through with some big dough to tape the show in Vegas, you know, and that was really a sign for me that they're totally into this and they're in for the long term. And when you look at any big corporation, you have to look at what have they done for you lately, and lately they've done a lot. I have to say that I feel the love. I think we all do, we feel very grateful to be sitting on a Direct TV month long concert. It came out great."[271]

Downloading continues to be a massive problem for recording companies and has been blamed for the steep decline in album sales and artist royalties. The major cause of concern leading up to the release of *Arrival* was Napster, a file sharing online service created in the US by Shawn Fanning. Launched in 1999, the service allowed all users to share music files, thus evading copyright laws. Inevitably musicians were furious because users shared the music online with other users, which meant they were not buying records so the artists did not get paid royalties. After a complicated legal wrangle, Napster was shut down in 2001.

Also, rather annoyingly for the band, an unknown (though said to be limited) quantity of inferior preview tapes of the album were allegedly handed out in Europe by Sony/Columbia representatives. They ended up on Napster where fans could share the tracks for free. The band tried to work this to their advantage by getting fans' reactions before the American release of the album.

In response to Napster, Neal Schon commented: "The whole ordeal with us with Napster was pretty shocking in the beginning… that they had gotten it from one of the execs at Sony, and it was passed on through somebody in Europe. I mean, the record was just done. It wasn't going to be out for months and here it was all over Napster. I knew that once the record would come out it would be all over Napster like everything else is, and I had my feelings about that too. I felt that it wasn't a bad thing but the artists do need to receive a residual and so do the companies, you know? I mean it's just like, you just can't get stuff for free like that when there's artists involved; this is how we make our living."[272]

"I can tell you that file sharing really hurts records," A&R boss John Kalodner said back in 2002 when asked about the reasons behind *Arrival's* low sales. "I can guarantee you that. There are probably other factors but I don't know them. File sharing is deadly to those kinds of records... records that are on the edge that sell 250,000 or whatever. It was right on the edge of doing well and then that 40% or 50% of music that gets stolen by file sharing is a significantly damaging amount. That definitely hurt that record."[273]

What surely whetted fans appetite was the reemergence of Steve Perry. To coincide with the release of *Arrival* and the tour, an episode of VH-1's popular series *Behind The Music* focusing on Journey was aired. It is no secret that most, if not all, the band members in Journey have signed some sort of confidentiality agreement which forbids them from talking to unofficial sources unauthorised by the band's management, or indeed talking about specific aspects of their career. Perry, who had apparently authorised Irving Azoff, Journey's manager, to allow the band to record a live DVD, release a new album and tour under the name Journey, surprised many by participating in the VH1 programme. Former manager Herbie Herbert, however, had never signed such a confidentiality agreement. "It was that ultimate editorial control," he says. "And so, when all of these other guys have signed this agreement, and all you can get out of them is this homogenised, pasteurised pulp – nothing with substance, all candy-coated – that is the worst thing you can get them to say. The most damning and incriminating thing is, 'By agreement I am not allowed to speak on those issues, or speak about those matters.' And then, off camera, everybody – Neal Schon and Ross Valory are saying, 'You really need to talk to Herbie, he didn't sign such an agreement.'"[274]

When the programme was aired it caused much contention between the band and Perry over a startling claim Perry made about feeling excluded from the other guys in the band. Indeed, the claim upset many longstanding fans because while they were writing and performing emotional, introspective and meaningful love songs, behind the scenes there appeared to be backbiting, arguing and divisions. For some fans this was not just hard to believe but appeared deceitful.

Herbie Herbert, who was also interviewed for the programme, explained:"I said this to this guy – maybe 25 times,'None of this is going to make it. I'm not going to give you anything that you can put in that VH-1 special.' I said: 'I'm going to tell the truth, and you haven't heard this yet.You know, you're not going to get much.'And, eight hours I was on camera – eight hours! Now, if you could add up all my segments, and they came to 30 seconds I'd be impressed. It probably was much more than that, but Perry went nuts.And, if you saw the very first promos for VH-1 that came out, it showed Steve Perry saying,'I never really felt like I was a part of the band.'Then it washed to me, where I'm saying, 'Yeah, that's like the Pope saying he never really felt Catholic.'

"Do you know how quick that was taken out? Perry launched like an MX missile when he saw that. He went crazy. That promo was eliminated and that little segment was taken out of VH-1. I mean, even ever so slightly disparaging – and that's not disparaging – that's just saying, 'That's like the Pope's not really Catholic!' Here he is, the Joe Montana of this team, and he never really felt like he was a part of the team. I'm just commenting on the absurdity of his comment. And, of course, the VH-1 guys wanted it because it was the only thing that gave the viewer [the idea that],'Well maybe there's going to be some meat and potatoes here. Maybe there's going to be some meat on the bone'."[275]

Ross Valory had to say this in response to VH-1's *Behind The Music* special on Journey: "There's so many ways the programme could have been presented. We did a lot of interviews. There's many, many, many hours of footage. Steve Smith spent much more time than he's represented for, in terms of interviewing. Even myself. There's so many ways it could have been done. But when you get down to it, it's an hour programme ... really 44 minutes. One could say it could have been done differently, should have been better, should have been more about the band and its history, or even more about what it's currently doing. I think it could have been focused differently, but nonetheless, it's had its influence, its positive effect. Generally, I'm fairly pleased with it."[276]

Valory had a point. Indeed, these programmes are often edited down to less than an hour, though possibly hundreds of hours of interviews and archive footage remained in the vaults. The programme makers go for a specific angle and focus on that aspect.

Herbie Herbert commented: "Pat Morrow [Journey's former tour manager] was on camera, god knows, six hours. Not one piece of footage of Pat was used. Pat was a huge, huge bone of contention between Perry and I. Pat went on to become a captain of industry with Nocturne, and is now successfully retired. And a lot of the problems that Steve had with Pat, Steve was right about. But, with a guy like Steve Perry, everything is a hang-up to him. This guy is the farthest thing from a hippie you could imagine. Zero love. Ya know, zero love."[277]

"Everyone thought we were this clean-cut band but that was a myth," said Neal Schon in 1997. "Behind the closed doors it was a very different story."[278]

Meanwhile, *Arrival* hit the shops. It opens with the strong and polished rock track 'Higher Place' which showed Journey fans that the band had not lost the ability to rock and that Augeri has a strong set of pipes. 'All The Way' is a good ballad but it comes in too early and would have been more effective further up the tracklisting. 'Signs Of Life' is a mid-tempo emotionally charged love song about moving on after a relationship, again demonstrating that Augeri knows his way around a love song and can nail down a rock song too. 'All The Things' is a sturdy mid-paced rock song with a surprisingly progressive riff while 'Loved By You' is a haunting, delicate ballad with some effective piano. 'Livin' To Do', another ballad, opens up with a tender guitar solo and much of the song is reminiscent of Schon's sixties blues influences. 'World Gone Wild' picks up the speed of the album, a strong rock song with some memorable keys and pounding drums. 'I Got A Reason' is one of the album's standout tracks, with an indelible groove and toe-tapping melody and Augeri's voice is on fine form. 'With Your Love' is a Jonathan Cain-led ballad that's just a little bit too sentimental and fails to match up to the heavyweight 'Faithfully'. 'Lifetime Of Dreams', a well-crafted ballad, is notable for its wonderful backing vocals and harmonies. 'Live And Breathe' begins with a brooding bass line and a gripping vocal performance; Schon brings in some heavy guitar during the chorus. 'Nothin' Comes Close' is a nifty track with some groove-laden guitar work and sturdy drumming. 'To Be Alive Again' is a fantastic and thoroughly enjoyable melodic rock song with an indelible melody. 'Kiss Me Softly' is a passionate ballad with some interesting arrangements while the final composition, 'We Will Meet Again', is an unconvincing way to end the album; the band should have closed with a melodic rock song just as they opened.

Though not without its flaws *Arrival* has more passion, charm and classic Journey moments than *Trial By Fire*. Though it has too many ballads and the tracklisting could have been more effective, there are lots of guitars and fantastic melodies. It suffers from being too long, but still deserves more credit then it gets; certainly with the benefit of hindsight it improves with age.

"[*Arrival*] was specifically written to try and get the themes and signatures from the Eighties," Ross Valory later reflected on the album. "In spite of how well it was written, performed, and recorded, it didn't make much of a dent. You can't add to the past that way, so we said let's just play what we want to play."[279]

"I have mixed emotions about *Arrival*," Augeri commented some years later. "I think that we were still under the record company's guidance and they were steering the band towards a certain sound. Perhaps in retrospect it's a snapshot of what the band were doing at that particular time… I would have preferred it to have been a little more concise. I would have loved to have had the ten best songs on there."[280]

Critical opinion was mixed. Andrew McNiece enthused on Melodicrock.com: "Another classic AOR record that is just short of a masterpiece. Another classy Journey record. As stated before, their most fresh and alive sounding record in years and musically some of their best work ever. Add to that, the best production ever… A minor point. In the long run, this is so much better than the Japanese release and it proves that the band will listen to their fans. Bravo."

European fans were eager to see Journey as the band had not toured the UK and the continent in over 20 years, but a proposed European tour with Styx never materialised. On June 2, 2001, the band kicked off a tour with Peter Frampton and former Bad English singer John Waite, opening in Las Vegas and winding up in Chula Vista, California, on August 18.

"He's a friend of ours from way back," said Jonathan Cain of John Waite, "and we just thought it made sense in a rock 'n' roll history sort of way, and he's available. We knew he was out there traveling... we hadn't spoken to John in years, and we were kicking it around. Supposedly The Baby's re-issue that's coming out on One Way really got everybody kind of thinking about, 'Hey what about...' and of course Bad English, and just the connection with our band. I think in a way we've come full circle, we really have. Journey has evolved back into a touring band and a rock band."[281]

"Well I didn't see much of them," John Waite commented. "I mean, Neal came out after the show on the last song and played with us most nights, but we were traveling on a different time schedule. We'd get there fairly early in the day and we would be the first on stage and then we'd be gone, you know. And then Frampton would go on, and then Journey would go on, but we were on a whole different schedule and we traveled in a whole different way."[282]

Waite continued: "I think the fact that Neal and I played together at the end of our set every night was sort of a sign that me and Neal are very good, you know, we always have been, and Deen actually bought me a guitar for my birthday, but I just don't get on with Jon."[283]

On the subject of Augeri as a frontman, John Kalodner said after the release of *Arrival*: "If Steve Perry wasn't going to sing, wasn't going to tour obviously somebody should go and sing the songs because 10,000 people who come see them want to hear those songs. There's an obvious desire for that. Steve Augeri, I like him and he's one of the nicer guys in the music business, really cool, nice to be around with good vibes, and I think the shows are pretty good but he isn't Steve Perry."[284]

On September 11, 2001, the world watched in horror as terrorists brought down the World Trade Centre in New York City and attacked elsewhere. In response to the attacks, Journey joined REO Speedwagon,

Styx, Bad Company, John Waite, Mark Farner, Survivor, Kansas, Eddie Money, Peter Frampton and Edgar Winter in a major fund-raising event held on October 20 and 21 at the Smirnoff Music Centre in Dallas, Texas, and the Hi-Fi Buys Amphitheatre in Atlanta, Georgia. Hosted by the comedian Drew Carey, the event raised $1 million for the victims and their families.

After the hectic schedule that the band committed to in the previous year, 2002 was fairly quiet. Neal Schon went off and formed Planet Us with Sammy Hagar, Deen Castronovo and bassist Michael Anthony, formally of Van Halen. Schon also co-wrote a couple of songs with famed British blues rockers Bad Company, while Jonathan Cain released an album titled *Animated Movie Love Songs*.

Journey fans were treated to the EP *Red 13* in November, the band's follow-up to *Arrival* with Augeri on vocals. Produced by Schon and Cain, *Red 13* was recorded at sporadic times throughout 2001 and 2002 at Wildhorse Studio in Novato, California. "We were really cutting corners and I think that it's much better than it actually sounds. I have been wanting to go back and have somebody remix that stuff," Schon said in 2005.[285]

It was an experiment for the band as it was released through their newly created label Journey Music and initially sold only through the band's official website. The online version of *Red 13* had artwork designed by Kelly McDonald but the retail version (only made available at Journey gigs) was designed by Journey fan Christopher Payne after the band had devised a competition for fans to come up with artwork for the EP. *Red 13* has become a sought-after collector's item after it was deleted in 2008. The EP contains: 'Intro/Red 13/State Of Grace', 'The Time', 'Walkin' Away From The Edge' and 'I Can Breathe'.

To promote the release the band had played a club date on July 17 at the Quest in Minneapolis. It was their first-ever club gig and proved that, despite their reputation, if they had a product to sell they would have to devise new ways of marketing their material, especially without the backing of a major label like Columbia.

Schon continued his collaboration with Planet Us in 2003 after the introduction of guitar wizard Joe Satriani, though the project would come to an abrupt end the following year. Journey fans did not go ignored as the band hooked up with Styx and REO Speedwagon for a summer tour under the moniker Classic Rock Main Event. Journey had their *Red 13* EP to promote, Styx had released *Cyclorama* and REO Speedwagon's last release was 2001's *Live: Plus*. Prior to the road jaunt, members of each band – Neal Schon, Steve Augeri and Jonathan Cain; Tommy Shaw and James Young of Styx; and Kevin Cronin and Dave Amato of REO Speedwagon – played a jam session together at a venue in New York.

European fans were ignored yet again as the band kicked off the tour on May 10 in Las Vegas and finished in Cincinnati, Ohio on August 2 after the tour was extended due to demand. Total album sales of the three bands topped a staggering 140 million. After a long stale period, classic rock in general was making a healthy comeback.

Though Journey made changes throughout the tour, here's one setlist they did play: 'Red 13 Intro/Separate Ways (Worlds Apart)', 'Stone In Love', 'Wheel In The Sky', 'Star Spangled Banner', 'Chain Reaction', 'Lights', 'Open Arms', 'Higher Place', 'Don't Stop Believin'', 'Ask The Lonely', 'Escape', 'Be Good To Yourself', 'Mother, Father' and 'Anyway You Want It' with an encore of 'Lovin', Touchin', Squeezin'' and 'Faithfully'.

Reviewing the show at Staples Centre in Los Angeles on May 20, Andrew McNiece wrote on his popular website Melodicrock.com: "The crowd especially seemed to really dig their set and really got into it, with some obligatory arm swaying, plenty of screaming and some rousing sing-a-longs during the set. Even in these days of anti-smoking and political correctness, a few lighters managed to make their way into the air during 'Lights' and 'Open Arms'. Great stuff! I think the band sensed the enthusiasm from the crowd, as Neal's rendition of '[The] Star Spangled Banner' was absolutely electric. You could see the smiles on their faces during several tracks, which is always good to see. It was a little sad to find I was the only one standing during 'Higher Place'. At least from where I was situated! The song is a dead-set, barnstorming rocker that was just a little lost on a crowd who wanted the hits. But that's what they got, with the rest of the set comprised of back catalogue classics. Steve Augeri put on a great show…"

Covering the show in Albany, New York on July 12, Richard and Laura Lynch wrote on SoundPress.Net: "Adding another patriotic flair to the evening was Neal Schon's solo version of 'The Star Spangled Banner' performed with fluid ease by the guitarist who started at seventeen years-old in Carlos Santana's band. But, when they tried to start 'Feeling That Way/Anytime' Jonathan Cain's equipment failure had the band scrambling to pull an audible of 'Where Were You', a concert rarity only recently re-added to the band's live repertoire. Still, Journey did not disappoint and their songs 'Stone In Love', 'Be Good To Yourself' and 'Lovin', Touchin', Squeezin'' were crowd pleasers. The band also introduced the new song 'State Of Grace' from their recent *Red 13*."

"There was so much speculation when we did that three-bill show a couple of years back with Styx and REO," Schon said in 2005. "REO fans were saying that Journey aren't selling any tickets, Styx management were saying they were selling all the tickets and Journey wouldn't be anything without them."[286]

Finishing off the year, November saw the release of the *Greatest Hits 1978–1997 – Music Videos And Live Performances* DVD in the US, while British fans had to wait until January. Though Neal Schon found time in 2003 to create his latest side-project Soul SirkUS (with an initial line-up of Deen Castronovo, bassist Marco Mendoza and singer Jeff Scott Soto) he still dedicated much of his time to Journey. In May, Japanese fans were treated to yet another compilation of Journey songs called *Open Arms – Greatest Hits*. But on June 11, the band kicked off yet another tour of the US called Summer Detour, which wound up on September 18.

Sarah Hunt of the website Digital Bits went to the band's first date of the tour at the Pechanga Resort in Temecula in California and praised drummer Deen Castronovo. She wrote: "Deen steps into the lead vocal role for a few classic songs in the current show – 'Suzanne', 'Keep On Runnin'' and 'Mother, Father', and darned if he doesn't nail 'em too! He and Augeri take turns on a few others, they actually have a great deal fun with this, and you'll enjoy watching (and listening) to them. The only drawback to this arrangement – if I had to mention one – is the lack of visual focus on the songs that Deen solos on lead vocals. It is tough to see him behind the drumset, but he sounds so good that you quickly get over it."

On November 27, 2003 the band joined REO Speedwagon and Styx for a tour of the Caribbean aboard Carnival's Triumph cruise ship. The ship set sail from Miami and over seven days visited such destinations as Cozumel in Mexico, Grand Cayman in Cayman Islands and Ocho Rios in Jamaica. Fans who had purchased a platinum package for the full seven days were able to meet members of the bands. For Journey, it was certainly an unusual way to end the year's touring schedule.

CHAPTER 8

All The Way:
Thirty Years Of Journey
(And Another New Singer)
(2005–2006)

"Steve [Perry] had been singing professionally for ten years and it was like a marshal hanging up his badge."

Jonathan Cain[287]

On January 21, 2005, Steve Perry and Journey reunited, albeit very briefly, to be inducted into the prestigious Hollywood Walk Of Fame in Los Angeles. The band was surprised when Steve Perry showed up to accept the honour with them. "Even though Neal had been on the radio [LA's KLOS] with a local team gently cajoling Steve to show," commented Ross Valory. "Apparently Steve called the guys back from the radio station and said: 'Yeah, you know, what's going on? Of course I'll be there.' Of course, we still didn't know when he was going to show. But he did. And he was in fine shape and fine spirits. He had some wonderful things to say in a prepared speech after following Neal and I. It was quite a pleasant surprise."[288]

Members of the band past and present turned up, including, of course, Steve Perry and Neal Schon, Jonathan Cain, Ross Valory, Steve Augeri, Robert Fleischman, George Tickner, Steve Smith and Aynsley Dunbar. Gregg Rolie failed to appear. After the ceremony Smith and Dunbar jammed together during a gig at the Hollywood House Of Blues. Of the unlikely reunion with Perry, Neal Schon said: "Life is too short – you need to get on with it. If you have problems, build a bridge and get over it. That's exactly where I'm at, and so I'm hoping that this is the beginning of a better relationship between Perry and ourselves."[289]

Robert Fleischman summed up his experience of re-connecting with some of his former bandmates: "It was a great day; everyone showed up except for Gregg and Herbie. The night before we stayed at the Hollywood Sunset Marquee and we all had a good time in the bar the next morning. We all got into the vans that took us to Hollywood Boulevard for the big ceremony. At the last minute Perry showed up. I don't think he had seen the band for quite some time. Everyone was excited, so was the crowd. There were so many people that it actually went into the street and stopped traffic! Johnny Grant, the Mayor of Hollywood, presented us with the awards. The crowd went wild. Perry gave a little speech and the rest of the band said their thanks. All the TV stations were there. I think that's when it all sunk in; this was real! Afterwards we had a luncheon then later on that night, Journey played at the House Of Blues. They asked me to come up and sing 'Wheel In The Sky'. It was so great to be back up on stage again. Soon afterwards, I put a band together called The Sky, and yes, I did speak to Steve. He lives in Hollywood and so do I, so we would run into each other now and then. It's always been good between us…"[290]

On the subject of Journey's failure to be inducted into the Rock 'n' Roll Hall Of Fame, Ross Valory said jokingly: "Similarly, we've yet to arrive in that city, somewhere in the midwest. Cleveland! Yeah, there's something going on there I understand. Apparently there's a Hall Of Fame there or something for bands of great notoriety. Unfortunately, they've forgotten about Journey. That's OK. The fans will get to them as well sooner or later. Cleveland, yeah right."[291]

Receiving the Walk Of Fame accolade was a triumphant start to a year that saw Journey commence work on a new album, to be called *Generations*, at the Record Plant in Sausalito, California, where they had recorded *Raised On Radio* back in the mid-Eighties. For whatever reason they chose not to work with producer Kevin Shirley, who had produced *Trial By Fire* and *Arrival*, instead hiring Kevin Elson. Of course, Elson had collaborated with the band on their biggest albums – *Departure*, *Escape* and *Frontiers* – and stayed with the band as their live engineer.

Whereas Augeri was co-credited as songwriter on some songs on *Arrival*, with *Generations* he was the sole author of 'Butterfly (She Flies Alone)' and co-writer on some other tracks. He explained in a 2005 interview: "So after the seventh year and no new record in sight for Journey, I decided I was going to start writing music just the same. Jon Cain suggested I pick up an Apple Powerbook, which has this Garage Band program in it, which is ideal for a technical moron such as myself – I mean a kid could sit down and write a record on it – I was like a kid in a candy store when I got it. I couldn't get away from it – it has all the great instrumentation and great drum loops and this and that. So I had all these songs bottled up in me and all these ideas and the moment I got my hands on it I started writing at this feverish pace. So it was during last year's tour that Neal took notice that I always had my head buried in the thing. So I laid some songs on him and he looked at me and to put it simply, I guess he was impressed with some of the musical ideas that I was coming up with. And I think the wheels started turning… Neal got the notion… at least with a small inkling of what I was doing, [and] that a new Journey album was in the works – at least a start or seed of it… So from that material we started building and having some writing sessions and it went from several songs of mine that were being considered, to you know… the usual…"[292]

"Steve and I really did a lot of work," said Cain, by now Journey's chief songwriter. "Neal was kind of gone. But I very carefully took his work and really honed in and did what I did on *Escape* with it. I tried to become that guy again. I was just there explaining that to them… it was great… we rekindled what we really do well together. He'll give me a track and let me work on it and I'll come back with you know… it's fun. We did it on the road…. we did it…"[293]

The band worked very quickly on the album for around 40 days throughout February and March, recording all the tracks within a week, rehearsing and recording live as they did in the old days, most notably on *Escape*. Mike Fraser who had worked with Bad English and Metallica was hired to record and mix the album in Vancouver where Fraser is based. "I think Kevin's a talented guy," Fraser says about Kevin Elson, "He's worked with Neal and the boys a lot and they all were on the same page about what kind of record they wanted to do. He's an easy going guy and a pleasure to work with. Lot's of great ideas, musically."[294]

Fraser remembers drummer Deen Castronovo during the recording and mixing stages: "Deen had a set of carbon steel drums that we thought we would check out. I couldn't believe how heavy each piece weighed! The small tom probably weighed 80lbs or more! I think we ended up using the kick drum from that set on a few tunes. Great sounding drum set but it was too 'live'-sounding and hard to contain."[295]

"Steve had a great set of pipes," Fraser says on Steve Perry's successor. "Oh man could that guy sing. Of course he's always going to be compared to Perry but I don't think that's fair. They are two different singers. It's the same as comparing Bon Scott with Brian Johnson, or Sammy Hagar with David Lee Roth. They come in and replace an established singer and always have to live in that shadow whether they're kicking ass or not."[296]

Fraser has some final words on the album: "Journey has spanned across a lot of different years with a bunch of personnel changes along the way. The early Journey years sounded somewhat different than the later Journey years... but it always has that thread of unmistakable Journey. *Generations* is a cool record in the fact that each guy in the band got to share some of the lead singing duties. It gave that record a great twist."[297]

"I found that *Arrival* had too many overdubs on it," Schon said in response to fans' initial criticisms of the album and how it compares to the new one. "Everything became meshy and you don't hear the air in the tracks anymore. The only thing I am disappointed with on this record is – somewhat – the drum sound from the Metallica room where we recorded... I imagined it was going to be a much bigger room sound. It ended up not sounding that big to me. I was in the room with Deen cutting the tracks, playing live and they sounded enormous. I don't know what happened. We went to analog tape, so they should have sounded even bigger. Pro Tools can make it sound real tiny. Had I known what Mike Fraser's studio was like in Vancouver, where he did *Back In Black* with AC/DC, we would have recorded there. That room was enormous and was actually cheaper than were we went – the Record Plant."[298]

However, in hindsight, Schon was not best pleased with the recording sound of *Generations*. He said: "I thought the vocals on it were so-so, and I thought it was not the writing that was at fault but the actual performances. I thought Steve didn't really have the voice that he had when we first got him, to perform on the songs, and I also thought that the sound of the record was not good. I was not happy with that at all. I mean we spent a frickin' small fortune on that record too – I didn't think the studio that we recorded it in sounded good and then I don't think the mixes ended up sounding right. I was not impressed with the sound quality at all."[299]

Jonathan Cain remarked: "I think *Generations* is a different time and place for us. I'm not going to compare the albums as there is great stuff on both albums. Everybody is different with what they like and I think… it certainly went down smoother from production and band stand point. We didn't have a record label in our face."[300]

"The recording of *Generations* is some of my proudest moments," Ross Valory enthused. "The music is strong, it's varied, it's surprisingly not necessarily what people would expect from Journey. After *Arrival*… we made a sincere and conscientious attempt at writing music that tied to our past influences and past styles. That threads, that signature… from *Arrival* to the songs we were most known for in the past. And it did absolutely no good. It didn't mean anything to anybody. In spite of what I believe and what you believe, ah, they were some quality songs and quality recordings representing the Journey style and all of a sudden nothing happened."[301]

Though the band had sold over 70 million albums worldwide since releasing their self-titled debut back in 1975 and were celebrating their 30th Anniversary in 2005 (even though they formed in 1973), they were without a record deal. They came up with a marketing idea that was to give away copies of the *Generations* CD to every ticket holder at most concerts during their summer tour. A global retail release with different packaging was planned after the tour finished.

Ross Valory explained: "The idea came from what Prince did last year. He was quite successful with it, despite the fact that his tickets are far more expensive than ours. We have a general agreement with the promoter at most venues. Some venues that's not possible. The politics of the economics are not set up for that, so just to let the fans know that it has to be advertised that way so they're not hoodwinked or disappointed or upset if they come to a show where there isn't a CD. The ones that are advertised with the CD/ticket are the [venues] that actually have it. If it's not advertised that way, usually a festival or fair, maybe other acts are included."[302]

Asked about fans putting the free CD on sale on eBay, Valory replied: "No we're not afraid. They've tried to put it up on eBay and it gets pulled off immediately. We got our eyes open. How we are getting around that is, people are coming to our show and getting the CD for what they pay for a ticket."[303]

Prior to the summer tour, Neal Schon said: "We're going to be able to play so much more material from the beginning, pre-Steve Perry days, and move on. We're probably going to end up doing a three-and-a-half-hour show, so I've invited all past members to come and sit in – including Steve Perry. We'll just have to wait and see if he shows up."[304]

Having just finished a tour with his side-project Soul SirkUS, Schon was eager to hit the road with his first love, Journey. In June the Recording Industry Association Of America announced that Journey had sold 41 million albums in the US alone. The band kicked off their 30th Anniversary tour - dubbed An Evening With Journey - in Irvine, California on June 26 and finished in Phoenix, Arizona on October 8. Augeri stopped drinking alcohol and caffeine and eating dairy products to look after his voice and body during the tour so he would be in peak condition; he reportedly spent two hours before each show warming up his vocals and body. However, Augeri experienced some teething trouble during the first two concerts. He said: "The simple reason is we are doing a three-hour show… I'm singing the absolute last quarter of the first set and then I sing the second set. So what happens is that I warm up – I don't have this lay-over period. I warm up, hit stage and I'm going. Now I have this period of time – 45 minutes – where I don't sing a note and I'm still trying to adapt to it. It's getting a little better as we go along but that is just the way it is. For seven years I never did anything like it, so I'm trying to teach an old dog new tricks."[305]

The band had committed to helping charities and the centerpiece of each concert was the appearance of a 30th Anniversary Journey Motorcycle, made by Arlen Ness Motorcycles, with artwork from Journey's back catalogue. Fans would have a chance at winning the bike by donating to the band's chosen charity: T.J. Martell Foundation, which helps research children's diseases. Another attraction on the tour was an interactive festival area known as Journeyville with continuous retrospective video footage (and stereo sound) from the band's history; it gave fans a chance to learn about and look into the band's past.

"This is something I have wanted to do for a long time," said Schon. "It wasn't an easy situation. Management weren't totally into it, our agent was not totally into it and I think a lot of promoters were not into it. They finally came around and agreed it would be really good."[306]

The setlist was an almost chronological tour through the band's history, including material from the three albums prior to Steve Perry joining in 1977. Many fans had not heard the band's music pre *Infinity* and some even assumed it was new material! "We did it because we hadn't played this stuff in a while and thought the fans would get behind it," Jonathan Cain explained at the time, "and also to show newer fans the evolution, if you will, of the band. Sometimes you forget where Journey came from, and it's actually shocked us the reaction of some of the people that show up."[307]

Cain sang many of the pre-Steve Perry songs when Gregg Rolie was in the band: "Yeah, I had to learn all this stuff and try to make it my own – it's a challenge every night – but it's fun. I'd sung with The Baby's way back when, but this *Generations* album was the first time I'd ever got to sing the lead on a Journey song, and now I'm singing a lot of the old stuff in the show and I find it suits me. There are no accidents, it was all meant to be, and in the show I get to sing and I get to play guitar too – and I'm doing a lot of that."[308]

Each concert was three-hours long with an intermission, and they did not downplay their biggest hits, which the band dubbed 'the dirty dozen'. On the opening night in Irvine the band played a hefty eight songs from *Generations*, which reportedly did not go down well with the fans, so they reduced the number of songs from the new album to three. Indeed, some of the earlier shows were not welcomed with open arms by fans of Journey's trademark AOR and melodic rock anthems. "We've had to balance it in terms of our studies, our own observing of the audience reaction," Ross Valory said at the time. "We've had to modify both sets, add a couple more familiar songs to the first set, and to reduce the number of *Generations* songs in the second set and add back in again more familiar songs just so we don't go over everybody's head because we can't forget this one thing: they are there to hear the songs that they love."[309]

Since 2004 when Deen Castronovo sang 'Mother, Father' and 'After The Fall', his vocal duties on some songs became a permanent fixture in the band's live shows. This lifted a massive weight off Augeri who would struggle through three hours of demanding Journey songs on a tight touring schedule. "It's a team and if someone goes down and if Stevie has a rough night I am there to pick up the slack whatever it takes," said the drummer/singer. "That's the best thing about this band – there is so much talent and there is so much ability in each member. I like the fact that we pull for each other and there's not like there is a lot of ego involved. And that's a blessing bro, because I have been involved in some bands where there is some heavy egos."[310]

"He's definitely a fucking trooper," Schon said of the band's frontman during the tour. "He goes out there and tries his hardest, you know. Luckily enough there is a lot of breathing time in the set with Deen singing and the rest of us singing. I think it's going to be fine. He's struggling with some mid-area stuff. I don't know that it's so much the high stuff, but his mid-range – something is bugging him right there. He's got his vocal coach coming out here and he'll be working with him, I'm sure he'll get back on path."[311]

Journey having some fun during time off in 1981

The great Gregg Rolie on stage in 1980. (CHRIS WALTER/PHOTOFEATURES)

Singer Steve Perry and guitarist Neal Schon live on stage in 1981. (BOB LEAFE/FRANK WHITE PHOTO AGENCY)

The iconic Steve Perry in 1981. (FRANK WHITE)

Close up of Jonathan Cain on stage; he would become Schon's most important ally. (LEGACY RECORDINGS)

The classic line-up: Neal Schon, Jonathan Cain, Ross Valory, Steve Smith and Steve Perry. (LEGACY RECORDINGS)

Jonathan Cain, Steve Perry and bassist Randy Jackson on stage in 1986 during the *Raised On Radio* tour.
(LARRY BUSACCA/RETNA PICTURES)

One time Journey bassist Randy Jackson in 1987. (CLAYTON CALL/REDFERNS)

Bassist Ross Valory, Jonathan Cain on keys and guitarist Neal Schon. (JANET MACOSKA/RETNA LTD.)

Journey live on stage circa 1982-3: Steve Perry, Neal Schon,
Steve Smith and Jonathan Cain. (PHOTOFEST)

Steve Augeri live on stage.

(TIM MOSENFELDER/GETTY IMAGES)

Jeff Scott Soto and Steve Augeri looking happy
together backstage at Firefest in England, 2009.

(COURTESY SUE ASHCROFT)

Bassist Ross Valory, singer Jeff Scott Soto and Jonathan Cain on rhythm guitar.

(TRACEY WELCH/RETNA PICTURES)

Journey stars past and present at the Hollywood Walk Of Fame in 2005. (TAMMIE ARROYO/AFF-USA.COM)

Yet another new singer: Arnel Pineda (centre) with bassist Ross Valory, guitarist Neal Schon (left) and drummer Deen Castronovo and keyboardist Jonathan Cain (right). (ROMEO GACAD/AFP/GETTY IMAGES)

Bassist Ross Valory still going strong on stage.
(SETTON/DALLE/RETNA PICTURES)

Neal Schon at the *Classic Rock* Roll Of Honour Awards in London, 2010. (BRIAN RASIC/REX FEATURES)

"You don't have to give Deen any tips, he's a natural," remarked Augeri. "I work constantly on retaining my voice and keeping it in good shape… I say that if anyone says I sound like Steve Perry, then I can just turn around and say take a listen to Deen because he's got him down to a tee….Thank god there's a Deen Castronovo in the band because there's no way on earth that I could do it [a three-hour show]."[312]

Not only had some fans noticed that Augeri was struggling through some shows but that Castronovo, on the other hand, looked like a clean bill of health and was singing pitch-perfect. "I'll tell you something… four or five years ago I wouldn't have been able to do it. I was pretty messed up on drugs and alcohol and the band had an intervention with me and got me on the straight and narrow. It's been great, I lost 60 pounds and that is the only way I could do it – off the drugs and alcohol and with the weight loss. I am able to do three hours with no problem."[313]

The band did continue to tweak the setlist throughout the tour, for variety more than anything else. "That's the beauty of it – we can screw around with it a bit, play 'Send Her My Love' on night, 'Message Of Love' another. I think as the fans get into the new album a little more they will dig it. It was amazing though, when we did 'Out Of Harms Way' it just killed them – they loved it live and I couldn't have been happier."[314]

The tour was interrupted and some shows cancelled in August when Jonathan Cain had an operation to have his appendix removed. Cain did, however, carry on in September despite not feeling fully recovered, though the concert length was shortened from three hours to ninety minutes.

Unfortunately European fans missed out again as Journey did not tour there in 2005. Ross Valory explained at the time: "It's been a long time since we've been to Europe and never really did a major tour there even though, at one point, we were popular enough to do so, but we declined. So it's time that we go back overseas, at least to Western Europe."[315]

Generations was released on August 29 in Europe via Frontiers, an Italian based record label dealing specifically with AOR and melodic rock; in the US the album was released through Sanctuary on October 4. The band's twelfth album and second one with Augeri peaked at a disappointing number 170 on the *Billboard* chart in the US and failed to make any impact in Britain, though it did chart in Sweden, Germany and Japan. It failed to spawn any hit singles, though 'Faith In The Heartland' was played briefly during an episode of NBC's *Football Night In America* later in the year.

Andrew McNiece wrote on melodicrock.com: "*Generations* sees Journey change tack a little, introducing a vocal role for all members. Whether that is entirely necessary or not, the majority of vocal performances on the album are excellent. *Generations* has all the ingredients required of a Journey album and a little extra punch, which fans were calling for. It cuts back the number of tracks on offer, which was probably *Arrival's* biggest problem.

"This album has some definite advantages over the previous album, but as discussed, also has a couple of detracting points, which I believe will split fans – with some preferring *Arrival* and others favoring *Generations*. Personally I prefer the US version of *Arrival* and the European release of Soul SirkUS' *World Play* overall. Rougher, tougher and more diverse than *Arrival*, *Generations* is an album that still rates as a must-buy for melodic rock fans, but it isn't a classic."

Generations opens with the sumptuous melodic rock track 'Faith In The Heartland' with lead vocals from Augeri. 'The Place In Your Heart' is another strong rock track with stern lead vocals from Augeri and strong guitar work from Schon, while 'A Better Life' proves that drummer Deen Castronovo can more than adequately sing a Journey ballad; it's a mellow song with some minor guitar work but an effective melody. 'Every Generation' features Jonathan Cain on lead vocals; it's a groovy, toe-tapping mid-paced song with a sing-along chorus. 'Butterfly (She Flies Alone)' is sung by Augeri who also adds additional guitar; it's not quite the ballad it could be but it does have an endearing quality and builds up to an effective crescendo. 'Believe' again has Augeri on lead vocals and additional guitar; it's a joyful song with an unforgettable melody and some good arrangements. 'Knowing That You Love Me' has Augeri singing lead vocals and it's a very Journey-esque power ballad with some exquisite guitar work and excellent backing vocals and harmonies. 'Out Of Harm's Way' opens with an aggressive guitar before the rest of the band join in and Augeri sings his heart out; it's a tough rock song that has a really catchy melody and chorus. 'In Self-Defense' stars Neal Schon on vocals and was originally including on 1982's *Here To Stay*, Schon's second album with Jan Hammer; it's a fast and furious rock song with pounding drums and speedy work on the fretboard. Schon is not a strong singer but for this type of song, his vocals work well. 'Better Together' is a blues-tinged rock song with Augeri returning to lead vocals; it's a slight departure for the band and harks back to some of Schon's blues-rock influences from the late sixties. 'Gone Crazy' is a boogie-woogie type rock song with Ross Valory on lead vocals; his vocals are slightly groggy but the song is fun though far from imaginative. The 9/11 inspired 'Beyond The Clouds' returns Augeri to lead vocals on what is essentially a typically sentimental ballad, but well-crafted nonetheless. The final track on the European version (added as bonus track) is 'Never Too Late', which has Castronovo on lead vocals and Cain on additional guitar; it's a better song to end the album with than 'Beyond The Clouds.' Start with a melodic rock track and finish with one.

Generations is a more varied album than *Arrival*, and harks back to *Escape* and *Frontiers* with some songs that sound experimental by the band's standards post-*Infinity*, and it has a definite live aura about it. Having the band share lead vocals throughout the album is a nice touch and was apparently inspired by Styx from the Classic Rock Main Event tour. Journey were so impressed how they shared lead vocals they decided to try it themselves. "It's a carry-over from a tradition we began last year in which everyone was singing at least a song or two," Ross Valory explained. "And we decided that since everyone has a good voice, we thought, 'Why not spread the talent on every set?' That is a departure as well. There were only a few albums where there were two singers, Steve Perry and Gregg Rolie. For the most part there was generally one lead singer. We have more than one here, why not display the talent?"[316]

Asked about some of the sombre themes the album hints at, Jonathan Cain explained: "You know, the US has had some things to deal with recently, and some things to soul-search, so there's a lot of that on the album too, I think; about being an American these days and looking at where the lines are drawn. 'Out Of Harm's Way' is basically our prayer for the soldiers over in the Middle East, and no matter what happens we hope they return safe."[317]

The quality of songs on offer are of a high standard, though some fans did make comments about the sound quality. Nevertheless, it remains a hugely enjoyable album. "I'm a bigger fan of British rock 'n' roll than American, any day of the week," Augeri enthused. "On *Generations* there is a lot of rock 'n' roll, and there is a lot of heavy rock 'n' roll, there's great guitar riffs and there's also some good power ballads in general. There's a great mixture."[318]

In November, Steve Perry made a brief return to the limelight to promote the *Live In Houston 1981: The Escape Tour* CD/DVD. He did a series of interviews that focused on the release, but he was also forthcoming about Journey's history. Asked if he felt emotional looking back at the footage, Perry replied: "It was too much of a heartache to look back. When I first heard the tapes and I remembered that show, it was too painful to think what it once was, but the only thing I could not do was... I'm a fighter for the music. I'm a fighter for the songs and a fighter for the performances, and I refuse to let them be evaporated into time. If I do anything, I'm going to fight for those performances to be heard and the band is out doing what they're doing and I was approached by Sony to do it, so I said absolutely, since I had produced the first compilation DVD. So, I got Allen Sides and we did the 5.1 and stereo mixes together then I did the editing. The interviews and all that was painful too. It was tough."[319]

"I swear to you that it was more a real labour of love insofar as I am the emotional protector of these songs in my heart," he continued, after being asked about returning to the band's music. "They mean too much to me still, they are like children to me and when any sort of representation goes out on them I am compulsively involved."[320]

After another busy year – and after eight years on the road – Augeri was starting to feel the strain. In 2006, they took a break for a few months, resuming touring in June with a visit to the UK for the first time since a London gig back in 1980. British fans had already shown their dedication to the band by setting up a Journey convention in 2004. Encouraged by an online petition at www.journey.co.uk to entice UK promoters to invest in a Journey tour, the band began the brief UK tour on June 2 at Edinburgh's Playhouse and played the packed Manchester Apollo on June 5; both shows had sold out and fans had reportedly travelled from around Europe to finally catch of a glimpse of the band live. However, there was no London date.

In Manchester, they played 'Separate Ways (Worlds Apart)', 'Only The Young', 'Faith In The Heartland', 'Stone In Love', 'Wheel In The Sky', 'Where Were You', 'Lights', 'Still They Ride', 'Feeling That Way', 'Anytime', 'Chain Reaction', 'Edge Of The Blade', 'Who's Crying Now', 'Mother, Father', 'Open Arms', 'Escape', 'Keep On Runnin'', 'Out Of Harm's Way', 'Faithfully', 'Don't Stop Believin'' and 'Any Way You Want It' with the encores 'Dead Or Alive' and 'Lovin' Touchin' Squeezin''.

Ian Harvey reviewed the gig for getreadytorock.com: "Augeri is in fine voice. He's ditched his rock T-shirt in favour of a red shirt and black waistcoat. We're sweltering in the crowd so goodness knows how hot he is on stage. I don't know how he does it but he doesn't even seem to break sweat as the band rocket through 'Only The Young' and 'Faith In The Heartland'."

The band also squeezed in a more-than-welcome appearance (as third band on the bill) at the Monsters Of Rock festival on June 3 at the Milton Keynes Bowl, headlined by veteran British rockers Deep Purple with Alice Cooper, Thunder, Queensrÿche, Ted Nugent and Roadstar also performing.

Journey then played Rock The Nation festival in Germany on June 7, followed a day later by an appearance at the enormously successful Sweden Rock festival, and then at Holland's Arrow Rock Festival. "We've been anxious to go to places outside of the United States for years and finally gotten the opportunity," said Ross Valory. "Certainly we have been welcomed over there, and we're looking forward to doing as much as possible."[321]

Back in the US, Journey undertook a joint headlining tour with Def Leppard, which began on June 23 in Camden, New Jersey. Def Leppard – often wrongly considered a heavy metal band because of their association with the New Wave Of British Metal – were far more suited to a band like Journey's fanbase than, say, Iron Maiden. Leppard's brand of commercial Americanised melodic rock has made them one of Britian's most successful rock bands, though their success in the US has far outweighed their popularity back home, or elsewhere for that matter. Jonathan Cain said in a press release: "[Def Leppard is] a band I've admired for a long time. We're honored to be performing with a band that received their Diamond Award at the same ceremony when we received our Diamond Award. So it seems fitting that we go out together after all these years and celebrate a lot of good years of rock 'n' roll."[322]

During the European dates and US tour that followed there were suggestions that Steve Augeri was not, in fact, singing live but had been using backing tapes to mask his deteriorating voice. It seemed to have began at Sweden Rock, after which fans started gossiping online about Augeri and alleging that he wasn't singing live. The forums soon became rife with fans lambasting Augeri. He was, to put it simply, getting roasted by Journey fans.

Had Augeri's run in the band come to a natural end? Was Journey's famously demanding back catalogue of songs just too much for him? Had Journey's grueling tour schedule proved too much for him between 1998 and 2006?

Former Journey manager Herbie Herbert says today, "Steve Perry is 65 years old now and if Steve Perry were in great shape, and was a great guy, and was completely willing to tour with Journey right now, or even the last ten years since 1999 when they started with Augeri, he would not be able to sing those songs in the original keys. Even if he was in the greatest of shape he'd be down a half step, maybe even a whole step, and so why they would not lower those keys for Augeri, I never quite understood... This is something Perry sang when he was a young guy, he was 30 and in great shape and you just can't do it 30 years later. They should have backed off the keys; and then they had Kevin Elson mixing who was my guy and Kevin got caught, I guess, up in Stockholm using a canned vocal off the hard drive but had mistakenly given the live vocal feeds to the radio booth and they kept going, 'Wait, this guy can't sing... He's terrible' and they go in the hall and it sounds perfect. How does that work? It's the hard drive; it's not really his real vocals. That causes problems. That's when they knew they had to shift gears from Augeri."[323]

The complicated situation became known as 'tapegate' and fans set up an online petition to oust Steve Augeri, who many claimed was past his peak and could no longer do justice to Journey's music. In a press statement the band announced that he was suffering from a chronic throat infection and had to step down as lead singer and quit the tour to recuperate. The band said: "Steve's been suffering with an acute throat condition since before we kicked off the tour with Def Leppard. We were hoping he'd be in a condition to handle the rigours of the road but unfortunately it appears to be a chronic condition requiring total voice rest. We all wish Steve a speedy recovery."[324]

Asked about the use of backing tapes on the Leppard tour, Ross Valory said after the tour was over: "This is another urban myth! It just didn't happen. The rumour got prominence because we were changing singers – Steve Augieri's voice did give out. It's a very difficult setlist. Not even Steve Perry could hold up very long, I believe, because these songs are very demanding of any singer… It turns out the person who stirred up the tape issue is not a journalist and didn't have the correct information. It appears to me some people have too much time on their hands, sometimes fans can be over-obsessed with the band of their dreams and they can get to be too imaginative or creative in order to provoke a response. It's like they're clutching at straws, and even inventing those straws! I don't, of course, wish to disparage the bulk of our fans."[325]

Augeri played his last show as Journey's frontman/singer on July 4 in Raleigh, North Carolina. Despite talk of Augeri possibly rejoining the band on tour at some point, he was replaced and is unlikely to ever front Journey again. "Steve [Perry] had to take a step back and re-evaluate his life and perhaps his health," Augeri explained in 2009. "I had to do the same. It was a mutual thing that we came across and I think, in the long run, certainly, it certainly worked out wonderfully for the band. For me, if you were to compare my health today to 2006, I'm a different… I'm physically regenerated. I mean, I can't say it any better. I was a physical mess and I needed to get away and unplug. The doctors told me that's what I needed to do. I did it and I'm so glad I did because, frankly, had I not, I may not... we wouldn't be having this conversation and I wouldn't have a voice to even speak to you one the phone."[326]

"I got to know Steve Augeri," said Kevin Chalfant, a friend of the band and former singer of The Storm, "and he's a great man and just a beautiful individual. You couldn't hate him. You can't hate him. I've had what happened to him happen to me where I'd be sick for an entire season. People would go, 'Oh he's washed up,' and all this and that, and then you know once you've had a season of rest you come back and you[re] stronger than you were.[327]

Nevertheless, Augeri made his mark in rock history and for that he must be applauded. After some time off he restarted Talisman and commenced work on his debut solo album. Looking back on the whole Journey saga, Augeri explained in 2009: "Of course I would have never been given this opportunity had it not been for the man who came before me. I owe Steve Perry for doing all the heavy lifting. It was a daunting task to walk in after someone of Mr. Perry's stature. He taught me to raise the bar for myself, and aim for new heights. But, like Steve before me, I too had reached a sign post and it was time to move on. For me though, it was a medical issue that was unpublished beyond just a vocal issue that brought about the end of my journey, pardon the pun. Doctors order if you will. What are you gonna do? *C'est la vie.*"[328]

Asked if he had any permanent damage to his vocal cords, the singer replied: "I was faced with the difficult decision to either take a break or fear damaging my voice permanently. Although it hurt beyond any pain you can inflict upon yourself, emotionally that is, in the long term it was the only way to go. I have my medical condition in check and have recovered vocally and then some."[329]

The band had some quick thinking to do as the tour was still in progression and proving to be very popular, so they hired Jeff Scott Soto. "Jeff approaches it differently: he has some of the common influences and roots that Steve Perry has," said Ross Valory. "He doesn't necessarily sing it like Steve Perry does but he has an affinity with singers like Sam Cooke and Sam & Dave, and he sings in a unique and original way."[330]

In melodic rock circles JSS, as he is referred to, is very popular from his work with Neal Schon in Soul SirkUS, as well as fronting the Yngwie Malmsteen Band, Axel Rudi Pell, Eyes, Talisman and Takara. Born on November 4, 1965 in Brooklyn, New York of Puerto Rican descent, JSS's singing heroes include Steve Perry and Freddie Mercury. After performing 'Dragon Attack' with Queen guitarist Brian May at the 2000 Freddie Mercury Birthday Party event in Reading, England, he was reportedly even in the running to front Queen before they hooked up with ex-Free and Bad Company singer Paul Rodgers. JSS was also involved in the music for the movie *Rock Star* as a member of the fictional band Steel Dragon with Zakk Wylde, Jeff Pilson, Jason Bonham and Miljenko Matijevic, with whom he shared lead vocals on the soundtrack. Though JSS has a dedicated fanbase the world over, he had never received a truly big break and was always hovering on the fringes of the mainstream despite an abundance of talent. Joining Journey finally gave him the potential to be a superstar.

However, the band and their management took some convincing from Schon who said: "Everybody was very skeptical at first… we ended up checking it out and it worked out fine. Management and promoters were scared and so were other band members, and they were waiting for tickets to get returned because the tour was pretty much sold out, especially the second leg. They were saying that tickets would be coming back because fans would be disappointed that it wasn't Steve, but I said: 'I don't think so.' It turned out that there were two tickets returned throughout the whole tour."[331]

Marco Mendoza, the bassist in Soul SirkUS, remembers, "For me in the back of my mind I'm like 'That's the perfect choice.' We started doing some Journey things in Soul SirkUS, not a whole lot but a few. Jeff is a chameleon, man; anything he can set his mind to do he can do. For me, I think they found themselves in a jam [and] he was the logical choice. I was talking to Jeff the day when he got the call – from Neal – when all this is going down and how they were caught up in some messy situation and they were stressing about it…"[332]

JSS made his singing debut with Journey on July 7 at Bristow in Virginia.

JSS: "Well, I'd known that Steve [Augeri] had had some issues even before I got the call in 2006. I'd heard a few troubling – I guess – bootlegs or even been to a couple of shows and spoken to Neal about it. Basically, the overall consensus was the guy needed a break; he needed a rest. He had been promised a break. To kind of take a year of and recharge, get reloaded again because that stuff will kill any singer. That catalogue took its toll on Perry eventually and he's the one who originated it. When they booked a tour for 2006 I knew Steve was going to have some troubles, some real troubles. And I was not wrong. It was basically after the European run and back into the US, I got a call from Neal saying, 'Man, I don't know how Steve's going to be able to make it through this tour.' It was almost a joking thing. 'Well, you never know bro' you might need to pack your bags and come out and sing with us…' Yeah, yeah, yeah right, like that's ever going to happen! It was mainly the fact that I knew the entire catalogue. I think that was one of the main reasons Neal could count on me. I literally had a few days notice: pack your bags and come out and save the tour. They were looking at other ideas to save the tour like Deen stepping forward and singing the set and the drum tech or bringing another drummer to get through the shows or Deen singing the whole set behind the drums which he didn't feel was an option: 'Guys, I'm not a singer, I'm a drummer who can sing.' He didn't want that pressure on himself. The only other option was to pull the plug on the tour. That would have meant even Def Leppard losing millions because it was a package tour. Again, it was two days notice: 'Can you come out and do this?' I said absolutely! I was more concerned about what Steve was going to feel. I didn't want him to feel like I was bulldozing my way in and saying, 'OK, it's my gig now'. I came in with all respect to every project and every aspect and, literally with a ten-minute soundcheck behind me, I went out there in front of my first audience with those guys in front of 22,000 people."[333]

Were Journey fans overly harsh towards Steve Augeri during the whole 'tapegate' scandal? JSS comments: "I don't think it's harsh. Any kind of disappointment especially amongst the diehard fans… There are ways to do things and there are ways that things are done especially in this business. There are a lot of cover-ups. Things that people do a certain way, they should or could be a little more honest about. That was them basically shooting themselves in the foot by just keeping things hush-hush and not really dealing with the problems at hand. I can understand why the fans were pissed off. They were pissed off that there was no real word. 'OK, Steve, you're voice is shot. Go home and we'll get this guy to fill in for you.' I've never really seen that done before. You can do that maybe with a bass player or a drummer but not the frontman."[334]

With no time to waste, the band with their new frontman launched right into it, as JSS explains: "I landed in Washington DC. They had two days off that week. It was agreed with Steve that he had to go home and rest... I literally landed that evening in DC with the guys just to say hello and welcome here and on the next day-off basically everybody's in there... They had their days off and I'm sitting around going, 'I'm wondering if somebody's going to give me a setlist... if we're gonna discuss what songs, if I know this, if I know that...' Not a single call the entire day. I didn't speak to a single bandmate. It wasn't until checkout time the next day heading to the bus, heading to the venue [that] I finally got a setlist and knew what I would be singing within the course of a few hours. One of the interesting parts of that is that, because it was a package tour, we would flip-flop on who was getting the full soundcheck and who would get a linecheck. That happened to be a Def Leppard's full-soundcheck day. Nobody bothered telling them, 'Guys, we're switching singers would you mind switching days so we could get a full soundcheck day?' As Joe Elliott found out later... he said, 'My God, of course we would have given you guys a full soundcheck day in a heartbeat. Nobody told us!' The band [Journey] came on, 'Who's this guy?!' They finished their soundcheck and we got a ten-minute linecheck. We went over three songs during that quick linecheck just to make sure I had levels so I could hear myself onstage. Within an hour-and-a-half we were on stage doing my first Journey gig."[335]

However, not all Journey fans felt JSS was the right man for the job. Herbert Herbert comments: "I think it was a mis-step to have Jeff Scott Soto there because he wasn't a tenor. You've gotta be a tenor to try to replace Steve Perry. He had a button he would hit to take his voice up an octave but it's an electronic octave, it wasn't right."[336]

"The register was much higher than he'd been singing for years," said Neal Schon, "even though he'd had the range before, but I knew that he would be able to nurture it and get up there to reach those notes, and after a while he did. Not immediately – but Jeff is a great musician and a great singer and the notes that he couldn't hit he would know what to substitute. That's what you do, you have to improvise when you can't quite hit everything that was there on the record – you substitute other notes for it. Every singer does it."[337]

The band's show in Nashville on July 16 was reviewed by Mike Farley at Bullz-eye.com: "Jeff Scott Soto was the front man for this legendary band. Soto was just an adequate fill-in, and was thankfully overshadowed by a band that was as tight as they have ever sounded, including spot-on harmonies. To his credit, Soto also was humble enough to thank the band for the opportunity, making reference to the fact that they were some of the greatest musicians on the planet."

Certainly JSS tried his best to fit in with the band both on- and off-stage. Was there a sense on the road that Journey was/is Jonathan Cain and Neal Schon's band?

JSS: "Oh, absolutely. Well, yes and no. For the most part it is their band. It's Neal's band first but it's Jonathan's band second, because obviously Jonathan is very instrumental in some of their biggest hits, whether it be as the main writer or the co-writer, even more so [than] when Gregg Rolie was in the band. You would think that Ross would have a little more say in that because he is, as much as Neal is, the original founding member of Journey and Ross pretty much has taken the backstage in letting Neal and Jonathan run the machine. And of course, Deen has always been kind of like Neal's boy. Neal knows he can count on Deen for everything, for whatever situation. Deen's just kind of there and he's happy to be there. He's not going to make waves. He's not going to try to say, 'Well, I've been here long enough I should speak my mind...'. He knows where his place is."[338]

On the subject of Steve Perry and whether or not the band continued to talk about him on the road or elsewhere, JSS recalls: "Yeah, we spoke about Perry a lot, and a lot of it was favourable, especially when they're talking about the good old days, the old stories. There were a few negative things in the sense of when business takes over and when there was a rift in the band that obviously separated [them], pushed them apart, and forced Perry to decide [that] he wanted to walk away and all those types of things. But aside from that, Perry was a favourable subject for conversation with everybody, and Jonathan couldn't say enough nice things about when they were writing this song or how Perry was effortless in doing this in the studio, and then how he would kick everyone out of the studio until he felt it was right and then he would bring them in and they would just go, 'My God, it sounds like magic'. That was refreshing in itself because going back to the fact that Perry's such a huge influence on me, I don't want to necessarily hear negativity. I want to hear that these guys actually did get along when they were creating all this magic."[339]

As a longstanding Steve Perry fan, would JSS like to see him back with Journey? It's a question that cannot be ignored and frequently crops up in any conversation about the elusive singer.

JSS: "Everybody would. I honestly know – and this is no revelation – Perry's voice is not what it used to be. He's even had to pull off his own solo tours for the sake of not being able to do what he used to be able to do… [He's had to] change the keys of things, to be able to get through certain songs. He's in his sixties now; he can't sing the way he did in his twenties or even thirties. For anybody to expect him to, you'd have to be extremely stupid because the voice changes, it matures, it lowers, it goes down. If anybody wants to just go back in to any old concert information from back in those *Escape* and *Frontiers* tours, those guys would be doing seven or eight nights in a row, one night off and then another fourteen nights in a row. They worked Perry to death. That guy wrote this stuff. He wrote this stuff [that] catered to his voice. But even his own catalogue was enough to eventually break his voice, to bring his range and his register down. You can hear it in the later recordings that they did in the band together. You can hear it on some of the live performances. You can hear it in his solo performances and solo albums. There's a reason why Perry's pulled out of the limelight. It's not that he's not interested in being a rock star or performing any more, it's that he has a certain level of what people expect of him. If he can't deliver that, of course, he's going to say, 'I don't want to get up there and people go, 'Oh, poor guy. He used to be so good'. He wants people to remember him the way they remember him. And I would be the same way. Once I couldn't do what people expected me to do, I'm not going to go out there and make an idiot out of myself. I'd rather just pull the reigns back and say, 'Hold on a second, I want people to remember how good I was not how shitty I am now'."[340]

The tour with Def Leppard proved so successful that it was extended and wound up in San Jan, Puerto Rico on November 19.[341]

"Journey really upped their game. They're a great band, and then, you know, we'd have to go on after that," said Def Leppard guitarist Phil Collen. "And if you're following 'Don't Stop Believin'", which was, like, a huge hit… you better be up to your game. So that just made us just raise the bar ourselves."[342]

"It was just great," said Ross Valory after the tour. "It was a co-headline. We agreed Journey would open because Def Leppard wanted to do a more elaborate stage production. Financially it was also a success. Madonna might have been making more money per show but I think we sold more tickets."[343]

Valory continued: "The Def Leppard/Journey tour won an award from *Pollstar* magazine for being the most creatively packaged… The interesting thing was the demographic of the audience: you'd have perhaps expected half the audience to be there for Def Leppard and half for Journey, but it didn't work out like that. It was more like one-third for us, one-third for Def Leppard and the other third were those who hadn't been to either band's gigs so we were courting the middle ground."[344]

JSS was made the official frontman for Journey on December 19, 2006.

"Once we knew it was going to be an official thing I don't remember signing a contract," JSS explains. "The only contract I signed initially was when I first joined them. It said I would be earning 'X amount' while I was touring and I was basically a hired guy, a hired musician. That contract lasted until the end of that Def Leppard tour and everything after that was an equal member of the band. There was more of an agreement just to make sure that I was protected on what I would be earning, what my rights would be. There was also kind of a gag order involved in the sense of I couldn't reveal or discuss the personal details of their lives and what's going on internally. Just to make sure they're protected themselves, protecting Steve Augeri, protecting Steve Perry's image. There's a security thing that they really want to make sure any outsiders coming in aren't just going to start blabbing their personal business. It's a natural thing to want to protect your own interest. Of course, that was part of the agreement there."[345]

It was the end of an eventful and some would say wholly unexpected year. But there were more surprises to come...

CHAPTER 9

Change For The Better:
Journey's Rebirth
(2007–2010)

"No, we didn't think it was the end, but we certainly didn't have any answers, immediate answers, until Neal just happened to be sitting on the Internet one night finding this guy in Manila singing Journey songs."

Ross Valory[346]

"It was extremely exhilarating, especially once it was official that I was the permanent band member at the latter part of 2006," says JSS on taking part in promotional photos and interviews as Journey's new frontman. "I really had to pinch myself because this is one of the biggest bands and influences in my life growing up as a teenager. I can't think of any bigger influence on me vocally than Steve Perry when I was growing up. To actually be fronting his band, it really was a dream come true. But on the other hand there was a lot of responsibility to go with that, especially because Perry's still existing and walking on the earth. It's not the same thing as a deceased singer or a singer who's obviously gone and not able to sing and there's just no way that singer will be able to front that band again like Queen or Bon Scott from AC/DC. It's a littler easier to step into that situation when the singer's gone from the face of the earth, but Steve Perry is very healthy and very capable of singing and living right down the street. Obviously you're going to get that backlash of 'Who is this guy? Why is he there? Why don't they just kiss and make up and get Perry back in?' That's a bit tough, but you go on with a thick skin and you know that that's going to occur."[347]

JSS and the band started to kick around ideas for a new Journey album as well as a proposed re-recording of some of their greatest hits. JSS: "We were actually discussing and humming out little ideas back and forth – I think it was on the third leg of the Leppard tour. It would have been in December of 2006. Neal and Jon were working on a few things individually and then collectively backstage. I didn't really feel it was my part to put my neck in unless asked, but sometimes I'd be working on stuff and humming stuff just to myself and kind of lightly they'd go, 'Oh, what is that?' I just kind of leaned over and hummed some ideas but I didn't want to say, 'Hey guys, mind if I sit in? Do you mind if I write with you?' We never got to that point on the actual tour. It wasn't until the beginning of 2007 that Neal and I got together in my house when he was visiting in LA for a couple of days. We just went into my home studio. He had a bunch of ideas. The same way he did with Soul SirkUS, he's got a bunch of ideas. Let's just put them down to drum loops and then let me just kind of toy around with them to see what I come up with, and we'll send them up to Jonathan to see what he wants to do and we'll see if we can start the process of songwriting then. We didn't really go any further than Neal putting some ideas down at my place; after that we were preparing for other things that were coming up and I was going to revisit those little ideas once I was done with the [forthcoming] Talisman tour."[348]

However, there were concerns that the band would sound like a Soul SirkUS clone. "It won't sound like Soul SirkUS!" Schon exclaimed, "It's going to sound like Journey – it doesn't sound like Soul SirkUS. I mean Soul SirkUS wasn't supposed to sound anything like Journey – it's so funny that people went, 'So that's what he sound like with that guy!'

but that's not necessarily true.... The new album is definitely going to sound like Journey – it's going to have big hooks and choruses and many memorable parts, much like our older hits. I think the only change will be that there will be more upbeat songs and a more live sound – I'm not saying heavy, but more upbeat, fun, party, and with a sound more like our live show."[349]

Journey kicked off 2007 in style by playing an 11-date tour of the UK, expanded from the eight originally planned. Asked if the few dates they played in 2006 gave promoters more confidence investing in Journey, Neal Schon said: "Completely! That was the break we'd been waiting for: finally some promoter stepped up to the plate and was not scared of us, or of losing his ass. It went very well so some other promoters took a look at that and now all over Europe we're the hot ticket."[350]

The tour began in Sheffield on March 1 and visited Newcastle, Glasgow, Nottingham, Manchester, Cardiff, Bournemouth, Birmingham and London before finishing back in Newcastle for a second show on March 15.

On the subject of the length of each set, Schon said: "We got so used to playing very long sets: the year before last we did three hours – which was my idea – and everybody hated me at the end of the tour. It was like, 'You asshole, what a terrible idea.' The fans loved it but then once you've played to them for three hours it's like they never want to hear anything else again. I think an hour-and-a-half or one hour forty-five is plenty."[351]

"I've loved Journey for many years," says the tour's support act, American Singer Danny Vaughn, after the Hammersmith Apollo show in London, which was attended by JSS's good friend, Queen guitarist Brian May, "and it was great to just watch them do their thing. Jeff spotted me and couldn't resist shoving the microphone in my face and giving me a few bars of 'Lovin' Touchin' Squeezin'.' I loved every minute of it."[352]

In London they blasted out 'Jerusalem/Rubicon', 'Stone In Love', 'Ask The Lonely', 'Wheel In The Sky', 'Keep On Runnin'', 'Who's Crying Now', 'Opened The Door', 'Mystery Mountain', 'Edge Of The Blade', 'Remember Me', 'Chain Reaction', 'Lights', 'Mother, Father', 'Open Arms', 'La Do Da', 'Line Of Fire', 'Send Her My Love', 'Lovin', Touchin',

Squeezin", 'Where Were You', 'Faithfully', 'Don't Stop Believin", 'Any Way You Want It' and the encore of 'Separate Ways (Worlds Apart)'.

Jason Ritchie wrote on getreadytorock.com: "The good thing about Journey is they have vocalists in abundance, which you need in a set lasting over two hours. Drummer Deen Castronova deftly handles 'Open Arms' (boy does he hit the Perry-like notes and phrasings spot on) and 'Mother, Father', which had me beaming from ear to ear to hear this gem played live… The band seemed to be enjoying themselves and sound-wise it was very good, bar a few times you couldn't hear Jon Cain's piano."

Asked about how he got the support gig playing an acoustic set, Vaughn says, "A stroke of luck, really. Jeff Scott Soto is a good friend of mine and we have worked together before. He had heard that Journey were looking for a low maintenance opening act for the European shows. I think they had an acoustic act already in mind but it didn't come through so Jeff was right there dropping my name. As it happens, I'm on Frontiers Records, the same label Journey themselves are using in Europe, plus I have some friends in their camp as well, so it was a very easy sell."[353]

On the subject of hanging out backstage, Vaughn remembers, "One of the first things that struck me was that this is touring, and the music business in general, at a whole different level from the circles I normally move in. These are the big leagues. The first time I met everyone, they all came piling into the backstage area from the tour bus and each guy went to a different corner or area of a room and whipped out their Mac PowerBooks and did whatever business each of them did. I wasn't even sure they were going to talk to anyone at first, it all looked so intense. But they were very welcoming and very friendly. And there was no 'us and them' separation just because we were the opening act. We all hung out at the same table and talked quite a bit at various times."[354]

"At the time it seemed like a really positive thing," says Vaughn on the relationship between JSS and Journey which he witnessed backstage. "Each member of Journey is very different from the other, and it takes time to get to know some of them, but they were all very cool and I saw no indication that they wouldn't be continuing on with Jeff. I thought he was a real asset to the band because of his huge stage presence. He's a very engaging performer and that added an extra charge to the whole group when they played."[355]

Even though the tour was very successful, opinion amongst fans seemed to be split about whether JSS was the right singer for Journey, despite his obvious talents. "I thought he was a great choice," says Vaughn. "And a courageous one, because he was not an obvious choice for the band. All I know is, I watched him sing what is, by far, the most difficult back catalogue of hit songs that any singer has to perform, night after night. He did an amazing job and he gave everything he had on stage. What more could you possibly ask?"[356]

Danny Vaughn recalls a couple of anecdotes from the tour: "We didn't travel in the same vehicles so we weren't around them except for show times or a little before. What really took me by surprise was when Jeff brought me to meet Deen on the first night. It turns out that Deen is a real aficionado of melodic rock and all of the bands that were around at the time, and he knew about [Vaughn's band] Tyketto, so that made me very proud... [Also] we were backstage at the first UK gig, and they had a small musical work-station set up by their dressing rooms where Jonathan and Neal could warm up before going on stage. There was a general conversation about what would be the first thing that they would play. Neal wanted to do something very English to get the crowd going. But he said that he didn't want to do 'God Save The Queen' because everyone had done that to death. Then he says, 'Hey, what's the name of that hymn, that really [old] English hymn?' Now as it happens, the only Englishman in the room was the fella playing guitar with me and he says, 'Do you mean "Jerusalem"?' Neal gets really excited. 'Yeah, yeah, that's it! How does it go?' So there we are, singing the first few lines to Neal and Jonathan: 'And did those feet, in ancient times, walk upon England's green and pleasant land'. Remember, this is all about 15 minutes before they are due to go on. So Neal and Jonathan get to work on it and the next thing you know, they are playing it loud and proud on stage. And it was absolutely amazing! As if they had been playing it for years. The hairs stood up on the back of your neck and everyone was up out of their seats."[357]

The band's intro tape was The Who's 'Won't Get Fooled Again', which some fans remarked was the band's dig at *Frontiers*, but it was all hearsay.

JSS: "People looked deeply into it. Neal just absolutely loved The Who; he loved that song. They were using that song when Augeri was actually in the band as well. That's why it's weird that people looked that deeply into it because if you listen to any bootlegs before Steve was out of the band you would hear that that song led into [their set]... When Daltry hits that big scream that was the cue for the lights to go down and the band [would come on]. Bands look for that one song to get everybody really pumped just before the lights are about to go down and that was the one for that particular tour. Once Daltry hits that blood-curdling scream, the audience, they're pumped up and they're ready to go, and bam – the lights go off and they're really into it. It worked. It was a very good little vehicle that they used."[358]

However, prior to the tour, Neal Schon said: "I think... *Frontiers* – I would not go back there! I think initially they did a great job with their packaging, but the problem with them is that they do a great job getting it out and promoting for the first month, and then as soon as they make their money back they drop the ball. I think any indie label – they don't have a lot of money to spend and they're looking to make their money back, or maybe double their money, and then the promotion stops and they just move on to the next thing."

Journey returned to the US for more concerts before JSS rejoined Talisman on some summer shows, including a spot at Sweden Rock. Everything seemed to be going fine between JSS and Journey, at least on the surface, but on June 12 it was announced through Journey's official website that JSS had been dropped from the band. He made his last performance for Journey in Leesburg, Virginia on May 12.

"Well, I was hearing rumours when I was on the Talisman tour that they were actually looking for someone else," says JSS in early 2010, "and it was strange... It was actually my webmaster that was getting these strange little things from fans all around saying, 'Is it true Jeff's not in the band anymore? Is it true Journey's looking for a new singer? Is Jeff going to be let go?' He was coming to me while I was on the Talisman tour in Europe saying, 'What's going on?' I said, 'I don't know. I spoke to Neal and... when I'm done with this we're going to get cracking on the album right away. They gave me their OK to go out and do this and get this out of the way because it meant a lot to me... to kind of close a chapter on this so I could get ready for the new chapter with them. I have no idea what you're talking about!' But, by the same token, when I did try to reach any of them to ask them if they knew what's going on, I didn't hear back from any of them! Of course... nobody was returning my calls. Nobody was picking up when I was trying to reach them, but management were the only ones who were assuring me that everything was fine and to finish my tour and when I got back we're going to resume.

"I thought, OK, well, if management say that, I guess we're all good. We're going to finish this massive tour, everybody's on holidays and doing their little things, so maybe that's why I can't reach them. It was the last night of the Talisman tour that I basically found out I was let go from the band from someone else who accidentally told me, thinking I already knew. And, of course, I'm sure they felt rotten basically serving me with my divorce papers. But once again management and everybody denied it – well, not everyone. No one in the band [did] because I still couldn't reach anybody. They didn't call me back. It was management who denied any of that was true, and it was no more than two days later that I got back to Los Angeles from Europe and I was given a call from management saying I was let go. I haven't spoken to any one of those guys from the band since. It's three years now and I haven't spoken to anybody since it occurred."[359]

"Well, I already had a previous relationship with Soul SirkUS so everything was fine," says JSS on the relationship he had with Journey's management. "It was not like they were kissing my arse, but it also wasn't like they were treating me like I was any kind of saviour. It was kind of a deep-playing field. I'd known them; they'd known me. Business resumed as usual from the end of the Soul SirkUS thing to the end of the Journey thing."[360]

Neal Schon said in a statement: "We appreciate all of Jeff's hard work and we can't thank him enough for stepping in when Steve Augeri got sick last year. He did a tremendous job for us and we wish him the best. We've just decided to go our separate ways, no pun intended. We're plotting our next move now."[361]

Jonathan Cain added: "We were lucky to have a friend who was already a Journey fan step in on a moment's notice during the Def Leppard tour to help us out. Jeff was always the consummate professional and we hope that he remains a friend of the band in the future. We just felt it was time to go in a different direction."[362]

"When we went to [record] some original material we found that that sound… it doesn't sound like Journey," bassist Ross Valory told the author in an interview for *Powerplay* magazine in late 2008. "He had a different voice; it certainly suited the performance [but] when it came to an overall decision, we decided to let him [Jeff] go."[363]

Jonathan Cain said at a later date: "There were little personality conflicts here and there. We just thought that, looking ten years forward, this wasn't our guy – and we wish him well."[364]

Asked, if in hindsight was it the right decision to have hired Jeff in the first place, Valory remarked: "We had to have somebody! We had a tour and a singer with no voice. It was absolutely the right, perfect decision… And that was on a probational standpoint. We just decided not to continue."[365]

Tyketto singer Danny Vaughn comments, "I have to say that, obviously, I am not privy to the inner workings of what went on between them. Jeff is way too much of a gentleman to 'kiss and tell'. So I don't know exactly how he was treated. My own feeling is that it's sad that they decided to get another singer… Jeff was doing an awesome job night after night and, as Jeff is my friend, I really had hoped that his ship had come in and he was going to go on with them."[366]

Some fans had predicted Journey would oust JSS, but others thought he added a neat touch to the band, a different angle to their music, as well as an abundance of energy, charisma and verve. However, his dismissal was not handled well according to some observers.

One such person was Brian May. "Well, yeah, Brian was one of the first people I spoke to," says JSS. "He was at the show in London and I have a very close friendship with Brian, both musically and as a friend.

I look up to him as a big brother basically. To be able to say Brian May is my big brother in itself is a very exciting idea. The fact is that he's just such a kind, humble person… he's just one of those people I just wish I knew more of in this world. I just feel like I can go to him [and talk about] the way I was feeling when it all went down. They let me go and people were telling me my face, my image was removed from the website and my things were removed like I never existed, all these different things, [and I] was going through such a horrible phase, and I knew I could call him and he would just speak to me with a very bring-me-back-down-to-earth kind of [attitude]. He knew I was angry. He knew I was hurt. He just had a way of helping me through everything. And within a couple of days he wrote to me and said: 'Listen, this is just bothering me and I would love to address it. Would you have a problem with it?' I said absolutely not…."[367]

May wrote a lengthy piece on his Soapbox (brianmay.com) on June 14, 2007, in which he sympathised with Soto, and mused on various options available to Journey. "I know in my heart Jeff would never have walked out on this – he is way too loyal," he wrote. "It saddens me that he seems to been shed like a used pair of boots… he deserves to be treated with respect."[368]

Talisman bassist Marcel Jacob, who died in 2009, was critical of the way Journey's management handled the situation in a lengthy screed on the Talisman blog: "Jeff's been my brother for a long time. I hurt almost as bad as he does. I feel very strongly that he's been used and wrongfully dismissed, [with] no warning, no second chance, for no proper reason given other than that Journey now wants to use a cover-band singer. How sad, screwing Jeff for that…"[369]

When asked about his thoughts on the whole Journey saga, JSS responds: "It was one of the highlights of my life, as much as it was one of the lowlights. It was something I was extremely proud of and extremely excited [about] and looking forward to moving forward with these guys and extending another chapter to their legacy. Of course I was gutted beyond words – and still even to this day – that we couldn't walk away with a hand-shake… just remaining as good friends and brothers and everything that I thought we had when I was out there with them. It's something that bothers me dearly because I'm a very peaceful person. I'm all about peace, love and harmony with everybody. I would still love to have that with them. I would hope that some day we could put whatever differences, whatever the reasons were that I was let go, whatever was the situation that got us to this point, I would hope that some day we could put them aside and just get along."[370]

"I don't think management really have anything to do with that," says JSS in response to the question of whether Journey's management would get in the way of a reconciliation between the singer and Journey. "That's something Neal personally has to focus on and deal with [and] once he's able to put that aside – I think he's very influential in what the others felt about me – and once we get past that, I think he'll be as influential in making sure that they don't feel that anymore. Again, to this day I still don't know what the reason is – or the reasons were – that I was let go, so hopefully we'll find out and make amends of things."[371]

Asked if he would he try to speak to them if he saw them socially, he replies, "I wouldn't so much try to speak with them. I would hope that they would extend the invitation or the kind gesture to come over and speak to me, because I had nothing to do with this little estrangement. I would love them to say, 'Hey, what's goin' on?' and kind of break the ice. Absolutely, Ross Valory came to a TSO [Trans-Siberian Orchestra] show back when we played San Jose a few months ago, and of course management and everybody around us, they were all nervous, they knew he was coming, they know he's a big fan, he came every year and they were worried about me. I said, 'Guys, I have absolutely no problem with Ross being there. He can come backstage; he can do the meet and greets, everything. I have no problem.' Remember: they're the ones that had a problem with me. And when he came backstage I was one of the first people he saw, he lunged straight for me, big hugs; it was like nothing had ever happened. I love the guy. If anybody, he and I hung out and got along the most especially onstage. He finally had somebody who would play off of him where for so many years he was just playing his bass and ignored. He loved that he had somebody interacting with him onstage. We got along great and we even spoke about that. He goes,

'I really missed you and I'm sorry the way it went down. You know obviously it was a decision beyond my control, but things work out for a reason. You look happy here and everybody's happy, and we left it at that."[372]

In mid-2007 Journey were once again without a singer. It seemed as though they could never recapture the majesty and success that they had achieved with Steve Perry, and many fans were probably wondering if perhaps, like Perry, they risked ruining their reputation by continuing and now should finally put the band to rest. Their legacy speaks for itself but after two singers post-Steve Perry, maybe it was time to pack it all in and move on to something else? "No, we didn't think it was the end," Ross Valory told the author in 2008, "but we certainly didn't have any answers, immediate answers…"[373]

Meanwhile, Neal Schon had been looking on YouTube, where he came across a singer from the Philippines named Arnel Pineda. Jonathan Cain was also on the hunt: "I had actually found a couple of guys I was interested in too – we were both kind of looking and putting the feelers out – he was kind of satisfied with someone he'd found, but we weren't totally sure, so we kept looking. I think [YouTube is] a legitimate place to find talent."[374]

Reportedly, the band even considered using Jeremy Hunsicker from an American Journey tribute band to front the real band: "We were writing with Jeremy just to check him out," Jonathan Cain explained, "and we actually wrote a song ['Never Walk Away'] with him that ended up on the album. Jeremy's a friend of the band and will continue to be – he's a really talented guy – we were thrilled to meet him and to write a song with him."[375]

The video Schon discovered featured Pineda singing 'Faithfully'. Schon was so impressed that on June 12 he apparently contacted Noel Gomez, who uploaded Pineda's videos, via YouTube, for details on how to get in touch with Pineda. Fast forward to August 12 and Pineda was flown to Marin County to audition over a two-day period for the job of Journey's new lead singer. Rehearsals apparently went exceedingly well and on December 5, Pineda was named as Journey's latest singer.

Neal Schon explained: "Well, when Arnel finally got his visa together, he came in and we rehearsed for three days and he auditioned live. He went better and better every day. The fourth day, we went into Jonathan's studio and we had a couple new songs that we were working on, 'Never Walk Away' and 'Where Did I Lose Your Love'. The music was already there, the demo was already there, the voice was just not on it. So we had Arnel listen to it. He just listened to it – never heard it before – and went out into the studio and started singing. We had to teach him the lines and the melody, but he got it so quickly. He's a natural in the studio. I was talking to Jon about it and was like… jeez. I mean, here he is, here's our guy! We both looked at each other and agreed and that was pretty much it. It was a done deal."[376]

Pineda – who was born on September 5, 1967 in Sampaloc, Manila – became the singer of a band called Ijos Band in 1982 during his teens. As an adult he built up a successful career in Asia and spent time living in Hong Kong with his band New Age. In 2006, he formed a band called The Zoo that played songs by Journey, Aerosmith and Survivor, and their videos were made available on the Internet.

Was there a chance that fans – certainly casual fans – would get slightly confused and frustrated with the band after having three singers in a decade? "I'm sure it has [confused them]," said Jonathan Cain, "and I hope our fans will bear with us because we're trying to give them the best Journey that we can be. I think with Arnel we've found our boy. He's a real tenor and he's been through a lot. Everything's going well vocally and I think he'll be our guy for a while, I can't see any more changes happening as he's doing such a good job."[377]

Some critics figured that finding their new singer on YouTube was nothing more than a marketing stunt. "This is a success story for YouTube: amazing band finds singer on YouTube!" Ross Valory told the author in 2008. "And it's been even notable to publications like *Rolling Stone* magazine, which never cared for Journey, even they covered the story. It's unusual, so it has given us spin for the naysayer's… the fashion in which we acquired Arnel has added to the magic and the excitement for what we're doing this year."[378]

Unfortunately, Arnel Pineda's recruitment inspired some racist comments on online forums. Jeff Scott Soto says, "We were born and raised in America and, regardless of our ethnicity, we're still American. For them to get somebody not only of Asian decent but not even from America to front the band, in that sense of what people are used to Journey being perceived as, I thought, 'Oh, jeez, it's going to take it to a karaoke level'. That was just my initial thoughts: I wasn't thinking about how I feel personally, I was thinking about what the general American and Joe Public was going to think. I was thinking of what the people were going to perceive, but obviously the challenge overcame all of that. I think Arnel's an amazing singer; he definitely stepped up to the [challenge]. It's the best thing they could have done for themselves. The whole story that goes with it; it's not like he was in another touring band or he was an established artist or whatever. The guy had an amazing Cinderella story behind it. That's kind of what they needed to get out of this little predicament they were in."[379]

Jonathan Cain said: "The people that say those kind of things are just small-minded people. I kind of suspected that something like that might come about, but in the end it's all about the heart and soul of the band and what makes it tick – and right now Arnel's making it tick."[380]

With material already in the pipeline for a new album, the band, with their new singer, began work on Journey's thirteenth studio album in November 2007 at The Record Plant in Sausalito in California. Most, if not all, of the non-vocal work was done before then; they had certainly laid down the demos. They also worked on re-recording some of Journey's well-known hits, with some recording done at Samsung Recordings in Seoul, South Korea. The band also reacquainted themselves with Kevin Shirley, who had most recently produced *Arrival* for the band.

"Kevin Shirley is a fine asset to this band," Ross Valory told the author in 2008. "He certainly knows how to view its history in terms of the greatest hits... When we re-recorded the greatest hits he was busy comparing the tracks with the original tracks to see that the arrangements, orchestration and approach was by the book, so to speak.

It was very astute of him to handle it that way; he's quite an asset to the band. He's one of the most important members."[381]

Kevin Shirley: "They originally called me to do a couple of tracks, they were doing this Wal-Mart package. I was kind of pleased they called since Neal [Schon] and I had had a little bit of a hiccup along the way [*Trial By Fire*] over something that was fairly insignificant, then they had gone on and done a couple of albums [sic] on their own, which I thought were fairly average. So, I was pleased by the call and we did a couple of songs and I was pretty focused on not doing something that was average. Then, the project went from two songs to four songs to 24 songs. It ended up being a lot of hard work."[382]

"We did it all in two months," Ross Valory explained to the author in 2008. "We actually recorded more songs than we kept. We recorded 26 or 27 songs, new and old and we kept 22 because there's all the mixing and mastering. It was done quite quickly and efficiently."[383]

However, there is still a fundamental feeling that Journey is definitely Schon and Cain's band. Asked if the band shares any collective influences, Valory told the author in 2008: "It's hard for me to say. I do have the opportunity to write and contribute and basically haven't for the most part in many years. Neal and Jonathan are, of course, the main writers. It would be better to ask them. They listen to so many different things."[384]

On February 21, Arnel Pineda made his live debut with Journey in front of 20,000 screaming fans at the Vina del Mar International Song Festival in Chile, and on March 6 they played a private live show at the Remax Convention at the MGM Grand in Las Vegas, which was followed two days later by a performance at Las Vegas' Planet Hollywood. The latter was recorded for a bonus DVD that came as part of a special package with the forthcoming new album.

Kevin Shirley explained: "That was a real piece of work. It was like the DVD was jinxed because just before they did all the line checks on the day of the show, they lost power and so they lost all the sync with the cameras and didn't re-sync them prior to the shoot. When I got the finals back, they just weren't good enough, and we were at test pressings by then, so they asked me if I could fix it. So, I went into the video studio, and if you can believe this, I sat there from eleven in the morning until six at night just moving frames around so that everything was back in sync – I mean, it was a live show and it was looking like it was mocked up dummy show. When I was done, I called home and said I was on my way and would pick up some dinner, and just then the computer crashed and the guy that was editing it hadn't saved it once during the entire project. What can you do? I walked around the block, had a beer and came back to do it again."[385]

They also made a high-profile appearance on the *Ellen Degeneres Show* in the US. "It seems like it's going to be very exciting! I've been working my butt off to get in shape again because I'm finally cordless again," Neal Schon explained, "so I want to be a little more mobile and move around a lot. Arnel is all over the place. It's sort of having the best of all worlds with Arnel. Once we settle in and we get into a groove and we start playing, I think it's really going to come more to life than that. But he's definitely a natural. From the four or five gigs that we've done so far, he's been different in every one of the gigs… really truly great, but just different. It's not like he's into a set thing where it's exactly the same every night. He just moves around differently. I think that's really cool. I love it."[386]

Asked if the band were hoping to emulate the success of such veteran rock bands as Def Leppard, Ross Valory explained to the author in an interview for *Powerplay* magazine: "Well, Journey has been quite successful in the last eight years having reformed without all the original members, and now, with Arnel, I think it's putting it over the top; I think we might have a good shot because we have airplay for new material, other than just the classic-rock airplay, and we might have a new shot at re-inventing ourselves, so to speak. We've been quite successful for the last decade performing the greatest hits, [but] we've had new music releases that basically didn't get any airplay or exposure. On this round, we're doing quite well having some airplay [and] having released an album that includes re-recordings of some of the greatest hits; it's like going around the back door. Whether it was intentional or not, everything is falling into place this year. Our new singer, our tour schedule, our album release: it's all doing quite well. It's hectic, but welcome hectic."[387]

The new album - titled *Revelation* - was released in the US on June 3, 2008 via a new deal the band had struck with Wal-Mart, and in Europe on June 6 via Frontiers with the bonus track 'Let It Take You Back'. Various packages were made available but the album with the second disc of re-recorded greatest hits (it is not the same tracklisting as the original 1988 release) and the live DVD proved popular.

What was their reasoning behind re-recording some of Journey's most well-known songs?

Ross Valory told the author in 2008: "That was a Wal-Mart proposal. That's what they wanted. They initially wanted a studio album, re-recorded greatest hits... and a DVD of some performance. We renegotiated one disc of greatest hits, one disc of new material and a complete HD DVD. It began with their requirements for what their deal called for. Then it was a matter for, OK, not only getting a singer for the band but a singer for the band that's capable for honouring and doing justice to recording eleven of Steve Perry's greatest hits with the band, you know. It turned out it was the perfect decision, the right singer, the right time, and so what we have as a result is some great material re-recorded, done justice."[388]

The songs they chose to re-record were: 'Only The Young', 'Don't Stop Believin'', 'Wheel In The Sky', 'Faithfully', 'Any Way You Want It', 'Who's Crying Now', 'Separate Ways (Worlds Apart)', 'Lights', 'Open Arms', 'Be Good To Yourself' and 'Stone In Love'.

Releasing the CD via Wal-Mart in the US meant fans could buy it only from the supermarket online store, or through the band's official site. They were not the only ones to strike such a deal: The Eagles and REO Speedwagon established the trend and AC/DC and Kiss followed with *Black Ice* and *Sonic Boom*, respectively. "Well, I think they [Wal-Mart] have a mailing list of 80 million people," said Jonathan Cain, "who will all be informed by e-mail. They have the biggest bricks-and-mortar warehouse in the world, you have the point of purchase everywhere in the stores, and you have hi-tech Internet engines which can either send it out mail order or from which you can digitally download it. You have all these different opportunities through Wal-Mart to get your music out to fans – and they're crazy about us, so what can I say? If you've got somebody that believes in you, it's better than a record company. We're very happy with what they're doing for us right now."[389]

On the subject of the Wal-Mart deal, Herbie Herbert says: "[It's] absolutely fucking brilliant… and it's surprising to me that so many corporations have decided that that's easy pickin'; let's just go pick off their superstars and do exclusive sale[s], whether it's Victoria's Secret and the Spice Girls or Bon Jovi or Journey or Eagles or AC/DC and Wal-Mart. They sell two CDs and a DVD for $11.99 or whatever on Journey. They make like two or three bucks; they have to pay for their promotion, marketing and manufacturing costs, but it's much more profitable per unit sold for the artist, and then they go out and, in the case of The Eagles, they sold three million double-live albums at Wal-Mart. Would they have been able to do that on any conventional label through conventional record retailers? I say the answer is, fuck no. If another retailer wanted to sell The Eagles record, they had to go to Wal-Mart and buy it… and then sell them at their store for a higher price. Probably 95% of all sales were right at Wal-Mart. I'd never even walked into a Wal-Mart in my life. It says a lot about how far in the toilet the record business really went."[390]

Revelation proved to be the band's biggest success in the United States since *Trial By Fire* back in 1996. It sold 107,000 in its first week of release, peaking at number 5 on the *Billboard* 200 album charts in the US and charted in Sweden, Germany, Netherlands, Switzerland, Norway and the UK. It was also nominated as *Classic Rock* magazine's 'Album Of The Year' in the UK. By November 2009, the album had sold a reported 800,000 in the United States. Critics and fans raved about the new CD.

Ben Ratliff wrote in the *New York Times*: "*Revelation* seems like a record to justify a tour… And though the album doesn't transcend this purpose, it is, actually, good. Mr. Pineda, who sings hard and with the appropriate vulnerability, gives it some distinction. Beyond that, the band seems to have taken rock vitamins: it feels alive."

"The whole album has a real familiarity to it," wrote Rob Evans in *Powerplay*. "It's almost like you are listening to Journey's greatest hits that never were. The band has obviously very consciously made the decision to emulate the sound that made them a household name in the

Eighties… While I personally preferred the variation that *Generations* offered, there is no denying that this is a superb album that deserves every accolade that is thrown at it."

Andrew McNiece enthused on Melodicrock.com: "I haven't always agreed with the decisions made by the band, but it is hard to argue any point when you are holding a disc of this quality. The new material is some of the best songs I have heard from the band in many years. No, it doesn't break any new ground, but it does continue the classic spirit of Journey in the very best way possible. Many fans don't want new ground – not from a band some 30 years old. I think the guys have done the best possible job in delivering a set of songs that is true to their Eighties sound, and, with some magic desk-jockeying by Kevin Shirley, has delivered a contemporary-sounding record that positively jumps thought the speaks with energy not heard since *Escape* and *Frontiers*."

Revelation opens with an instantly catchy melodic rock track, 'Never Walk Away', which is pure uncontaminated Journey. 'Like A Sunshower' is a beautifully crafted ballad with an excellent lead vocal performance and infectious chorus. 'Change For The Better' harks back to the *Escape* album, a fantastic rock track with a toe-tapping chorus that screams for the live stage. 'Wildest Dreams' is a pounding electric riff-driven track with a fierce lead vocal performance and some sturdy drums. 'Faith In The Heartland' is a re-recording from the *Generations* album that Steve Augeri sang; this version is just as heartfelt as the original though better recorded. 'After All These Years' is a compassionate ballad with some delicate keys that recall 'Faithfully'. 'Where Did I Lose Your Love' is a strong melodic rock track with all of Journey's trademarks and, as such, it works wonderfully. 'What I Needed' slows the tempo down somewhat; it's a slow, soft song that builds up to a powerful crescendo and has a heartfelt vocal performance from Pineda. 'What It Takes To Win' doesn't quite work as well as the other rock tracks, but there's some interesting guitar work throughout. 'Turn Down The World Tonight' is a simply wonderful ballad that shows just how good a singer Pineda is; Cain's piano is affectionate and the melody is undeniably dulcet. Finally, 'The Journey (Revelation)' is an instrumental piece that adds an interesting aspect to the album. The bonus track on the European version, 'Let It

Take You Back,' is a nifty mid-paced rocker with some groovy guitar work, a memorable guitar solo in the middle and a fun melody.

Revelation is the album Journey fans had been waiting for since *Frontiers* back in 1983; it really is that good. It contains all the traits that make a classic Journey album. There is very little at fault and from start to finish it never bores. There are even rock tracks and ballads to please all Journey fans and the band's performance cannot be faulted at all. The band had this kind of album in them all along; it just took a long time for them to make it. Arnel Pineda gives a simply intoxicating vocal performance on every track: the band had certainly made the right choice and, vocally, Pineda is the best singer the band have had - besides Steve Perry, of course.

"I really like 'Wildest Dreams' a lot," Ross Valory told the author in an interview for *Powerplay* magazine. "It's a really up-tempo rocker. It fits the balance for all those ballads that we're known for. Speaking of ballads, one of the two singles released to radio is 'After All These Years'; that's a fine ballad. In my estimate, I think it's as good as 'Faithfully' or 'Open Arms', our more famous tunes."[391]

He continued: "There's quite a variety to it, yes. Ballad and powerful rock 'n' roll. Very few bands really do both. Still, it always has been a variation in talent and approaches to material for the band, but there's quite a bit of musicianship and variety that makes up Journey."[392]

The rest of 2008 was spent touring. The band kicked off a UK tour on June 17, and wound up on June 28 in Newcastle. Reviewing the Manchester Apollo show on June 19, Rob Evans wrote in *Powerplay*: "It was obvious right from the moment that Arnel Pineda walked on stage and opened his mouth that Neal Schon and the Journey collective had made the right choice. Having seen the band with Augeri in 2006, I thought they were perfect, if lacking a little bit of onstage charisma and camaraderie. In 2007, with Jeff Scott Soto, they left me stone cold… In 2008, Arnel Pineda has brought to the band a sense of fun, charisma and camaraderie that has been lacking since the Perry years."

Andy Nathan reviewed the London Hammersmith Apollo show for getreadytorock.com and said: "Not only did Neal Schon give a masterclass with his fluent guitar runs and extended solos, that pushed songs to their limit while maintaining complete control, he visibly seemed to be enjoying himself, which is not always the case. Furthermore, as well as impressing with his powerhouse drumming, Deen Castronovo also impressed with his own Perry impressions during 'Keep On Runnin'' and 'Open Arms,' giving Arnel a well-deserved rest."

On July 9 in Denver, Colorado, they began a tour of the US with Heart and Cheap Trick. Reviewing the Las Vegas show on July 18, Judith Reeves wrote on getreadytorock.com: "The band belted out as many hits, it seemed, as they could get out in the time they had, so not much talking and a lot of playing – which is fine by me… The encore brought out 'Escape' from the album of the same name and, interestingly, Jon Cain's first album with the band. Finishing with 'Faithfully', Journey clearly achieved what they had set out to do… play their best live set yet. And that's saying something when every live set is as good as Journey play."

During the tour the band celebrated Pineda's birthday during a show at the Molson Theatre in Toronto. They wound up the successful road jaunt on October 4.

However, was it already too much for him? He told *Rolling Stone*, in a now famous article: "It's very, very sad. There are days I just break down and cry. This is a job I'm doing for my family. That's all the consolation I'm getting."[393]

He continued: "It's all buses, stage, microphone. I never really get to go around and walk. They wake me up for soundcheck, then I wait until the show at nine. It's a fantastic job, but at the same time it's a curse… I told Neal that the only thing that will make me quit this is if I get sick. I guess that's the same reason Steve Perry bailed out."[394]

Herbie Herbert, Journey's former manager, says, "The material is hard on any singer. There was an article in *Rolling Stone*. I never even pay attention, I don't go to any shows, I don't read anything, but there was one article with Arnel Pineda where he was saying, 'I cry myself to sleep and I'm so homesick, I might not even do another tour' and all that. I said something that I would normally never say which is, 'That's the gayest shit I've ever heard.' It was. There is one thing that is the glue on situations like this and it's the money. The guy's making such big money now, he'll probably go for as long as he possibly can. These guys have all set themselves up with lifestyles that need to be constantly fed for a long time and I think he's the most popular of the replacement singers."[395]

Jeff Scott Soto says, "It's unfortunate how that was perceived as well. When I read it I knew exactly how he would have meant it with the limited English. It was as a very innocent statement: 'Of course I miss my family. Of course this is so overwhelming. I've never done anything like this, and to all of a sudden be launched into this limelight like this, and the expectations, and this that and the other. Of course it's very overwhelming. Sometimes I sit in my bed and go, "Oh my God, I wish I could just go home and kind of hide".' Everybody I've spoken to took it the wrong way. I've stood up for Arnel. I absolutely understood what he meant by what he said. I defended him just saying, it was just an innocent comment. 'This is unbelievable, this is great. Sometimes I feel like I don't deserve this.' The guy is so humble. He's such a kind, calm human being. For anybody to take what he said the wrong way you have to really be stupid. Everyone did. The media just blew it up in to something it wasn't. The poor guy, he was ridiculed, or the band were ridiculed, for the decision to take him instead of looking at the face value of what he said."[396]

Kevin Shirley commented: "He's [Pineda] great. He's raw, but he's a singer of untapped depth. I am a little concerned that he doesn't have the experience to control his voice over a long tour. Journey material is the toughest a tenor could have. Even Steve Perry, in his day, couldn't handle the present material with its added grit, as well as the soaring ballads, on an extended tour. I hope Arnel keeps some reserve and doesn't blow it out in the excitement of the big gigs – but he's the real deal. He could be one of the greats."[397]

Some fans and critics had begun calling Pineda a Steve Perry clone. In response to this, Jonathan Cain said: "I don't think he sounds like Steve. I think he's got a different, more husky tenor than Steve Perry. And we dig it. He's got a little bit more of rock edge to his sound, a little bit more brassy. When you have a catalogue like ours, you're going to be looking for someone who can pull off the material. I don't think he sounds that much like Steve Perry. He does his own take on Steve Perry. Tenors singing in that register are going to give you that sound. We wanted somebody who is his own self. There are plenty singers out there that are true Steve Perry clones. They look like Steve, they move like Steve; they're in Journey tribute bands. What we do is very tricky. Our vocalist has got to rock and croon and Arnel can do both. Things on the new album Steve Perry wouldn't touch. Arnel's not a clone. He's Filipino. He comes from the street. He was homeless. He's a 100 percent authentic dude. That's what we were looking for."[398]

The following year, 2009, was set up as another busy one for Journey with their new frontman. They performed at the Super Bowl XLIII pre-game show in Tampa, Florida on February 1 and on March 14 they played to 30,000 fans in Manila in the Philippines, a show that was recorded for a future DVD release. On May 23 they kicked off a summer tour in Sacramento, California, and flew over to Ireland to play at gig at Dublin's O2 Arena with fellow melodic rock legends Def Leppard and Whitesnake. Aidan Coughlan wrote in the *Irish Independent*: "Following a resurgence in popularity, thanks largely to the use of 'Don't Stop Believin'' in *The Sopranos* series finale, Journey seem to be the crowd-pleasers of the night. Energetic, they garner some fine singalongs as the evening swings into motion."

On June 15 they played a stunning though brief set at the Download festival at Donington in England, performing 'Separate Ways (Worlds Apart)', 'Stone In Love', 'Ask The Lonely', 'Change For The Better', 'Wheel In The Sky', 'Faithfully', 'Don't Stop Believin'', and 'Any Way You Want It'. *NME* reported on their website: "Iconic rock band Journey sparked a huge crowd singalong during their afternoon set on the main stage on the last day of Download (June 14). Coming onstage at 2.30pm the band finished their set with classic Eighties hits 'Don't Stop Believin'' and 'Any Way You Want It', both of which the vast crowd eagerly sang along with…"

By October, the band had well and truly made a major comeback, and with the American release of *Live In Manila* DVD, Journey fans were more than content with the band's new singer. They even performed 'Don't Stop Believin'' on the *Oprah Winfrey Show*. Certainly the use of 'Don't Stop Believin'" on mega-hit American TV musical *Glee* and elsewhere added to the band's rising profile.

Neal Schon kept busy, forming a new band and playing a small tour of the East Coast of the United States in early 2010. It was a more relaxed year for Journey as they began work on a new album - their first concept album - with Kevin Shirley at Fantasy Studios in Berkeley, where they recorded *Escape* and *Frontiers*. Shirley reported on his website Caveman's Diary (www.cavemanproductions.com):"The new Journey album record-ing is almost finished – we have a few lead vocals to do, Neal (Schon) wants to do a few segues and we'll get to those and the mix in November, and I think that should wrap it up for an early 2011 release." Neal Schon told *Classic Rock* magazine's Dave Ling in May:"We're going to be here [in the studio] for a little bit over a month. Overdubs and vocals are going really well. Kevin has to run off to another project, so we will come back and sing some more in November. The material is extremely strong."

To keep Journey fans in Europe happy, *Live In Manila* was released to excellent reviews. "Whilst it's never going to rival the *Live In Houston* DVD from the Perry era," wrote Rob Evans in *Powerplay*, "it is an entertaining way to spend a couple of hours, as you get to witness the bundle of energy that is Arnel Pineda in all his glory. He truly is a superstar in his home country and this DVD captures the fervour; don't get me wrong, it's a very polite fervour, [but it] greets him when he hits the stage and for the ensuing next couple of hours. The stage show is a big, grandiose affair that brings to mind the Houston show, but that's where the similarities end because as good as Arnel is, and he is bloody good, he's no Steve Perry."

Jeb Wright wrote on classic rock revisited.com:"More than two hours long, *Live In Manila* shows Journey returning to vocalist Arnel Pineda's homeland, a place where the singer used to live on streets. The DVD is a testament to tenacity and shows Arnel returning in triumph as the singer for one of the most popular bands in history… This DVD is a testament to life after Perry. The band tried a few times and were simply not able to get it quite right. This time, however, the rock gods seem to have given them a gift. Everything has fallen into place for Journey, including a number one DVD and a platinum-selling album."

In November, it was announced that Journey would perform their biggest tour of the UK in their 30-plus year career in a triple band package that included Foreigner and Styx. The tour was planned for June 2011 and they would hit the following venues: Wembley Arena, Birmingham NIA, Newcastle Metro Radio Arena, *Manchester Evening News* Arena and Glasgow SECC. It had taken some time but Journey were finally getting the success they deserved in the UK.

The band were going steady and the internal politics appeared, at least on the surface, to have been sorted out. The notion that Steve Perry would rejoin Journey is quite obviously little more than a fantasy that will doubtless never be realised. In order to preserve his legacy, Perry must continue to maintain a low-key profile. It is apparent that former and current longstanding members of Journey still harbour some ill feelings towards Perry. They have their reasons. Behind the scenes, Perry was quite obviously in control during their peak years right up until *Raised On Radio*, which has his stamp all over it. And, reading between the lines from the making and subsequent release of *Trial By Fire*, it is obvious that Perry had some kind of hidden agenda. But in the new millennium it is an entirely different story; Journey is Neal Schon and Jonathan Cain's band – they call the shots. No question. However, the way they treated Augeri and Soto was certainly met with dubious frowns by dedicated and knowledgeable fans.

With Journey's famously difficult back catalogue of songs to sing on stage, time will tell if Arnel Pineda has longevity with the band. Jeff Scott Soto says, "I think Arnel's humble enough to know his place in the band. And I have a feeling, just from my experiences with them and my experiences in general in this business, that when you get into a situation of that level – [with] the corporation side of things – you kind of have to expect what your boundaries are. I think Arnel's accepted it and he knows that – he's in his forties now – this is a situation [where] he's not going to look a gift horse in the mouth. He's going to take it for what it is and still make it last as long as the band is going to last. As long as the band is still interested in him I think it's going to work, it's going to last. They could be successful with future endeavours; they had the Cinderella story to come out of the shoot with. With that, there was a renewed interest in Journey, but I don't know if that's going to be enough to sustain them. Maybe it will; it's really hard to tell. There are so many predictions of what was going to happen that didn't happen, that, if anything, they showed that the renewed interest and success was a middle finger to everybody who said they're not going to work out."[399]

Will Pineda burn out after a couple of albums? Or does he have the vocal and physical strength to carry on for a lot longer? Time will tell...

Afterword

BY JEFF SCOTT SOTO

Journey for me was one of those bands that came along and stung me by surprise like a wasp. I wasn't into rock so much in 1979 when I first heard 'Any Way You Want It', but the song was so infectious, it forced me to want more!

Realising I had already heard hits from their back catalogue, I dove into their past albums, becoming a life-long fan as well as discovering the most inspiration vocally from the voice, Steve Perry. No other vocalist had ever given me so much in terms of soul and emotion, but then his range made him second to none. Sam Cooke was one of my heroes growing up, and through his influence on Perry I found a contemporary hero to learn from, and Journey's music gave me the education and tools to create on my own from there, something which can still be heard through a lot of my work today.

Working with Neal for a short time in Soul SirkUS got me closer to the genius that he is as a guitarist, a natural-born artist, but to later grace the stage with him and the others who for so many years taught me the essence of song and style was an experience I will forever hold dear... My eleven months as their front man is a proud memory in my professional career.

Kudos to nearly 30 years of one of the greatest bands in the world!

Jeff Scott Soto
August, 2010
www.jeffscottsoto.com

Endnotes

FOREWORD

1 Ross Valory quote, author interview, *Powerplay*, 2008.

INTRODUCTION

2 Herbie Herbert quote, author interview, 2010.

CHAPTER 1

3 Gregg Rolie quote, Martin Popoff interview, *Classic Rock Revisited*, 2009.

4 Herbie Herbert quote, author interview, 2010.

5 Gregg Rolie quote, *Nightwatcher's House Of Rock* interview, houseofrockinterviews.blogspot.com, 2009.

6 Gregg Rolie quote, Martin Popoff interview, *Classic Rock Revisited*, 2009.

7 Gregg Rolie quote, *Nightwatcher's House Of Rock* interview, houseofrockinterviews.blogspot.com, 2009.

8 Neal Schon quote, Rick Landers interview, *Modern Guitars Magazine*, 2005.

9 Neal Schon quote, Rick Landers interview, *Modern Guitars Magazine*, 2005.

10 Neal Schon quote, Boni Johnson interview, *Record Review*, 1979.

11 Neal Schon quote, Courtney Grimes interview, *Modern Guitars Magazine*, 2005

12 Neal Schon quote, Courtney Grimes interview, *Modern Guitars Magazine*, 2005.

13 Herbie Herbert quote, author interview, 2010.

14 Herbie Herbert quote, author interview, 2010.

15 Herbie Herbert quote, author interview, 2010.

16 Herbie Herbert quote, author interview, 2010

17 Herbie Herbert quote, Liz Lufkin interview, *BAM Magazine*, 1979.

18 Herbie Herbert quote, author interview, 2010.

19 Gregg Rolie quote, *Nightwatcher's House Of Rock* interview, houseofrockinterviews.blogspot.com, 2009.

20 Prairie Prince quote, Billy Amendola interview, *Modern Drummer Magazine*, 2010. *("I'm also on a live recording of their very first shows opening for Santana in '73.")*

21 Aynsley Dunbar quote, Liz Derringer interview, *Super Rock Magazine*, 1978.

22 Aynsley Dunbar quote, Liz Derringer interview, *Super Rock Magazine*, 1978.

23 Gregg Rolie quote, Liz Lufkin interview, *BAM Magazine*, 1979.

24 Spelled 'Nite' on the actual album.

25 Gregg Rolie quote, Deane Zimmerman interview, *Hit Parader*, 1978.

CHAPTER 2

26 Neal Schon quote, Boni Johnson interview, *Record Review*, 1979

27 Neal Schon quote, Alex Pappademas interview, *GQ*, 2008.

28 Ross Valory quote, Michael Goldberg interview, publication unknown, 1979.

29 Herbie Herbert quote, Andrew McNiece interview, Melodicrock.com, 2008.

30 Ross Valory quote, Carl Arrington interview, *Circus*, 1980.

31 Herbie Herbert quote, author interview, 2010.

32 Herbie Herbert quote, author interview, 2010.

33 Robert Flesichman quote, author interview, 2010.

34 Richard Fleischman quote, author interview, 2010.

35 Robert Fleischman quote, author interview, 2010.

36 Jimi Jamison quote, author interview, 2010.

37 Robert Fleischman quote, author interview, 2010.

38 Robert Fleischman quote, author interview, 2010.

39 Robert Fleischman quote, author interview, 2010.

40 Robert Fleischman quote, author interview, 2010.

41 Robert Fleischman quote, author interview, 2010.

42 Robert Fleischman quote, author interview, 2010.

43 Herbie Herbert quote, author interview, 2010.

44 Robert Fleischman quote, author interview, 2010.

45 Robert Fleischman quote, author interview, 2010.

46 Robert Fleischman quote, author interview, 2010.

47 Robert Fleischman quote, author interview, 2010.

48 Steve Perry interview, interviewee unknown, *Rock Magazine!*, 1984

49 Steve Perry quote, Craig Anderton interview, *Modern Recording*, 1980.

50 Steve Perry quote, interviewee unknown, *Circus*, 1983.

51 Steve Perry quote, Rich Sutton interview, *Songs Hits*, 1984.

52 Herbie Herbert quote, author interview, 2010.

53 Neal Schon quote, Liz Lufkin interview, *BAM Magazine*, 1979.

54 Gregg Rolie quote, Deane Zimmerman interview, *Hit Parader*, 2010.

55 Herbie Herbert quote, author interview, 2010.

56 Steve Perry quote, Deane Zimmerman interview, *Hit Parader*, 1978.

57 Joe Chiccarelli quote, author interview, 2010.

58 Joe Chiccarelli quote, author interview, 2010.

59 Gregg Rolie quote, Deane Zimmerman interview, *Hit Parader*, 1978.

60 Joe Chiccarelli quote, author interview, 2010.

61 Neal Schon quote, Boni Johnson interview, *Record Review*, 1979.

62 Ross Valory quote, Michael Goldberg interview, publication unknown, 1979.

63 Herbie Herbert quote, author interview, 2010.

64 Herbie Herbert quote, Andrew McNiece interview, melodicrock.com, 2008.

65 Neal Schon quote, Liz Lufkin interview, *BAM Magazine*, 1979.

66 Herbie Herbert quote, author interview, 2010.

67 Herbie Herbert quote, author interview, 2010.

68 Steve Perry quote, Mitch Lafon interview, *BW&BK*, 2005.

69 Herbie Herbert quote, Andrew McNiece interview, melodicrock.com, 2008.

70 Ross Valory, Carl Arrington interview, *Circus*, 1980.

71 Steve Smith quote, interviewee unknown, 'The Psychology Of Drumming', thedrumninja.com, 2010.

72 Herbie Herbert quote, author interview, 2010.

73 Herbie Herbert quote, author interview, 2010.

74 Steve Perry quote, Liz Lufkin interview, *BAM Magazine*, 1979.

75 Steve Smith quote, Liz Lufkin interview, *BAM Magazine*, 1979.

76 Steve Perry quote, Boni Johnson interview, *Record Review*, 1979.

77 Steve Perry quote, Deane Zimmerman interview, *Hit Parader*, 1979.

78 Gregg Rolie quote, Deane Zimmerman interview, *Hit Parader*, 1978.

79 Herbie Herbert quote, author interview, 2010.

80 Steve Smith quote, interviewee unknown, *BAM Magazine*, 1980.

81 Gregg Rolie quote, Liz Lufkin interview, *BAM Magazine*, 1979.

82 Herbie Herbert quote, Andrew McNiece interview, melodicrock.com, 2008.

83 Steve Perry quote, Chuck Speake interview, *Voice Magazine*, 1980.

84 Steve Perry quote, Deane Zimmerman interview, *Hit Parader*, 1979.

85 Steve Perry quote, Michael Goldberg interview, publication unknown, 1979.

86 Neal Schon quote, Alex Pappademas interview, *GQ*, 2008.

87 Herbie Herbert quote, author interview, 2010.

88 Steve Perry quote, Jeff Tamarkin interview, *Record Review*, 1981.

89 Geoff Workman quote, Craig Anderton interview, *Modern Recording*, 1980.

90 Kevin Elson quote, Craig Anderton interview, *Modern Recording*, 1980.

91 Kevin Elson quote, Craig Anderton interview, *Modern Recording*, 1980.

92 Steve Smith quote, Deane Zimmerman interview, *Hit Parader*, 1980.

93 Herbie Herbert quote, interviewee unknown, *BAM Magazine*, 1980.

94 Steve Perry quote, Chuck Speake interview, *Voice Magazine*, 1980.

95 Ricky Phillips quote, author interview, 2010.

96 Ricky Phillips quote, author interview, 2010.

97 Steve Perry quote, Jeff Tamarkin interview, *Record Review*, 1981.

98 Steve Smith quote, interviewee unknown, *BAM Magazine*, 1980.

99 Steve Smith quote, Robyn Flans interview, *Modern Drummer*, 1986.

100 Steve Perry quote, Chuck Speake interview, *Voice Magazine*, 1980.

101 Herbie Herbert quote, author interview, 2010.

102 Gregg Rolie quote, *Nightwatcher's House Of Rock* interview, houseofrockinterviews.blogspot.com, 2009.

103 Steve Perry quote, interviewee unknown, *Rockline Magazine*, 1981.

104 Ross Valory quote, Jon Sutherland interview, *Record Review*, 1983.

105 Herbie Herbert quote, author interview, 2010.

106 Jonathan Cain quote, David Huff interview, *Jam Magazine*, 1981.

107 Gregg Rolie quote, Martin Popoff interview, *Classic Rock Revisited*, 2009.

108 Ricky Phillips quote, author interview 2010.

109 Gregg Rolie quote, *Nightwatcher's House Of Rock* interview, houseofrockinterviews.blogspot.com, 2009.

110 Herbie Herbert quote, Matthew Carty interview, *Castles Burning* (http://members.cox.net/mrcarty/page2.html), 2001.

111 Ross Valory quote, Charley Crespo interview, *Hit Parader*, 1981.

112 Gregg Rolie quote, Morley Seaver interview, antimusic.com/rocknworld.com, year unknown.

113 Jonathan Cain quote, interviewee unknown, *Tiger Beat Presents Rock*, 1983.

CHAPTER 3

114 Neal Schon quote, interviewee unknown, *Melody Maker*, 1980.

115 Ross Valory quote, Sylvia Simmons interview, *Kerrang!*, 1981.

116 Steve Perry quote, Andy Secher interview, *Hit Parader*, 1981.

117 Herbie Herbert quote, author interview, 2010.

118 Stanley Mouse quote, author interview, 2010.

119 Herbie Herbert quote, author interview, 2010.

120 Ross Valory quote, Jon Sutherland interview, *Record Review*, 1983.

121 Jonathan Cain quote, Andy Secher interview, *Hit Parader*, 1983.

122 Neal Schon quote, Sylvia Simmons interview, *Kerrang!*, 1981.

123 Steve Perry quote, Andy Secher interview, *Hit Parader*, 1981.

124 Steve Perry quote, Rob Evans interview, *Powerplay*, 2006.

125 Jonathan Cain quote, Sylvia Simmons interview, *Kerrang!*, 1981.

126 Jonathan Cain quote, Andy Secher interview, *Hit Parader*, 1982.

127 Herbie Herbert quote, author interview, 2010.

128 Herbie Herbert quote, interviewee unknown, *BAM Magazine*, 1980.

129 Ross Valory quote, Debbie Seagle interview, antimusic.com/ rocknworld.com, 2005.

130 Ross Valory quote, Debbie Seagle interview, antimusic.com/ rocknworld.com, 2005.

131 Herbie Herbert quote, author interview, 2010.

132 Steve Perry quote, interview with Dick Clark, 1996.

133 Herbie Herbert quote, author interview, 2010.

134 Herbie Herbert quote, Andrew McNiece interview, melodicrock.com, 2008.

135 Jonathan Cain quote, Andy Secher interview, *Hit Parader*, 1983.

136 Neal Schon quote, Andy Secher interview, *Hit Parader*, 1983.

137 Ross Valory quote, Jon Sutherland interview, *Record Review*, 1983.

138 Keith Olsen quote, author interview, 2010.

139 Jonathan Cain quote, Brett Ryder interview, mckinneynews.net/ pegasusnews.com, 2009.

140 Neal Schon; Andy Secher interview, *Hit Parader*, 1983.

141 Jonathan Cain quote, interviewee unknown, *16 Magazine*, 1983.

142 Jonathan Cain quote, interviewee unknown, *16 Magazine*, 1983.

143 Jonathan Cain quote, Jon Sutherland interview, *Record Review*, 1983.

144 Jonathan Cain quote, Andrew McNiece interview, melodicrock.com, 2001.

145 Steve Smith quote, Robyn Flans interview, *Modern Drummer*, 1986.

146 Steve Smith quote, Robyn Flans interview, *Modern Drummer*, 1986.

147 Ross Valory quote, Jon Sutherland interview, *Record Review*, 1983.

148 Steve Smith quote, Andy Secher interview, *Hit Parader*, 1983.

149 Steve Perry quote, Andy Secher interview, *Hit Parader*, 1983.

150 Herbie Herbert quote, Carl Arrington interview, *Circus*, 1983.

151 Neal Schon; Andy Secher interview, *Hit Parader*, 1983.

152 Neal Schon quote, Hank Thompson interview, *Hit Parader*, 1984.

153 Herbie Herbert quote, Matthew Carty interview, *Castles Burning* (http://members.cox.net/mrcarty/page2.html), 2001.

154 Herbie Herbert quote, Carl Arrington interview, *Circus*, 1983.

155 Nightmare Spokesperson quote, *BOP* magazine, 1983.

156 Herbie Herbert quote, author interview, 2010.

157 Steve Perry quote, Rob Evans interview, *Powerplay*, 2006.

158 Steve Perry quote, Rob Evans interview, *Powerplay*, 2006.

159 Herbie Herbert quote, Matthew Carty interview, *Castles Burning* (http://members.cox.net/mrcarty/page2.html), 2001.

CHAPTER 4

160 Herbie Herbert quote, author interview, 2010.

161 Herbie Herbert quote, author interview, 2010.

162 Herbie Herbert quote, Matthew Carty interview, *Castles Burning* (http://members.cox.net/mrcarty/page2.html), 2001.

163 Neal Schon quote, Hank Thompson interview, *Hit Parader*, 1984.

164 Steve Perry quote, Jodi Summers Dorland interview, *Hit Parader*, 1985.

165 Steve Perry quote, Jodi Summers Dorland interview, *Hit Parader*, 1985.

166 Jonathan Cain quote, Ted Greenwald interview, *Keyboard Magazine*, 1986.

167 Steve Perry quote, Laura Gross interview, *Faces Rocks*, 1987.

168 Steve Perry quote, Rich Sutton interview, *Song Hits*, 1986.

169 Randy Goodrum quote, author interview, 2010.

170 Herbie Herbert quote, author interview, 2010.

171 Herbie Herbert quote, author interview, 2010.

172 Steve Smith quote, Robyn Flans interview, *Modern Drummer*, 1986.

173 Steve Perry quote, Rich Sutton interview, *Song Hits*, 1986.

174 Jonathan Cain quote, Laura Gross interview, *Faces Rocks*, 1987.

175 Herbie Herbert quote, Andrew McNiece interview, melodicrock.com, 2008.

176 Ross Valory quote, David Randall interview, getreadytorock.com, 2007.

177 Steve Smith quote, Robyn Flans interview, *Modern Drummer*, 1986.

178 Larrie Londin quote, James Bryan Fox interview, www.techtrek.com, 1991.

179 Steve Smith quote, Robyn Flans interview, *Modern Drummer*, 1986.

180 Steve Smith quote, Robyn Flans interview, *Modern Drummer*, 1986.

181 Jonathan Cain quote, Rich Sutton interview, *Song Hits*, 1986.

182 Jonathan Cain quote, Ted Greenwald interview, *Keyboard Magazine*, 1986.

183 Herbie Herbert quote, author interview, 2010.

184 Herbie Herbert quote, author interview, 2010.

185 Jonathan Cain quote, Rich Sutton interview, *Song Hits*, 1986.

186 Jonathan Cain quote, Bruce Britt interview, *LA Daily News*, 1993.

187 Neal Schon quote, Andrew McNiece interview, melodicrock.com, 2001.

188 Herbie Herbert quote, Andrew McNiece interview, melodicrock.com, 2008.

189 Randy Jackson quote, Bryan Alexander and Mark Gray interview, *Rolling Stone*, 2008.

190 Herbie Herbert quote, author interview, 2010.

191 Herbie Herbert quote, Andrew McNiece interview, melodicrock.com, 2008.

192 Steve Perry quote, Laura Gross interview, *Faces Rocks*, 1987.

193 Steve Smith quote, Robyn Flans interview, *Modern Drummer*, 1986.

194 Steve Perry quote, Alex Pappademas interview, *GQ*, 2008.

195 Steve Perry quote, Alex Pappademas interview, *GQ*, 2008.

CHAPTER 5

196 Steve Perry quote, author unknown, *USA Today*, 1996.

197 Herbie Herbert quote, Andrew McNiece interview, melodicrock.com, 2008.

198 Herbie Herbert quote, Andrew McNiece interview, melodicrock.com, 2008.

199 Ron Wikso quote, author interview, 2010.

200 Ron Wikso quote, author interview, 2010.

201 Ron Wikso quote, author interview, 2010.

202 Herbie Herbert quote, author interview, 2010.

203 Neal Schon quote, Lee-Anne Goodman interview, *Calgary Herald*, 1997.

204 Herbie Herbert quote, author interview, 2010.

205 Kevin Chalfant quote, Kimmo Toivonen, rockunited.com, 2001.

206 Herbie Herbert quote, author interview, 2010.

207 Herbie Herbert quote, Andrew McNiece interview, melodicrock.com, 2008.

CHAPTER 6

208 Steve Perry quote, interviewee unknown, cavemanproductions.com, year unknown.

209 Steve Perry quote, author unknown, *Billboard Magazine*, 1996.

210 Herbie Herbert quote, author interview, 2010.

211 Steve Perry quote, Mitch Lafon interview, *BW&BK*, 2005.

212 Ross Valory quote, Hugh Ochoa interview, *Modern Guitars*, 2005.

213 Steve Smith quote, Robyn Flans, *Modern Drummer*, 1997.

214 Steve Smith quote, Robyn Flans, *Modern Drummer*, 1997.

215 Steve Perry quote, author unknown, *USA Today*, 1996.

216 Steve Perry quote, author unknown, *USA Today*, 1996.

217 Steve Perry quote, interviewee unknown, *St. Louis Dispatch*, 1997.

218 Neal Schon quote, Andrew McNiece interview, melodicrock.com, 2001.

219 Steve Smith quote, Robyn Flans, *Modern Drummer*, 1997.

220 Steve Perry quote, author unknown, *USA Today*, 1996.

221 Kevin Shirley quote, interview by Bryan Reesman, mixonline.com, 2002.

222 Jonathan Cain quote, Andrew McNiece interview, melodicrock.com, 1997.

223 Steve Smith quote, Robyn Flans, *Modern Drummer*, 1997.

224 Steve Perry quote, author unknown, *USA Today*, 1996.
225 Ross Valory quote, interviewee unknown, Cavemanproductions. com, year unknown.
226 Neal Schon quote, interviewee unknown, Cavemanproductions. com, year unknown.
227 Kevin Shirley quote, interview by Bryan Reesman, mixonline. com, 2002.
228 Neal Schon quote, Andrew McNiece interview, melodicrock.com, 2001.
229 Steve Perry quote, author unknown, *USA Today*, 1996.
230 Steve Perry quote, interviewee unknown, *St. Louis Dispatch*, 1997.
231 Steve Perry quote, Alex Pappademas interview, *GQ*, 2008.
232 Ross Valory quote, Debbie Seagle interview, antimusic.com/ rocknworld.com, 2005.
233 Steve Perry quote, Mitch Lafon interview, *BW&BK*, 2005.
234 Steve Perry quote, Mitch Lafon interview, *BW&BK*, 2005.
235 John Kalodner quote, Andrew McNiece interview, melodicrock.com, 2002.
236 Jonathan Cain quote, Andrew McNiece interview, melodicrock.com, 1997.
237 Herbie Herbert quote, author interview, 2010.
238 Herbie Herbert quote, author interview, 2010.
239 Steve Perry quote, author unknown, *USA Today*, 1996.
240 Ross Valory quote, David Randall interview, getreadytorock.com, 2007.
241 Neal Schon quote, Andrew McNiece interview, melodicrock.com, 1998.

CHAPTER 7
242 Jonathan Cain quote, Andrew McNiece interview, melodicrock.com, 1997.
243 Herbie Herbert quote, Andrew McNiece interview, melodicrock.com, 2008.
244 Kevin Shirley quote, Tom Watson interview, *Modern Guitars*, 2008.

245 Steve Perry quote, Geoff Edgers interview, *The Boston Globe*, 2005.

246 Jonathan Cain quote, Andrew McNiece interview, melodicrock.com, 1997.

247 Steve Perry quote, Rob Evans interview, *Powerplay*, 2006.

248 Steve Perry quote, Alex Pappademas interview, *GQ*, 2008.

249 Herbie Herbert quote, author interview, 2010.

250 Steve Perry quote, Geoff Edgers interview, *The Boston Globe*, 2005.

251 Steve Perry quote, Mitch Lafon interview, *BW&BK*, 2005.

252 Neal Schon quote, Andrew McNiece interview, melodicrock.com, 2001.

253 Herbie Herbert quote, author interview, 2010.

254 Neal Schon quote, Andrew McNiece interview, melodicrock.com, 1998.

255 Steve Augeri quote, Andrew McNiece interview, melodicrock.com, 2001.

256 Steve Augeri quote, Andrew McNiece interview, melodicrock.com, 2001.

257 Steve Augeri quote, Andrew McNiece interview, melodicrock.com, 2001.

258 Ross Valory quote, Hugh Ochoa interview, *Modern Guitars*, 2005.

259 Steve Augeri quote, Andrew McNiece interview, melodicrock.com, 2001.

260 Neal Schon quote, Andrew McNiece interview, melodicrock.com, 1998.

261 Neal Schon quote, Andrew McNiece interview, melodicrock.com, 1998.

262 Jonathan Cain quote, Andrew McNiece interview, melodicrock.com, 2001.

263 Steve Augeri quote, Andrew McNiece interview, melodicrock.com, 2001.

264 Kevin Shirley quote, Tom Watson interview, *Modern Guitars*, 2008.

265 Neal Schon quote, Andrew McNiece interview, melodicrock.com, 1998.

266 Ross Valory quote, Debbie Seagle interview, antimusic.com/ Rocknworld.com, 2005.

267 Jonathan Cain quote, Andrew McNiece interview, melodicrock.com, 2001.

268 Neal Schon quote, Andrew McNiece interview, melodicrock.com, 2001.

269 Ross Valory quote, Hugh Ochoa interview, *Modern Guitars*, 2005.

270 John Kalodner quote, Andrew McNiece interview, melodicrock.com, 2002.

271 Jonathan Cain quote, Andrew McNiece interview, melodicrock.com, 2001.

272 Neal Schon quote, Andrew McNiece interview, melodicrock.com, 2001.

273 John Kalodner quote, Andrew McNiece interview, melodicrock.com, 2002.

274 Herbie Herbert quote, Matthew Carty interview, *Castles Burning* (http://members.cox.net/mrcarty/page2.html), 2001.

275 Herbie Herbert quote, Matthew Carty interview, *Castles Burning* (http://members.cox.net/mrcarty/page2.html), 2001.

276 Ross Valory quote, Don Zulacia interview, livedaily.com, 2001.

277 Herbie Herbert quote, Matthew Carty interview, *Castles Burning* (http://members.cox.net/mrcarty/page2.html), 2001.

278 Neal Schon quote, Lee-Anne Goodman interview, *Calgary Herald*, 1997.

279 Ross Valory quote, George Dionne interview, BlogCriticsMusic (http://blogcritics.org/music), 2005.

280 Steve Augeri quote, Rob Evans interview, *Powerplay*, 2005.

281 Jonathan Cain quote, Andrew McNiece interview, melodicrock.com, 2001.

282 John Waite quote, Andrew McNiece interview, melodicrock.com, 2001.

283 John Waite quote, Andrew McNiece interview, melodicrock.com, 2001.

284 John Kalodner quote, Andrew McNiece interview, melodicrock.com, 2002.

285 Neal Schon quote, Rob Evans interview, *Powerplay*, 2005.

286 Neal Schon quote, Andrew McNiece interview, melodicrock.com, 2005.

CHAPTER 8

287 Jonathan Cain quote, Bruce Britt interview, *LA Daily News*, 1993.

288 Ross Valory quote, Hugh Ochoa interview, *Modern Guitars*, 2005.

289 Neal Schon quote, 'Journey in LA' *Rolling Stone*, 2005.

290 Robert Fleischman quote, author interview, 2010.

291 Ross Valory quote, Hugh Ochoa interview, *Modern Guitars*, 2005.

292 Steve Augeri quote, Andrew McNiece interview, melodicrock.com, 2005.

293 Jonathan Cain quote, Andrew McNiece interview, melodicrock.com, 2005.

294 Mike Fraser quote, author interview, 2010.

295 Mike Fraser quote, author interview, 2010.

296 Mike Fraser quote, author interview, 2010.

297 Mike Fraser quote, author interview, 2010.

298 Neal Schon quote, Andrew McNiece interview, melodicrock.com, 2005.

299 Neal Schon quote, Phil Ashcroft interview, *Fireworks*, 2007.

300 Jonathan Cain quote, Andrew McNiece interview, melodicrock.com, 2005.

301 Ross Valory quote, Andrew McNiece interview, melodicrock.com, 2005.

302 Ross Valory quote, George Dionne interview, BlogCriticsMusic (http://blogcritics.org/music), 2005.

303 Ross Valory quote, George Dionne interview, BlogCriticsMusic (http://blogcritics.org/music), 2005.

304 Neal Schon quote, 'Journey in LA' *Rolling Stone*, 2005.

305 Steve Augeri quote, Andrew McNiece interview, melodicrock.com, 2005.

306 Neal Schon quote, Andrew McNiece interview, melodicrock.com, 2005.

307 Jonathan Cain quote, Phil Ashcroft interview, *Fireworks,* 2005.

308 Jonathan Cain quote, Phil Ashcroft interview, *Fireworks,* 2005.

309 Ross Valory quote, Debbie Seagle interview, *antimusic.com/rocknworld.com*, 2005.

310 Deen Castronovo quote, Andrew McNiece interview, melodicrock.com, 2005.

311 Neal Schon quote, Andrew McNiece interview, melodicrock.com, 2005.

312 Steve Augeri quote, Rob Evans interview, *Powerplay*, 2005.

313 Deen Castronovo quote, Andrew McNiece interview, melodicrock.com, 2005.

314 Jonathan Cain quote, Andrew McNiece interview, melodicrock.com, 2005.

315 Ross Valory quote, Hugh Ochoa interview, *Modern Guitars*, 2005.

316 Ross Valory quote, Hugh Ochoa interview, *Modern Guitars*, 2005.

317 Jonathan Cain quote, Phil Ashcroft interview, *Fireworks,* 2005.

318 Steve Augeri quote, Rob Evans interview, *Powerplay*, 2005.

319 Steve Perry quote, Mitch Lafon interview, *BW&BK*, 2005.

320 Steve Perry quote, Rob Evans interview, *Powerplay*, 2006.

321 Ross Valory quote, author interview, *Powerplay*, 2008.

322 Jonathan Cain quote, press released published on livedaily.com, 2006.

323 Herbie Herbert quote, author interview, 2010.

324 Press statement as referenced on heavymetaladdiction.com.

325 Ross Valory quote, David Randall interview, getreadytorock.com, 2007.

326 Steve Augeri quote, Andrew McNiece interview, melodicrock.com, 2009.

327 Kevin Chalfant quote, Andrew McNiece interview, melodicrock.com, 2008.

328 Steve Augeri quote, Mark Balogh interview, rockeyez.com, 2009.

329 Steve Augeri quote, Mark Balogh interview, rockeyez.com, 2009.

330 Ross Valory quote, David Randall interview, getreadytorock.com, 2007.

331 Neal Schon quote, Phil Ashcroft interview, *Fireworks*, 2007.

332 Marco Mendoza quote, author interview, 2010.

333 JSS quote, author interview, 2010.

334 JSS quote, author interview, 2010.

335 JSS quote, author interview, 2010.

336 Herbie Herbert quote, author interview, 2010.

337 Neal Schon quote, Phil Ashcroft interview, *Fireworks*, 2007.

338 JSS quote, author interview, 2010.

339 JSS quote, author interview, 2010.

340 JSS quote, author interview, 2010.

341 Melodicrock.com's Andrew McNiece spent time on the road with both bands in October. His diary can be viewed at this link: http://www.melodicrock.com/Journey-LA2006/tourdiary.html.

342 Phil Collen quote, *Launch Radio Networks*, quoted on ultimate-Guitar.com, 2006.

343 Ross Valory quote, David Randall interview, getreadytorock.com, 2007.

344 Ross Valory quote, David Randall interview, getreadytorock.com, 2007.

345 JSS quote, author interview, 2010.

CHAPTER 9

346 Ross Valory quote, author interview, *Powerplay*, 2008.

347 JSS quote, author interview, 2010.

348 JSS quote, author interview, 2010.

349 Neal Schon quote, Phil Ashcroft interview, *Fireworks*, 2007.

350 Neal Schon quote, Phil Ashcroft interview, *Fireworks*, 2007.

351 Neal Schon quote, Phil Ashcroft interview, *Fireworks*, 2007.

352 Danny Vaughn quote, author interview, 2010.

353 Danny Vaughn quote, author interview, 2010.

354 Danny Vaughn quote, author interview, 2010.

355 Danny Vaughn quote, author interview, 2010.

356 Danny Vaughn quote, author interview, 2010.

357 Danny Vaughn quote, author interview, 2010.

358 JSS quote, author interview, 2010.

359 JSS quote, author interview, 2010.

360 JSS quote, author interview, 2010.

361 Neal Schon quote, statement referenced on blabbermouth.net, 2007.

362 Jonathan Cain quote, statement referenced on blabbermouth.net, 2007.

363 Ross Valory quote, author interview, *Powerplay*, 2008.

364 Jonathan Cain quote, Phil Ashcroft interview, *Fireworks*, 2008.

365 Ross Valory quote, author interview, *Powerplay*, 2008.

366 Danny Vaughn quote, author interview, 2010.

367 JSS quote, author interview, 2010.

368 Brian May quote, taken from his website www.brianmay.com, 2007.

369 Marcel Jacob quote, referenced on komodorock.com, 2007.

370 JSS quote, author interview, 2010.

371 JSS quote, author interview, 2010.

372 JSS quote, author interview, 2010.

373 Ross Valory quote, author interview, *Powerplay*, 2008.

374 Jonathan Cain quote, Phil Ashcroft interview, *Fireworks*, 2008.

375 Jonathan Cain quote, Phil Ashcroft interview, *Fireworks*, 2008.

376 Neal Schon quote, Valerie Nerres interview, *All Access Magazine*, 2008.

377 Jonathan Cain quote, Phil Ashcroft interview, *Fireworks*, 2008.

378 Ross Valory quote, author interview, *Powerplay*, 2008.

379 JSS quote, author interview, 2010.

380 Jonathan Cain quote, Phil Ashcroft interview, *Fireworks*, 2008.

381 Ross Valory quote, author interview, *Powerplay*, 2008.

382 Kevin Shirley quote, Tom Watson interview, *Modern Guitars*, 2008.

383 Ross Valory quote, author interview, *Powerplay*, 2008.

384 Ross Valory quote, author interview, *Powerplay*, 2008.

385 Kevin Shirley quote, Tom Watson interview, *Modern Guitars*, 2008.

386 Neal Schon quote, Valerie Nerres interview, *All Access Magazine*, 2008.

387 Ross Valory quote, author interview, *Powerplay*, 2008.

388 Ross Valory quote, author interview, *Powerplay*, 2008.

389 Jonathan Cain quote, Phil Ashcroft interview, *Fireworks*, 2008.

390 Herbie Herbert quote, author interview, 2010.

391 Ross Valory quote, author interview, *Powerplay*, 2008.

392 Ross Valory quote, author interview, *Powerplay*, 2008.

393 Arnel Pineda quote, Andy Greene article, *Rolling Stone*, 2008.

394 Arnel Pineda quote, Andy Greene article, *Rolling Stone*, 2008.

395 Herbie Herbert quote, author interview, 2010.

396 JSS quote, author interview, 2010.

397 Kevin Shirley quote, Tom Watson interview, *Modern Guitars*, 2008.

398 Jonathan Cain quote, Brett Ryder interview, mckinneynews.net/pegasusnews.com, 2009.

399 JSS quote, author interview, 2010.

APPENDIX 1

Selective Discographies (UK)

If the discographies of every member of Journey past and present were included in this section, it would be unnecessarily long, so the author has had to be restrictive. The following discography is a selective list of UK-only releases (unless stated otherwise) and focuses almost exclusively on Journey, together with arguably the most integral members of the band: Neal Schon, Jonathan Cain and of course, Steve Perry. There is also a bit at the end detailing certain albums from other members of the band and associated projects...

JOURNEY
STUDIO ALBUMS (CDs)

JOURNEY
Columbia, 1975
Of A Lifetime/In The Morning Day/Kohoutek/To Play Some Music/
Topaz/In My Lonely Feeling/Conversations/Mystery Mountains

LOOK INTO THE FUTURE
Columbia, 1976
On A Saturday Night/It's All Too Much/Anyway/She Makes Me

(Feel Alright)/You're On Your Own/Look Into The Future/Midnight Dreamer/I'm Gonna Leave You

NEXT
Columbia, 1977
Spaceman/People/I Would Find You/Here We Are/Hustler/Next/ Nickel And Dime/Karma

INFINITY
Columbia, 1978
Lights/Feeling That Way/Anytime/La Do Da/Patiently/ Wheel In The Sky/Somethin' To Hide/Winds Of March/Can Do/Opened The Door

EVOLUTION
Columbia, 1979
Majestic/Too Late/Lovin', Touchin', Squeezin'/City Of The Angels/ When You're Alone (It Ain't Easy)/Sweet And Simple/Lovin' You Is Easy/Just The Same Way/Do You Recall/Daydream/Lady Luck

DEPARTURE
Columbia, 1980
Any Way You Want It/Walks Like A Lady/Someday Soon/People And Places/Precious Time/Where Were You/I'm Cryin'/Line Of Fire/ Departure/Good Morning Girl/Stay Awhile/Homemade Love/Natural Thing★/Little Girl★
★Bonus Tracks, 2006 Reissue

ESCAPE
Columbia, 1982 (USA: 1981)
Don't Stop Believin'/Stone In Love/Who's Crying Now/Keep On Runnin'/Still They Ride/Escape/Lay It Down/Dead Or Alive/Mother, Father/Open Arms/La Raza Del Sol★/Don't Stop Believin' (Live)★/ Who's Crying Now (Live)★/Open Arms (Live)★
★ Bonus Tracks, 2006 Reissue

FRONTIERS
Columbia, 1983
Separate Ways (Worlds Apart)/Send Her My Love/Chain Reaction/ After The Fall/Faithfully/Edge Of The Blade/Troubled Child/ Back Talk/Frontiers/Rubicon/Only The Young★/Ask The Lonely★/ Liberty★/Only Solutions★
★ Bonus Tracks, 2006 Reissue

RAISED ON RADIO
Columbia, 1986
Girl Can't Help It/Positive Touch/Suzanne/Be Good To Yourself/Once You Love Somebody/Happy To Give/Raised On Radio/I'll Be Alright Without You/It Could Have Been You/The Eyes Of A Woman/Why Can't This Night Go On Forever/Girl Can't Help It (Live)★/I'll Be Alright Without You (Live)★
★ Bonus Tracks, 2006 Reissue

TRIAL BY FIRE
Columbia, 1996
Message Of Love/One More/When You Love A Woman/If He Should Break Your Heart/Forever In Blue/Castles Burning/Don't Be Down On Me Baby/Still She Cries/Colours Of The Spirit/When I Think Of You/Easy To Fall/Can't Tame The Lion/It's Just The Rain/Trial By Fire/Baby I'm Leaving You/I Can See It In Your Eyes★
★ Bonus Track, 2006 Reissue

ARRIVAL
Columbia, 2001
Higher Place/All The Way/Signs Of Life/All The Things/Loved By You/Livin' To Do/World Gone Wild/I Got A Reason/With Your Love/ Lifetime Of Dreams/Live And Breathe/Nothin' Comes Close/To Be Alive Again/Kiss Me Softly/We Will Meet Again
NOTE: The originally released Japanese version (2000) contains a different tracklisting.

GENERATIONS

Frontiers, 2005

Faith In The Heartland/The Place In Your Heart/A Better Life/Every Generation/Butterfly (She Flies Alone)/Believe/Knowing That You Love Me/Out Of Harms Way/In Self-Defense/Better Together/Gone Crazy/Beyond The Clouds/Never Too Late★

★Bonus Track, 2005 Original Release

REVELATION

Frontiers, 2008

Disc 1: Never Walk Away/Like A Sunshower/Change For The Better/ Wildest Dream/Faith In The Heartland/After All These Years/Where Did I Lose Your Love/What I Needed/What It Takes To Win/Turn Down The World Tonight/The Journey (Revelation)/Let It Take You Back★

Disc 2: Only The Young/Don't Stop Believin'/Wheel In The Sky/ Faithfully/Any Way You Want It/Who's Crying Now/Separate Ways (Worlds Apart)/Lights/Open Arms/Be Good To Yourself/Stone In Love

★Bonus Track

NOTE: Disc 2 is a collection of re-recorded greatest hits with Arnel Pineda. A triple package was also released containing a DVD of the band's latest line-up recorded on March 8, 2008 in Las Vegas.

LIVE ALBUMS (CDs)

CAPTURED

Columbia, 1981

Majestic/Where Were You/Just The Same Way/Line Of Fire/Lights/ Stay Awhile/Too Late/Dixie Highway/Feeling That Way/Anytime/Do You Recall/Walks Like A Lady/La Do Da/Lovin', Touchin', Squeezin'/ Wheel In The Sky/Any Way You Want It/The Party's Over (Hopelessly In Love)

GREATEST HITS LIVE

Columbia, 1998

Don't Stop Believin'/Separate Ways (Worlds Apart)/After The Fall/Lovin', Touchin', Squeezin'/Faithfully/Who's Crying Now/Any Way You Want It/Lights/Stay Awhile/Open Arms/Send Her My Love/Still They Ride/Stone In Love/Escape/Line Of Fire/Wheel In The Sky/Fireworks★

★Hidden Track

LIVE IN HOUSTON 1981 – THE ESCAPE TOUR

Columbia, 2005

Escape/Line Of Fire/Lights/Stay Awhile/Open Arms/Mother, Father/ Who's Crying Now/Where Were You/Dead Or Alive/Don't Stop Believin'/Stone In Love/Keep On Runnin'/Wheel In The Sky/Lovin', Touchin', Squeezin'/Any Way You Want It/The Party's Over (Hopelessly In Love)

NOTE I: After 'Mother, Father' there is a Jonathan Cain piano solo; after 'Where Were You' there is a Steve Smith drum solo; after 'Keep On Runnin'' there is a Neal Schon guitar solo.

NOTE II: This concert was initially filmed for MTV. Confusingly, it was issued as a CD/DVD set in 2005, and in 2006 a separate CD and DVD was released. The DVD omits 'The Party's Over (Hopelessly In Love)'

COMPILATIONS/COLLECTIONS (CDs)

IN THE BEGINNING

Columbia, 1980

Of A Lifetime/Topaz/Kohoutek/On A Saturday Night/It's All Too Much/In My Lonely Feeling/Mystery Mountain/Spaceman/People/ Anyway/You're On Your Own/Look Into The Future/Nickel And Dime/I'm Gonna Leave You

GREATEST HITS

Columbia, 1998

Only The Young/Don't Stop Believin'/Wheel In The Sky/Faithfully/I'll

Be Alright Without You/Any Way You Want It/Ask The Lonely/Who's Crying Now/Separate Ways (Worlds Apart)/Lights/Lovin', Touchin', Squeezin'/Open Arms/Girl Can't Help It/Send Her My Love/Be Good To Yourself/When You Love A Woman★
★Bonus Track, 2006 Reissue

TIME3
Columbia, 1992
Disc 1: Of A Lifetime/Kohoutek/I'm Gonna Leave You/Cookie Duster★/Nickel And Dime/For You★/Velvet Curtain/Feeling That Way★/Anytime/Patiently/Good Times★/Majestic/Too Late/Sweet And Simple/Just The Same Way/Little Girl+/Any Way You Want It/Someday Soon/Good Morning Girl
★ Previously Unreleased
+ Alternative Version
Disc 2: Where Were You/Line Of Fire/Homemade Love/Natural Thing★/Lights (Live)/Stay Awhile (Live)/Walks Like A Lady (Live)/Lovin', Touchin', Squeezin' (Live)/Dixie Highway (Live)/Wheel In The Sky (Live)/The Party's Over (Hopelessly In Love) (Live)/Don't Stop Believin'/Stone In Love/Keep On Runnin'/Who's Crying Now/Still They Ride/Open Arms/Mother, Father
★ Previously Unreleased
Disc 3: La Raza Del Sol★/Only Solutions+/Liberty★/Separate Ways (Worlds Apart)/Send Her My Love/Faithfully/After The Fall/All That Really Matters★/The Eyes Of A Woman/Why Can't This Night Go On Forever/Once You Love Somebody/Happy To Give/Be Good To Yourself/Only The Young/Ask The Lonely+/With A Tear★/Into Your Arms★/Girl Can't Help It+/I'll Be Alright Without You+
★ Previously Unreleased
+ Alternative Version

THE ESSENTIAL JOURNEY
Columbia 2001
Disc 1: Only The Young/Don't Stop Believin'/Wheel In The Sky/Faithfully/Any Way You Want It/Ask The Lonely/Who's Crying Now/

Separate Ways (Worlds Apart)/Lights/Lovin', Touchin', Squeezin'/ Open Arms/Girl Can't Help It/Send Her My Love/When You Love A Woman/I'll Be Alright Without You/After The Fall
Disc 2: Chain Reaction/Message Of Love/Somethin' To Hide/Line Of Fire (Live)/Anytime/Stone In Love/Patiently/Good Morning Girl/ The Eyes Of A Woman/Be Good To Yourself/Still They Ride/Baby I'm Leavin' You/Mother, Father/Just The Same Way/Escape/The Party's Over (Hopelessly In Love) (Live)
NOTE: A Limited Edition triple-disc set was also released. The third disc contained just eight tracks.

DON'T STOP BELIEVIN': THE BEST OF JOURNEY
Camden, 2009
Disc 1: Don't Stop Believin'/Who's Crying Now/Be Good To Yourself/ Open Arms/Separate Ways (Worlds Apart)/Faithfully/Only The Young/ Ask The Lonely/Nickel And Dime/Wheel In The Sky/Lovin', Touchin', Squeezin'/Walks Like A Lady/The Party's Over (Hopelessly In Love)/ Stone In Love/Still They Ride/Only Solutions/Send Her My Love/ After The Fall
Disc 2: Suzanne/Girl Can't Help It/Why Can't This Night Go On Forever/Mystery Mountain/Message Of Love/Can't Tame The Lion/ If He Should Break Your Heart/All The Way/Of A Lifetime/In My Lonely Feeling/Conversations/On A Saturday Night/I'm Gonna Leave You/Spaceman/People/Feeling That Way/Chain Reaction
NOTE: This was a UK-only release.

EPs (CDs)

CASSETTE EP
Columbia, 1982
Don't Stop Believin'/Who's Crying Now/Open Arms/Lovin', Touchin', Squeezin'

RED 13
Journey Music, 2001
Intro: Red 13/State Of Grace/The Time/Walkin' Away From The Edge/I Can Breathe
NOTE: This EP was sold exclusively through the band's website.

SINGLES
This is a selective list of singles released by Journey in North America and/or elsewhere. Only a handful of them charted in the UK; they are marked ★ ...

To Play Some Music (1975)
On A Saturday Night (1976)
She Makes Me (Feel Alright) (1976)
Spaceman (1977)
Wheel In The Sky (1978)
Anytime (1978)
Lights (1978)
Just The Same Way (1979)
Lovin', Touchin', Squeezin' (1979)
Too Late (1979)
Any Way You Want It (1980)
Walks Like A Lady (1980)
Good Morning Girl (1980)
The Party's Over (Hopelessly In Love) (Live) (1981)
Don't Stop Believin' (1982)★ (UK Chart: #62)
Open Arms (1982)
Still They Ride (1982)
Who's Crying Now (1982)★ (UK Chart: #46)
Stone In Love (1982)
Separate Ways (Worlds Apart) (1983)
Faithfully (1983)
After The Fall (1983)
Send Her My Love (1983)

Only The Young (1985)
Be Good To Yourself (1986)★ (UK Chart: #90)
Suzanne (1986)
Girl Can't Help It (1986)
I'll Be Alright Without You (1986)
Why Can't This Night Go On Forever (1987)
Who's Crying Now (Reissue) (1989)★ (UK Chart: #83)
Lights (Live) (1993)
Natural Thing (1993)
When You Love A Woman (1996)
Message Of Love (1996)
Can't Tame A Lion (1996)
If He Should Break Your Heart (1996)
Higher Place (2001)
All The Way (2001)
With Your Love (2001)
The Place In Your Heart (2005)
After All These Years (2008)
Never Walk Away (2008)
Where Did I Lose Your Love (2008)

VHS/DVD COMPILATIONS

Frontiers And Beyond (1984) (VHS, Compilation)
Raised On Radio (1986) (VHS, Documentary)

DVD CONCERTS

JOURNEY 2001
Columbia, 2001
Separate Ways (Worlds Apart)/Ask The Lonely/Stone In Love/Higher Place/Send Her My Love/Lights/Who's Crying Now/Open Arms/Fillmore Boogie/All The Way/Escape/La Raza Del Sol/Wheel In The

Sky/Be Good To Yourself/Any Way You Want It/Don't Stop Believin'/ Lovin', Touchin', Squeezin'/Faithfully

NOTE: There is a Neal Schon guitar solo after 'Ask The Lonely' and there is a Jonathan Cain piano solo after 'Who's Crying Now'.

GREATEST HITS 1978–1997 (MUSIC VIDEOS AND LIVE PERFORMANCES)

Columbia, 2003

Don't Stop Believin' (1981: Live, Escape Tour, Houston, TX)/Wheel In The Sky (1978: Music Video)/Faithfully (1983: Music Video)/Any Way You Want It (1981: Live, Escape Tour, Houston, TX (P.A. Board Mix))/ Separate Ways (Worlds Apart) (1983: Music Video)/Lights (1978: Music Video)/Lovin', Touchin', Squeezin' (1979: Music Video)/Be Good To Yourself (1986: Live, Raised On Radio Tour, Mountain Aire Festival, Angels Camp, CA)/When You Love A Woman (1996: Music Video)/ Who's Crying Now (1981: Live, Escape Tour, Houston, TX (P.A. Board Mix))/Send Her My Love (1983: Music Video)/Girl Can't Help It (1986: Live, Raised On Radio Tour, Mountain Aire Festival, Angels Camp, CA)/Open Arms (1981: Live, Escape Tour, Houston, TX (P.A. Board Mix))/Just The Same Way (1980: Music Video)/Stone In Love (1981: Live, Escape Tour, Houston, TX)/Feeling That Way (1978: Music Video)/After The Fall (1983: Music Video)/I'll Be Alright Without You (1986: Live, Raised On Radio Tour, Atlanta, GA)

LIVE IN HOUSTON 1981 – THE ESCAPE TOUR

Columbia, 2006

Escape/Line Of Fire/Lights/Stay Awhile/Open Arms/Mother, Father/ Who's Crying Now/Where Were You/Dead Or Alive/Don't Stop Believin'/Stone In Love/Keep On Runnin'/Wheel In The Sky/Lovin', Touchin', Squeezin'/Any Way You Want It

LIVE IN MANILA

Image Entertainment, 2009

Disc 1: The Journey/Majestic/Never Walk Away/Only The Young/Ask The Lonely*/Stone In Love/Keep On Runnin'+/After All These Years/

Change For The Better/Wheel In The Sky/Lights/Still They Ride+/
Open Arms/ Mother, Father+/ Wildest Dream
Disc 2: When You Love A Woman/Separate Ways (Worlds Apart)/What
I Needed/Edge Of The Blade/Where Did I Lose Your Love/Escape/
Faithfully/Don't Stop Believin'/Any Way You Want It/Lovin', Touchin',
Squeezin'/Turn Down The World Tonight/Be Good To Yourself
★ Neal Schon guitar solo 'Skylight' follows…
+ Deen Castronovo on lead vocals
NOTE: The 2008 Revelation triple CD package contains an exclusive
live DVD. See the LIVE ALBUMS heading for information.

LIVE IN TOKYO (LIVE FROM THE ESCAPE TOUR 1981)
Showtime Movies, 2009
Where Were You/Line Of Fire/Don't Stop Believin'/Stone In Love/
Keep On Runnin'/When The Love Has Gone/Who's Crying Now/Lay
It Down/Dead Or Alive/Turn Around Tokyo/Lights/Stay Awhile/Too
Late/Dixie Highway/Lovin' You Is Easy/La Do Da/ The Party's Over
(Hopelessly In Love)/Wheel In The Sky/Lovin', Touchin', Squeezin'/
Any Way You Want It
NOTE: There is a Jonathan Cain piano solo after 'Lay It Down'; there
is a Neal Schon guitar solo after 'Stay Awhile' and 'Lovin' You Is Easy';
there is a Steve Smith drum solo after 'La Do Da'.

MOVIE SOUNDTRACKS

DREAM, AFTER DREAM
Columbia, 1980
Destiny/Snow Theme/Sand Castles/A Few Coins/Moon Theme/
When The Love Has Gone/Festival Dance/The Rape/Little Girl

MOVIE SOUNDTRACK APPEARANCES
Caddyshack (1980) – Any Way You Want It
Heavy Metal (1981) – Open Arms
The Last American Virgin (1981) – Open Arms

Tron (1982) – Only Solutions, 1990s Theme
Two Of A Kind (1983) – Ask The Lonely
Risky Business (1983) – After The Fall
Vision Quest (1984) – Only The Young
White Water Summer (1987) – Be Good To Yourself
North Shore (1987) – Happy To Give
The Wedding Singer (1998) – Don't Stop Believin'
Armageddon (1998) – Remember Me
Charlie's Angels: Full Throttle (2003) – 'Any Way You Want It'
Talladega Nights: The Ballad Of Ricky Bobby (2006) – Faithfully
I Now Pronounce You Chuck And Larry (2007) – Open Arms
Yes Man (2008) – Separate Ways (Worlds Apart)
Bedtime Stories (2008) – Don't Stop Believin'

NOTABLE TV SOUNDTRACK APPEARANCES
Scrubs (2003) – Don't Stop Believin'
Family Guy (2005) – Don't Stop Believin'
The Sopranos (2006) – Don't Stop Believin'
Glee (2009) – Don't Stop Believin'

PROMO VIDEOS
Wheel In The Sky (1978)
Feeling That Way (1978)
Lights (1978)
Just The Same Way (1979)
Lovin', Touchin', Squeezin' (1979)
Any Way You Want (1980)
Who's Crying Now (1981)
Stone In Love (1981)
Don't Stop Believin' (1981)
Open Arms (1982)
Separate Ways (Worlds Apart) (1983)
Faithfully (1983)

After The Fall (1983)
Send Her My Love (1983)
Be Good To Yourself (1986)
Girl Can't Help It (1986)
I'll Be Alright Without You (1986)
When You Love A Woman (1996)

TRIBUTE ALBUMS

TRIBUTE TO JOURNEY (VA)
Mausoleum, 2006
Separate Ways (Worlds Apart) (Kelly Hansen)/Any Way You Want It (Alex Mitchell)/Faithfully (Marq Torien)/Don't Stop Believin' (Eric Dover)/Open Arms (Jizzy Pearl)/Girl Can't Help It (John Corabi)/Only The Young (Mark Knight)/Lovin', Touchin', Squeezin' (Chaz West)/Wheel In The Sky (Kelly Hansen)/Be Good To Yourself (Ralph Saenz)/Who's Crying Now (Kory Clarke)/Lights (Stevie Rachelle)

AN '80S METAL TRIBUTE TO JOURNEY (VA)
Cleopatra (Import), 2006
Don't Stop Believin' (Mickey Thomas)/Who's Crying Now (Bobby Kimball)/Send Her My Love (Kip Winger)/Open Arms (Tommy Shaw)/Any Way You Want It (VA)/Faithfully (Robin McAuley)/Wheel In The Sky (Kelly Hansen)/Girl Can't Help (John Corabi)/Only The Young (Mark Knight)/Lovin', Touchin', Squeezin' (VA)/Lights (Stevie Rachelle)/Separate Ways (Worlds Apart) (Kelly Hansen)

FLY2FREEDOM (KEVIN CHALFANT)
Clique, 2007
Don't Stop Believin'/Separate Ways (Worlds Apart)/Who's Crying Now/Stone In Love/Any Way You Want It/Stone In Love/Feeling That Way/Anytime/Just The Same Way/Lights/Where Were You/Open Arms/Send Her My Love

NEAL SCHON

A comprehensive albeit selective list of his work outside Journey.

SOLO – STUDIO ALBUMS (CDs)

LATE NITE
Columbia, 1989
Le Dome/Late Nite/Softly/The Theme/I'll Be Waiting/I'll Cover You/
Rain's Comin' Down/Smoke Of The Revolution/Inner Circles/Steps/
Blackened Bacon

BEYOND THE THUNDER
Higher Octave, 1995
Big Moon/Bandalero/Cool Breeze/Zanzibar/Send Me An Angel/
Boulevard Of Dreams/Espanique/Caribbean Blue/Someone's Watching
Over Me/Iguassa Falls/Deep Forest/Call Of The Wild

ELECTRIC WORLD
Virgin, 1997
Night Spirit/N.Y.C./Highway 1/Electric World/Gypsy Dance/My
Past Life/Memphis Voodoo/Breaking Waves/Midnight Express/Living
Desert/The Dragon/Medicine Man/The Emperor/Emerald Forest/
One And Only/High Mileage/Scram/Mandolin Sky/Eye On The
World/All Our Yesterdays/A Prayer For Peace

PIRANHA BLUES
Blues Bureau, 1999
Whiskey Women Blues/Gotta Get Back To You/Lonesome Road/Hole
In My Pocket/Walkin' Out The Door/I'm In Love/Love Trance/Slow
Down/Play The Blues/Girl Like You/Hey Hey Babe/Blues For Miles

VOICE
High Octane, 2001
Caruso/Hero/(Everything I Do) I Do For You/Killing Me Softly/From
This Moment On/Why/I Can't Make You Love Me/Con Te Partiro/
My Heart Will Go On/A Song For You

I ON U
Favoured Nations, 2005
Blue Passion/I On U/Timeless Motion/Chamber/Urban Angel/Moon Dust/Loner's Dream/Burning Bridges/Highland/It Will Happen/ Taken There/Father

WITH JAN HAMMER – STUDIO ALBUMS (CDs)

UNTOLD PASSION
Columbia, 1981
Wasting Time/I'm Talking To You/The Ride/I'm Down/ARC/It's Alright/Hooked On Love/On The Beach/Untold Passion

HERE TO STAY
Columbia, 1982
No More Lies/Don't Stay Away/(You Think You're) So Hot/ Turnaround/Self Defense/Long Time/Time Again/Sticks And Stones/ Peace Of Mind/Covered By Midnight

COMPILATIONS/COLLECTIONS (CDs)

NO MORE LIES: THE NEAL SCHON AND JAN HAMMER COLLECTION
Razor & Tie, 1998
Miami Vice Theme/Wasting Time/I'm Talking To You/I'm Down/ Arc/It's Alright/Hooked On Love/On The Beach/Untold Passion/No More Lies/Don't Stay Away/(You Think You're) So Hot/Turnaround/ Self Defense/Long Time/Time Again/Sticks And Stones/Peace Of Mind/Covered By Midnight

WITH SAMMY HAGAR – LIVE ALBUM (CD)

THROUGH THE FIRE
Geffen, 1984
Top Of The Rock/Missing You/Animation/Valley Of The Kings/Giza/

Whiter Shade Of Pale/Dot And Dirty/He Will Understand/My Home Town

WITH BAD ENGLISH – STUDIO ALBUMS (CDs)

BAD ENGLISH
Epic, 1989
Best Of What I've Got/Heaven Is A 4 Letter Word/Possession/Forget Me Not/When I See You Smile/Tough Times Don't Last/Ghost In Your Heart/Price Of Love/Ready When You Are/Lay Down/The Restless Ones/Rockin' Horse/Don't Walk Away

BACKLASH
Epic, 1991
So This Is Eden/Straight To Your Heart/Time Stood Still/The Time Alone With You/Dancing Off The Edge Of The World/Rebel Say A Prayer/Savage Blue/Pray For Rain/Make Love Last/Life At The Top

COMPILATIONS/COLLECTIONS (CDs)

GREATEST HITS
Sony, 2003
Time Stood Still/Straight To Your Heart/When I See You Smile/So This Is Eden/Forget Me Not/Price Of Love/Time Alone With You/Heaven Is A 4 Letter Word/Possession/Savage Blue/Don't Walk Away/Ghosts In Your Heart/Rebel Say A Prayer/Pray For Rain

SINGLES (CDs)
Forget Me Not (1989)
When I See You Smile (1989)★ (UK Chart: #61)
Price Of Love (1989)★ (UK Chart: #80)
Heaven Is A 4 Letter Word (1990)
Possession (1990)
Straight To Your Heart (1991)

VHS/DVD COMPILATIONS
Bad English (1990) (VHS, Compilation)

WITH HARDLINE – STUDIO ALBUMS (CDs)

DOUBLE ECLIPSE
MCA, 1992
Life's A Bitch/Dr. Love/Rhythm From A Red Chair/Change Of Heart/
Everything/Takin' Me Down/Hot Cherrie/Bad Taste/Can't Find My
Way/I'll Be There/31-91/In The Hands Of Time/Love Leads The Way

SINGLE (CD)
Can't Find My Way (1992)

WITH ABRAXAS BLUES – STUDIO ALBUM (CD)

ABRAXAS POOL
Miramar, 1994
Boom Ba Ya Ya/A Million Miles Away/Baila Mi Cha-Cha/Waiting
For You/Going Home/Szaba/Guajirona/Cruzin/Don't Give Up/Ya
Llego/Jingo

WITH SOUL SIRKUS – STUDIO ALBUM (CD)

WORLD PLAY
Frontiers, 2005
World Play/Highest Ground/New Position/Another World/Soul Goes
On/Alive/Periled Divide/Peephole/Abailar To Mundo/Friends To
Lovers/Praise/My Sanctuary/Coming Home/My Love, My Friend/
Close The Door/James Brown
NOTE: The European release came with a bonus DVD of music videos
for 'New Position' and 'Another World,' behind-the-scenes footage and
an interview with the band.

JONATHAN CAIN

Jonathan Cain joined Journey in 1980. This is a selective discography of his solo albums.

WINDY CITY BREAKDOWN

Bearsville/Wounded Bird, 1977

Windy City Breakdown/Lay Low Joe (Holiday On Ice)/Rock It Down/ Moon Child/Rollercoaster Baby/Spinning My Wheels/Go Now/Your Lady Or Your Life

BACK TO THE INNOCENCE

Intersound, 1995

Something Sacred/Full Circle/Hometown Boys/Back To The Innocence/ Summer Of Angry Son/What The Gypsy Said/Women Never Forget/ My Old Man/The Great Divide/When The Spirit Comes/Family Hand-Me-Downs/The Waiting Years/Distant Shores/Little River

NOTE: This is the European tracklisting which differs from the American release.

PIANO WITH A VIEW

Higher Octave, 1995

Elegance On The Catwalk/Winds Of Carnivale/Interlude: Just Between Lovers/Tell It To My Heart/Lady By The Bay/Into The Intimacy/From The First Look/Passion Dance/Piano With A View/From Wings Of Love/After The Tears/The Way That I Want You/Isle Of Fantasy

BODY LANGUAGE

Higher Octave, 1997

Paradiso/Body Language/Moonlight At Marbella/Crazy With The Heat/Even In My Wildest Dreams/Melt Away/I'll Always Remember/ Cry For Love/Eyes Of Chacmool/Daydream/With Your Love

FOR A LIFETIME

Higher Octave, 1998

For a Lifetime/Open Arms/A Day To Remember/Song Of Calabria/

Just To Love You/One Look/Blue Nocturne/China Moon/Precious Moments/Olema Waltz/A Wish For Christmas/Waves And Dreams/ Bridal March

NAMASTE
Wildhorse, 2001
When Ever We Say Goodbye/El Matador/I Tell Myself/Namaste'/ Everytime It Rains/Does It Feel Like Love/In Over My Head/A Walk In The Jungle/Faces Of Mardi Gras/In The Rapture

ANIMATED MOVIE LOVE SONGS
One Way, 2002
A Whole New World/Colours Of The Wind/Beauty And The Beast/ Can You Feel The Love Tonight/A Dream Is A Wish Your Heart Makes/ Somewhere Out There/My Funny Friend And Me/Reflection/ Someday My Prince Will Come/Part Of Your World/You'll Be In My Heart/Remember Me This Way/Looking Through Your Eyes/Soon/ Bella Notte

BARE BONES
AAO, 2004
Who's Crying Now/Bare Bones/On The Rocks/Imagine This/ Rochambo/Lost In A Kiss/Love Lines/A Sight For Sore Eyes/Guilty Pleasures/Sometimes She Breaks/Bumpin'/Tongued Tied/Reflections N.Y.C.

WHERE I LIVE
AAO, 2006
Where I Live/Can She Say/Sometimes She Breaks/Between A Heartache And A Song/Fragile World/Shine On Chicago/Pride Of The Family/Half Full/Letting Me Down/Before Brando/Man's Best Friend/Faithfully (with Mica Roberts)

COMPILATIONS/COLLECTIONS (CDs)

ANTHOLOGY
One Way, 2001
Something Sacred/Full Circle/Back To The Innocence/Hometown Boys/Just The Thought Of Losing You/Lose Myself In You/Faithfully/Wish I Was There With You/Waiting Years/Little River/Baptism Day/When The Spirit Comes/Summer Of An Angry Son/Women Never Forget/Waiting On The Angels/My Old Man/Family Hand-Me-Downs/Distant Shores/The Time It Takes

STEVE PERRY
Steve Perry is certainly not as prolific as his former bandmates, so what follows is a small but detailed list of his solo work...

STUDIO ALBUMS (CDs)

STREET TALK
Columbia, 1984
Oh Sherrie/I Believe/Go Away/Foolish Heart/It's Only Love/She's Mine/You Should Be Happy/Running Alone/Captured By The Moment/Strung Out/My My My★+/Harmony★/Makes No Difference★/Don't Tell Me Why You're Leaving★/If Only For The Moment, Girl★
★Bonus Tracks, 2006 Reissue

FOR THE LOVE OF STRANGE MEDICINE
Columbia, 1994
You Better Wait/Young Hearts Forever/I Am/Stand Up (Before It's Too Late)/For The Love Of Strange Medicine/Donna Please/Listen To Your Heart/Tuesday Heartache/Missing You/Somewhere There's Hope/Anyway/If You Need Me, Call Me★/One More Time★/Can't Stop★/Friends Of Mine★/Missing You (Live)★
★Bonus Tracks, 2006 Reissue

COMPILATIONS/COLLECTIONS (CDs)

GREATEST HITS + FIVE UNRELEASED
Columbia, 1998
Oh Sherrie/Foolish Heart/She's Mine/Strung Out/Go Away/When You're In Love (For The First Time)★/Against The Wall★/Forever Right Or Wrong (Love's Like A River)/Summer Of Luv★/Melody/Once In A Lifetime, Girl★/What Was/You Better Wait/Missing You/I Stand Alone/It Won't Be You+/If You Need Me, Call Me★+
★Previously Unreleased
+Demos

PLAYLIST: THE VERY BEST OF STEVE PERRY
Sony Legacy, 2009
Oh Sherrie/When You're In Love (For The First Time)/Somewhere There's Hope/You Better Wait/What Was/Go Away/Against The Wall/She's Mine/Melody/Foolish Heart/For The Love Of Strange Medicine/Summer Of Luv/Strung Out/Missing You (Live)

SINGLES
Don't Fight It (with Kenny Loggins) (1982)
Oh Sherrie (1984)
She's Mine (1984)
Strung Out (1984)
Foolish Heart (1984/85)
You Better Wait (1994)
Missing You (1994)

OTHER ALBUMS OF INTEREST

A selective list of albums some of the most important albums (former and current) Journey musicians have been involved with...

THE BABYS (FEATURING JONATHAN CAIN)

HEAD FIRST
Chrysalis, 1976
Love Don't Prove I'm Right/Everytime I Think Of You/I Was One/White Lightening/Run To Mexico/Head First/You Got It/Please Don't Leave Me/California
NOTE: Rock Candy Records reissued a remastered version of this album in 2009.

UNION JACKS
Chrysalis, 1980
Back On My Feet Again/True Love Confessions/Midnight Rendezvous/Union Jack/In Your Eyes/Anytime/Jesus, Are You There?/Turn Around In Tokyo/Love Is Just A Mystery
NOTE: Rock Candy Records reissued a remastered version of this album in 2009.

THE STORM (FEATURING ROSS VALORY, STEVE SMITH AND GREGG ROLIE)

THE STORM
Interscope, 1991
You Keep Me Waiting/I've Got A Lot To Learn About Love/In The Raw/You're Gonna Miss Me/Call Me/Show Me The Way/I Want You Back/Still Loving You/Touch And Go/Gimme Love/Take Me Away/Can't Live Without Love

EYE OF THE STORM
Music For Nations, 1996
Don't Give Up/Waiting For The World To Change/I Want To Be The One/To Have And To Hold/Livin' It Up/Love Isn't Easy/Fight For The Right/Give Me Tonight/Soul Of A Man/What Ya Doin Tonight?/Come In Out Of The Rain/Long Time Coming

NOTE: This album was originally recorded for Interscope in 1993 but shelved. It was released by Music For Nations in Europe in 1996 and Miramar Records in the USA in 1998. Steve Smith was not involved in this, their second and final album. Neither did he perform live with the band.

ROBERT FLEISCHMAN

VINNIE VINCENT INVASION (WITH VINNIE VINCENT)
Capitol, 1986
Boyz Are Gonna Rock/Shoot U Full Of Love/No Substitute/Animal/ Twisted/Do You Wanna Make Love/Back On The Streets/I Wanna Be Your Victim/Baby-O/Invasion
NOTE: This is a Vinnie Vincent album with Fleischman on vocals.

STEVE AUGERI

SHINE (WITH TYKETTO)
Music For Nations, 1995
Jamie/Rawthigh/Radio Mary/Get Me There/High/Ballad Of Ruby/ Let It Go/Long Cold Winter/I Won't Cry/Shine

SKYSCRAPER (WITH TALL STORIES)
Frontiers, 2009
Tomorrow/Clementine/Original Sin/All Of The World/Pictures Of Summer/River Rise/No Justice/Eternal Light/Stay/You Shall Be Free/ Superman

JEFF SCOTT SOTO

ESSENTIAL BALLADS (SOLO)
Frontiers, 2006
If This Is The End/As I Do 2 U/Holding On/Send Her My Love/Lonely Shade Of Blue/This Ain't The Love/Don't Wanna Say Goodbye/4U/

Still Be Loving U/Till The End Of Time/Sacred Eyes/By Your Side/ Beginning 2 End/Through It All★/Last Mistake★/Another Try★
★Bonus tracks on the Locomotive Records version
NOTE: Both versions feature a cover of Journey's 'Send Her My Love'.

ARNEL PINEDA

ZOOLOGY (WITH THE ZOO)
MCA, 2007
Gimik/I Gave It All/Pain In My Heart/Paumanhin/So Wrong/Manhid/ Soulmate/Too Satisfied/Hiling/Ewan Ko Ba/Gimik (M5 version)/I Gave It All (acoustic version)/Gimik (acoustic version)
NOTE: This album was released in the USA in 2008.

APPENDIX 2

Where Are They Now?

Many musicians have passed through Journey's ranks during their long history, some of whom were not in the band long enough to record any material, some only as hired session musicians, some as touring musicians, and some as both session and touring musicians. Journey fans argue about whether or not certain players were actually members of the band rather than temporary "hired hands". Nevertheless, the following list is an attempt to clarify the line-up history simply because some members of Journey – including their first proper lead singer Robert Fleischman – never actually recorded an album with them. The following list of former members of Journey is a story in itself...

GEORGE TICKNER (Rhythm Guitarist, 1973–1975)
As well as playing rhythm guitar and co-writing songs on Journey's self-titled debut album, Tickner is credited as a co-writer of some songs on both *Look Into The Future* ('You're On Your Own,' 'I'm Gonna Leave You') and *Next* ('Nickel And Dime.') After leaving Journey he enrolled at Stanford Medical School and later co-founded a recording studio called The Hive with Ross Valory. He formed a short-lived band called VTR with Valory and Stevie "Keys" Roseman hence the name VTR.

Their sole album *Cinema* featured contributions from Neal Schon, Steve Smith and Prairie Prince. He attended Journey's induction into the Hollywood Walk Of Fame in 2005 along with many other former members from their past.

GREGG ROLIE (Keyboardist/Vocalist, 1973–1980)
A key member of Journey in their earliest days to the beginning of their most commercially successful years in the late Seventies, Gregg Rolie is still spoken of in revered tones by fans. When Steve Perry joined in 1977, Rolie's voice was quickly overshadowed and their sound changed massively from jazz fusion-type rock to more simple commercial rock. He was a keyboardist, lead singer, songwriter and producer on every Journey album from *Journey* to *Departure* and can be heard on the 1981 live album *Captured*. After he left the band in 1980 he pursued a solo career and formed the Gregg Rolie Band who regularly tour and record; he also formed The Storm with Ross Valory and Steve Smith and Abraxas Pool with Neal Schon. He remains one of the most respected musicians in his field.
Visit www.greggrolie.com.

AYNSLEY DUNBAR (Drummer, 1974–1978)
Liverpool-born drummer Aynsley Dunbar was a member of Journey from their self-titled debut album to *Infinity*. He left as they shifted gears from jazz rock to melodic rock and AOR. He joined Jefferson Starship in 1978 and following that stint (he played on three albums from 1977 to 1982) his credits include Whitesnake, UFO and Jake E. Lee. He has certainly not faded from view.
Visit www.aynsleydunbar.com.

ROBERT FLEISCHMAN (Lead Vocalist 1977)
Robert Fleischman was the band's first properly appointed lead singer, and was in the band between the albums *Next* and *Infinity*, although he did not record an album with them. He was quickly dropped. He co-wrote 'Wheel In The Sky', 'Anytime', 'Winds Of March' and sang 'For You'. He was briefly involved in the English band Asia but is best known for his collaborations with ex-Kiss guitarist Vinnie Vincent. He

has worked on TV and film soundtracks. In 2009, Fleischman formed a new rock band called The Sky.

Visit www.robertfleischman.com.

STEVE SMITH (Drummer, 1978–1985 and 1995–1998)

After his initial departure from Journey in 1985, Smith continued to play drums and record. He is credited as the drummer on some tracks in the sleeve notes to 1986's *Raised On Radio*. He formed a jazz band called Vital Information and worked with Steps Ahead. He also founded The Storm with Ross Valory, Kevin Chalfant and Gregg Rolie. He left The Storm after their self-titled debut album (1991). He reunited with Journey in 1995 for the album *Trial By Fire*, but left after Steve Perry departed for the second (and final) time in 1998. Smith has also worked on some of Neal Schon and Jonathan Cain's solo projects. In 2002, Smith was voted into the Modern Drummer Hall Of Fame. These days he continues to play in the jazz scene and is regarded as one of the most talented drummers on the jazz circuit. In 2003, Steve Smith & Buddy's Buddies *Very Live At Ronnie Scott's, Set One & Set Two* were released.

Visit www.vitalinformation.com.

RANDY JACKSON (Bassist, 1985–1987)

A respected musician, songwriter and producer, Randy Jackson was hired by the band during the *Raised On Radio* era to help fill the gap after the departures of Ross Valory and Steve Smith. He not only contributed bass and backing vocals to the album but also toured with the band, so he can justifiably claim to be a former member (despite debate amongst some quarters of the bands fanbase). After Journey, he continued to work as a session musician with a host of artists, but is these days best known as a judge on the massively popular TV show *American Idol*. He has since become a household name in America and is known abroad. On *American Idol* he often refers to his Journey days.

STEVE AUGERI (Lead Vocalist, 1998–2006)

After Steve Perry left Journey for the second and final time, New Yorker Steve Augeri was hired by the band. He sang on two albums – *Arrival* and *Generations* – as well as the 2002 EP Red 13. Augeri is also featured on the live DVD, Journey 2001. After his controversial departure from Journey in 2006, he released an album in 2009 with Tall Stories called *Skyscraper*. He also played live with the band, including a performance at 2008's Firefest festival in Nottingham, England. In 2010, he announced details of his first solo album and tour.

Visit www.steveaugeri.com.

FORMER SESSION MUSICIANS

STEVIE "KEYS" ROSEMAN (Keyboardist, 1980)
A revered name in the Californian music scene since the Sixties, Roseman filled the gap between the departure of Gregg Rolie and the arrival of Jonathan Cain. Roseman's keys can be heard on the track 'The Party's Over (Hopelessly In Love)' which is on the live album *Captured*. Post-Journey, he founded the band VTR with Valory and Tickner. He also played on Neal Schon's 1999 solo opus *Piranha Blues*.

LARRIE LONDIN (Drummer, 1985-1986)
Londin was hired to work on some tracks on the *Raised On Radio* album after the departure of Steve Smith, and he also played on Steve Perry's debut solo album *Street Talk*. He had previously toured with Elvis Presley and worked as a session player with many popular artists, including Diana Ross, B.B. King, Martha Reeves, Jerry Lee Lewis, Lionel Richie and The Four Tops. He died in 1992 of a heart attack at the relatively young age of 48.

BOB GLAUB (Bassist, 1986)
As with Larrie Londin and Randy Jackson, Bob Glaub was hired by the band to play on *Raised On Radio*, released in 1986 and produced by Steve Perry. As a session player he has worked with an eclectic range of artists, including Rod Stewart, Bonnie Raitt, Donna Summer and The Bee Gees.

FORMER TOURING MUSICIANS

PRAIRIE PRINCE (Drummer, 1973-1974)
Though Prairie Prince was a founding member of Journey, he left the band before they recorded their 1975 self-titled debut. Post-Journey he is best known for working with Todd Rundgren as well as Tom Waits, George Harrison and Brian Eno. He toured with The New Cars between 2005 and 2007, and in 2010 he also toured with Neal Schon. He remains a member of the San Francisco rock band The Tubes. Prince has also worked as a graphic artist; amongst the concepts in his portfolio is the album cover for Todd Rundgren's 1981 solo album *Healing*. Visit www.prairieprince.com.

MIKE BAIRD (Drummer, 1986-1987)
Mike Baird joined Journey as their replacement for Steve Smith and toured with them supporting *Raised On Radio*. He remains best known for playing with Rick Springfield and Eddie Money throughout the Eighties. He has also played drums for Michael Bolton, Airborne, Airplay, Hall & Oates, Kenny Logins and Richard Marx.

JEFF SCOTT SOTO (Singer, 2006-2007)
Like Robert Fleischman, Jeff Scott Soto (JSS) was only in Journey for a few months, and though he toured with them he was "let go" before he actually recorded any music with the band. Unlike Fleischman, JSS didn't write any material with Journey. JSS had already made a name for himself in the AOR/melodic rock scene prior to his stint in Journey and afterwards he continued to spread his wings. In 2008, he released a solo album (his fourth) called *Beautiful Mess* on the Italian label Frontiers. The funk-rock flavoured album received mostly good reviews. He also released a live album in 2009 called *One Night In Madrid*. JSS also found time to team up with a several revered musicians for an ambitious project called W.E.T; their self-titled debut album received positive reviews and they went on tour. If that wasn't enough, he sang on Trans-Siberian Orchestra's fifth album *Night Castle* (2009) and also toured extensively

with the band from 2008 onwards. Though melodic rock fans know how extremely talented he is, JSS has yet to receive his long overdue 'big break'.

Visit www.jeffscottsoto.com

APPENDIX 3

Steve Perry Solo

Steve Perry is far from prolific. For much of the late Nineties and into the new millennium he appeared to be in semi-retirement. He has two solo albums to his credit along with a compilation with five previously unreleased tracks and a second collection of combined material. Besides those albums, he has dabbled in bits and pieces here and there. He sang backing vocals on the 1980 Sammy Hagar track 'Run For Your Life' and duetted with Kenny Logins on the 1982 hit single 'Don't Fight It', which featured on Loggins' *High Adventure* album. "Doing that song was a fun experience," he said, "I learned from Kenny that each song doesn't have to be a hit. Our attitude was, if we didn't come up with something we liked, we wouldn't record it."[1]

In 1985, he sang vocals on the utterly dreadful USA For Africa charity single 'We Are The World' and sang 'If Only For The Moment' for the accompanying charity album. In 1987, he contributed to the Clannad album *Sirius* and in May 1998 he recorded two tracks ('I Stand Alone' and 'United We Stand') for the animated movie *Quest For Camelot*. Along the way he has also worked with Jon Bon Jovi, Sheena Easton, David Pack, the band Orson and others.

However, Perry is best known for his two solo albums of non-Journey work. In 1984, he said: "It's just the beginning. I feel like I've been set free for the first time. Freedom is an amazing thing. Once you get it, you don't want to give it up. I'm really feeling the freedom – it's this incredible thing rushing through me."[2]

There were plenty of lyrics on Perry's debut solo album, *Street Talk* – a name original given to Perry's pre-Journey outfit Alien Project. "They were always fun, as we wrote at my 15-acre 'retreat' in the Angeles National Forest," recalls Bill Cuomo of some of the songwriting sessions he was involved in. "I had built a dome house with a small studio in Mile High and it was very conducive to working. We were only six miles from Mountain High Ski Resort, so the scenery was very inspiring. Steve had a unique way of writing in that he heard the 'phonetics' in his head when he sketched out a melody – he knew where he wanted to hear certain sounds of words in the lyric and would insert them in the hummed melody at key points. We still have some great unfinished ideas 'in the can.'"[3]

Randy Goodrum co-wrote the bulk of the album's tracks. He says: "A lot of times Steve and I would chat a bit, and inside the discussion would be a premise that would arise. Steve and I have written many songs and the process can vary. Sometimes a melody, a groove, a musical or verbal phrase will start the ball rolling."[4]

One of the album's most notable songs was a gem called 'Foolish Heart'. "This was our first co-write," says Goodrum today. "I had a little start, more like a vamp, as illustrated in the intro and the first part of the verse. I put this together before I left CT [Connecticut] just to have something, a snippet of a song, just to get the ball rolling in case Steve didn't already have something to work on. I purposely wrote the little snippet in my style and not a Journey type of start."[5]

"Well, we rehearsed for approximately two weeks beforehand," says Bill Cuomo today, "which really helped us make good time in the studio. I don't think it took more than two to three weeks to finish tracking, along with my overdubs, once we settled on the band line up. We rehearsed for a week initially and tried recording a tune or two, but the chemistry wasn't quite right for Steve. I survived 'the band change' and appeared with the second line up that appears on the CD."[6]

Of those rehearsals, Cuomo recalls, "Sometimes he [Perry] would speak about the band [Journey] during rehearsal in one of his famous Neal Schon imitations. He had Neal down pat and would crack us up. I still have all the rehearsal tapes."[7]

Randy Goodrum remembers one important anecdote leading up to the recording of the album. "One story stands out: after we had written all the songs then the process [began] of figuring out who the musicians would be used in the recording process. Bill Cuomo and I had been in the writing process with Steve and we both were working session players, also our keyboard parts were essential on many of the songs, so we were fundamental. Steve chose the amazing Michael Landau for guitar, and one my all-time favorite bass players, Bob Glaub. The part that took the longest to figure out was the drummer."

"Steve booked Amigo Studio in North Hollywood for rehearsals and auditions," continues Goodrum. "He went through several 'well-known' drummers and just didn't feel like any of them were quite what he was looking for. I remember one day in particular Steve was trying to explain to a drummer what kind of feel he wanted on a song that Steve and I wrote, 'She's Mine'. During the conversation Steve asked if he could sit behind the drums and illustrate what he was looking for. That's when realised for the first time that Steve was an actual real-life drummer. After Steve played a couple of bars a light went off in my head. After the drummer left I told Steve that I knew the drummer he needed to use. Steve said to call him and have him come over a play. I said that there were two problems; he lives in Nashville, and he's rather blunt, and either you and he will be instant friends or it'll be over in an instant. Steve said make the call. I called Larrie Londin and told him what was up and Larrie flew in the next day.

From the first minute Steve and Larrie were friends; however next came the 'audition'. Bear in mind, with the drummer auditions that preceded Larrie's, Steve had worked, sometimes for hours, with each drummer and still wasn't getting what he wanted. The song we decided to try Larrie on was 'She's Mine'. Larrie counted it off and halfway through the second bar Steve looked over to me and gave me the thumbs-up and said, 'He's the one!'

"Almost every track on *Street Talk* is a first-take, largely due to the amazing anchor that Larrie laid down. Larrie was one of the greatest session drummers of all time. Don't just take my word for it, ask anyone that ever worked with him."

Indeed, Perry roped in the talents of a number of studio musicians, namely, drummers Craig Krampf – who was a member of Alien Project in the seventies – and Larrie Londin, bassist Bob Glaub, Chuck Domanico, Kevin McCormick and Brian Garfalo, guitarists Michael Landau, Waddy Wachtel, Craig Hull and Billy Steele, saxophonist Steve Douglas and keyboardists Steve Goldstein, Sterling Smith, Bill Cuomo, Randy Goodrum and Duane Hitchings. The array of musicians gave the album the sound Perry strove for, but there was still a band sound to the material.

Street Talk was recorded at Record One Studios in Los Angeles and produced by Perry himself. "It was easy for me to separate myself from Journey during the recording of *Street Talk*. When you're in a band everybody has a say in what's happening, but I didn't have to compromise here," Perry said.[8]

"Yes, Steve was very 'on top of it' regarding arrangement, structure etc.," recalls Bill Cuomo, "but was always open to trying different things. I also remember his keen sense of vocal harmonies that he would work out while writing."[9]

"Steve has a specific sound for each track that I've ever worked on with him," says Randy Goodrum. "He, however, has a very open mind and is ready to hear any suggestion that would make it more interesting or better... He works very hard and stays very focused. He is what some might consider a perfectionist. I like working with people like that."[10]

"The actual recording at Record One was only a week or two, it went down pretty fast," Michael Landau remembers. "We mostly came up with our own parts, and he [Perry] would sometimes change a few things. He definitely knew what he like guitar-wise when he heard it; we connected pretty quickly, he liked the tones I was getting... He was confident as a producer, occasionally there were some doubts as an artist, like most artists go through. He kept it upbeat and fun, no drama... I was 26 years old when we did that record; it was a great time for everyone and I can't stress enough of what a cool guy Steve was during the recording of the record, he's the real deal."[11]

Landau continues: "Steve was always a very nice, approachable guy, no rock-star crap. I was always very impressed by that. I could tell right from the beginning that he just wanted to make some good music, which he did in my opinion."[12]

On the recording of one of the album's finest songs, Goodrum remembers, "The only song in *Street Talk* that used a drum machine was 'Foolish Heart'. There was a haunting, dreamy quality about the Linn Drum program that was more appropriate than the live band version that we cut. Steve and I both programmed that part. After all, Steve is a drummer and has brilliant ideas about drum grooves and fills."[13]

"Journey's stuff is very melodic and polished," Perry once said. "What I sing on my solo album is much more gutsy. The Journey sound doesn't allow me to do this kind of singing. I wanted to do stuff that had the flavour of the early Motown era."[14]

Perry kept his distance from Journey. "I think at the time he was happy just to be in a fresh environment," says Michael Landau. "Bands can have a lot of built-up baggage."[15]

On his keyboard contributions, Bill Cuomo says, "It was fun. I originally laid out the intro and outro for 'Oh Sherrie' on my eight track at home. For the studio I had to re-create those parts and make them better – I didn't have the tools available that we have today, so I basically started from scratch. It worked out OK though. I also used a Fender Rhodes Chroma for a lot of tracking, which Steve really loved (as I did) but getting it repaired was always a problem. Unfortunately that synth didn't survive. On 'Go Away' I laid out some solo guitar ideas on my JX-3P for Michael Landau, but Niko Bolas [engineer] liked them so much we ended up using the synth through my amp for the solo licks."[16]

"I remember Larrie Londin having the studio savvy to relieve tension," Cuomo remembers. "We were in the middle of something that we couldn't quite get right and Larrie decided to be the 'de-fuser' by remarking, 'Hey Niko [Bolas], want to see my socks?' while we were in the control room listening to playback. He then dropped his summer shorts down around his ankles (exposing his socks) which busted everyone up and got us all in a lighter mood. After that I think Michael Landau coined the phrase, 'take it downstairs'. Larrie was just fantastic all the way around. He also came up with that great 'slap sound' you hear on 'Oh Sherrie'. Larry had this idea and was strong enough to be able to bang two fairly large pieces of 2" x 4" together, without mashing his fingers, to achieve that."[17]

Did Steve Perry hang out with his hired musicians?

Bill Cuomo: "Yes, during the writing phase Steve, Craig [Krampf] and I got plenty of time to chit-chat and hang out. Steve is a fun person and he has many culinary gifts as well. It was fun to turn him loose in my kitchen as he made a mean salad, Portuguese style. One funny instance at my house I have to mention. He was fascinated with a pet I had raised from three months of age, an Alaskan Grey Timber Wolf [called Wolfgang]. I remember Steve really pissing off my wolf one day – so much so, that he could never get near him again. I had fed Wolfgang a large slab of beef and cautioned Steve to keep his distance from the cage while Wolfgang was eating, as he didn't like to be disturbed. Anyway, Steve decided to sneak up behind the cage wall (despite my warning) in order to watch Wolfgang eat and thought he might be able to get close without Wolfgang knowing it. Well, that failed. Wolfgang lunged at Steve, completely airborne, and hit the chain link fence so hard I thought it would give way. Snarling and growling with a bloody mouth (from the fresh beef), Wolfgang looked like Cujo on steroids as he went to take a chunk out of Steve. Needless to say, Steve got the crap scared out of him and remarked that he had never before looked into an animal's eyes knowing that the animal was fully intent on killing him. He couldn't get over that and couldn't get near the wolf again after that."[18]

Street Talk[19] emerged in April 1984 and was a massive success for the singer and spawned his biggest hit single 'Oh Sherrie', which was penned for his then-girlfriend Sherrie Swafford. It peaked at number three in the *Billboard* Hot 100 and the video, which also featured Swafford, was played regularly on MTV. On the subject of Sherrie and the trappings of fame, Perry once said: "I don't get mobbed. Most people don't bother us. Sherry [sic] and I go out to dinner and most people are pretty good.

But there are some people who'll come up, and you'll be coming from the plate to your mouth and with the fork, and there'll be a piece of paper with a pencil thrown under your face and you go, 'Ah' – and they go, 'Aren't you Steve Perry?' And I actually go, 'Not while I'm eating.'"[20]

'Foolish Heart' peaked at number 18; 'She's Mine' peaked at 21 and 'Strung Out' peaked at 40 in the US. The album was dedicated to Richard Michaels, the bassist from Alien Project who died in a road accident. Perry did not tour to support the album. But was it the success Perry had hoped for? *Street Talk* certainly had an impact on the future of Journey.

Herbert Herbert was managing Perry at the time of *Street Talk*, and the song 'Oh Sherrie'. "He really had a gun to Journey's head right then," said. "He had me, and I was just committed, I'm going to make this happen because as a manager it was going to be a very rewarding thing for me. In view of the failures of virtually every major artist coming out of a major group, [I wanted] to have success [for Steve] on his own. The members of Pink Floyd, or Hall & Oates, or the Cars, or any band that was huge… Aerosmith or any of these guys, they do solo records and it's a dud. Phil Collins at that point had failed to go gold on *Face Value* and the one record that had come out as a solo record that had done extraordinarily well, virtually the same time, was *Bella Donna* [by] Stevie Nicks. She did triple platinum and we did more than double platinum in just America alone on Steve Perry's *Street Talk*. And I can tell you honestly, he denigrated me at every possible opportunity and said that I sandbagged him… the record should have been much bigger than *Escape*… [But that shows a] total ignorance of the concept of branding and what we had built over so many years. That was 1984. We had incorporated Journey, or Nightmare, to furnish the services of Journey in March of 1973. So here's eleven years of building a brand and a business and he wants to eclipse it with his first release. And if he doesn't I have failed, even though there is a history of nothing but abject failure on solo projects."[21]

"The success of *Street Talk* is the most satisfying thing I've ever experienced," Perry enthused, whatever he might have said to his manager, "because I co-coordinated the whole product myself. I financed the project, I booked the studio, I co-produced the record, found the musicians and wrote the material."[22]

Most of the reviews were favourable, though some did voice complaints. Pete Bishop wrote in *The Pittsburgh Press*: "Don't expect much tough "street talk"… And don't expect much in the way of rampaging rock 'n' roll. Perry's tack largely is easier-beat rock and ballads, perhaps his voice is huskier than usual and showing signs of strain."

Michael DeGagne says on allmusic.com: "Steve Perry does a respectable job in producing the album, and the overall package comes off rather clean and bright. *Street Talk* proves that Perry's songwriting and vocal prowess is worthy of its acclaim, but the musicianship that accompanies him throughout the album is noticeably weaker than what he is used to."

The album blends Perry's love of R&B, soul and Motown, and is a world away from Journey. Some of the ballads are more akin to Phil Collins' solo material from the same era. It's an enjoyable album with some excellent tracks though rock fans will find little comfort here.

"It is an honest album," he admitted. "It's a very honest project. And it's not like a glass table. It's more like a nice wood table. You know, it's got structure to it; you can't see through it… it's got something to look at, something to see."[23]

Street Talk was such a success that Perry began work on a follow-up in the mid-Eighties with the title *Against The Wall*. However, with the death of his 89-year-old mother, he returned to Journey for the *Raised On Radio* album. In the sleeve notes to the reissue of his second solo album, *For The Love Of Strange Medicine*, Perry attributes the shutting down of *Against The Wall* to a rift between himself and Sony Music after they bought Columbia Records (who had released *Street Talk* and all of Journey's albums featuring Perry). Sony decided not to release *Against The Wall* and it remained unfinished.

Fans had to wait ten years for a follow up to *Street Talk*, though Perry had been working on demos, including material with Extreme guitarist Nuno Bettencourt, which was not released: "Seeing the passion in other people and realising I had it in me again… People like Nuno helped me to believe in it all again," he said.[24]

Much of what Perry recorded was not released though some did end up on the second solo album. He said: "I have a lot of stuff laying around. Some of it's demo form, but the performances are great, if not the quality. See, the first time the brush touches the canvas is the way it's supposed to be."[25]

As for the lengthy gap: "I didn't sing for quite some time and I recorded some music, but the six or seven years when I didn't make any music I had nothing to say. Why make a record if you have nothing to say? So I had to wait until I got to a point where I really had something in my heart and that's when this record started coming out."[26]

For The Love Of Strange Medicine[27] was produced at various studios in California and features production credits from James "Jimbo" Barton and Tim Miner, as well as Perry himself.

Tim Miner: "Steve called my manager… (I was signed to Motown at the time.) My manager said: 'A Steve Perry called you today.' I said: 'The Journey Steve Perry?' He said: 'I don't know.' I returned the call thinking it was one of my friends just playing a joke on me. When Steve answered I put him through a series of questions to make sure it was him. It was pretty funny. I wanted so bad for it to be him because he was one of my heroes. Anyway, he stated that his guitar player Lincoln Brewster had given him my Motown CD for Christmas and he loved the last song 'Forgive Me'. He asked if we could re-cut it with some lyric changes and I suggested that we just write something new."[28]

"The album only took eight months to make, it took longer for me to find the honesty in myself to decide whether I needed to make a record or not, and if I was going to make one then it had to be from the honesty passion inside," Perry explained.[29]

The singer roped in some other notable talent, including keyboardist Paul Taylor – formerly of the melodic hard rock band Winger – drummer Moyes Lucas and bassist Mike Porcaro, best known for playing in the AOR outfit Toto. Several other musicians were also involved in the album. Tim Miner co-wrote the album's biggest hit 'Missing You', as well as several songs that were shelved. He says, "['Missing You'] was the first song we wrote together. We wrote it in LA at his home studio. It was very easy working with him and it took all of an hour to write it. Me at the piano and Steve with pen and paper. Same process for 'Anyway'."[30]

He continues: "The tracking was easy and fast. We recorded the basic rhythm tracks for 'Missing You' and 'Anyway' in one day. I have always played most all of the instruments on every artist I produce and singing the background vocals was a dream. Here I am standing at the mic next to freakin' Steve Perry!... We recorded the basic tracks in LA then we went to Dallas – where I lived at the time – and recorded the Dallas Symphony [Orchestra]. We continued to write in Dallas and that's where and when we wrote 'Anyway'. The recording of his lead vocals was an adventure. We recorded leads in LA, San Francisco then Dallas. There are two kinds of singers. One who loves everything they do and one who hates everything they do. Steve is the latter. I have produced artists who think every note coming out of their mouth is life-changing when it's terrible. Steve would sing the most amazing vocal on the very first take and wouldn't like any of it. He felt that if he didn't work really hard and long on the lead, then it must not be good enough. I don't mind working hard on lead vocals but when you're a great singer like Steve, your first, second or third takes are usually the magic. After that it starts to lose the lustre, vibe, feeling, etc. I'm a singer... and I have produced and worked with Al Green, Gladys Knight, Whitney Houston, Boys II Men, Take 6 and Brian McKnight to name a few, all great singers, so I know when a lead vocal is magical. Steve was very hard on himself. I'm very good at separating [the past] with the project at hand. The lead vocals could have been done in about 20 minutes instead of five months. It was the only time in the production process that we didn't see eye to eye."[31]

For The Love Of Strange Medicine went on to sell 500,000 copies in the US by September of 1994, and had a hit single with 'You Better Wait' which peaked at number 29 in the *Billboard* Hot 100. 'Missing You' was also released as a single but it only reached 74 in the *Billboard* Hot 100.

For The Love Of Strange Medicine is not as upbeat and pop-oriented as *Street Talk* but it is not to be discarded; there are some excellent tracks and Perry's voice is in fine shape. Over-produced in parts and over-sentimental, it is still a worthwhile effort. It does, however, deserve more attention.

Michael DeGagne says on allmusic.com: "Tracks such as 'Donna Please' and 'Listen To Your Heart' try hard to rekindle Perry's Journey-esque magic, but it's nowhere to be found. Instead, his lyrics fall off into thin air without making any impact, along with commonplace radio harmonies that have long since lost their Eighties lustre."

Though the album was not the big success *Street Talk* was, and Perry had been out of the spotlight for a while, what certainly aided the album's sales was a tour of the US. Perry kicked off kicked off the *For The Love Of Strange Medicine* tour (supported by English-born, Canadian singer-songwriter Sass Jordan) in Milwaukee, Wisconsin on October 21, 1994 and finished in Fresno, California on March 15, 1995.

Sass Jordan: "He was a fabulous host, so to speak, very friendly and generous with his time and stories... Steve is a very pleasant person to hang out with, and we used to sing together in the dressing rooms sometimes. He would tell me stories and give me advice... The interesting thing to me is that I continue to receive e-mails from fans that saw me perform on that tour, who loved it. It was the same as most tours... travel, sleep, sound-check and do press – radio stations, morning shows, phoners... I guess it was pretty high profile – people love Steve Perry! It was a really good experience, and especially great for me, as he is one of the singers that I grew up idolising, and to get to sing with him was a real dream come true."[32]

However, some shows were cancelled and perhaps it was obvious to many that Perry's voice had passed its peak and that the vocal registers he was once famous for hitting were now beyond him. His band was drummer Moyes Lucas, guitarist Lincoln Brewster, keyboardist/guitarist Paul Taylor and bassist Todd Jensen. They did play some Journey songs, including, 'Wheel In The Sky', 'Lovin, Touchin', Squeezin'', 'Separate Ways (Worlds Apart)', 'Faithfully' and 'Don't Stop Believin''. Writing about one performance, *Entertainment Weekly* said: "Opening with a power outage onstage, Steve Perry seemed unflustered as the technical difficulties were repaired, and cruised right into a few Journey classics, then it was on to a couple of previous solo hits, with 'Oh Sherrie' getting the crowd to know this was going to be one kick-butt show... The show was great, spotlighting old and new, and there are certain voices that are always recognisable, and one of those is Steve Perry."

Gerry Gittelson wrote in *FactorX* in January 1995: "It took about half the set for Steve Perry to really get going… His vocals were loud and clear; he was nailing these songs to the floor, then stomping 'em with his boots."

It proved to be Perry's only solo tour.

Finally, in 1998 Perry treated his fans to the reasonably comprehensive *Greatest Hits + Five Unreleased*. The unreleased tracks were: 'When You're In Love (For The First Time)', 'Against The Wall', 'Summer Of Luv' and 'Once In A Lifetime, Girl' from the *Against The Wall* sessions, the writing demo 'It Won't Be You' from *For The Love Of Strange Medicine* sessions, and the unreleased Alien Project demo 'If You Need Me, Call Me'.

In 2009 a compilation – no doubt to capitalise on the resurgence of interest in all things Journey – called *Playlist: The Very Best Of Steve Perry* was released with the following tracks: 'Oh Sherrie', 'When You're In Love (For The First Time,)' 'Somewhere There's Hope', 'You Better Wait', 'What Was', 'Go Away', 'Against The Wall', 'She's Mine', 'Melody', 'Foolish Heart', 'For The Love Of Strange Medicine' 'Summer Of Luv', 'Strung Out' and a live version of 'Missing You'.

Perry has hinted that there may be a new solo in the foreseeable future. "I've never stopped writing or recording music," he said, "I'll always have that burning within me. I've been hanging with some friends in the studio recently tracking some live stuff. Being with them and the feel of working with other musicians again is certainly enticing."[33]

Drummer Russ Miller recorded drums tracks with Perry in early 2010. "We did full sessions. The way Brian [West, co-producer] works is to have some of the tracks with all programmed drums. Some tracks would have combinations of live and programmed drums in different sections. Then, of course some with just me on acoustic drums all the way through… We did the drum tracks at RMI Studios in Chatsworth, California. I do a lot of records and movie sessions there. I keep a super high-end Yamaha drum kit in the room that is always mic'd up and ready to roll."[34]

"We had a great time," he continues, "I will never forget Steve standing in front of the drums, singing the chorus of songs while I played right into him, working out my part to help support and lift his vocal. He sounds amazing!"[35]

The question on every fans lips is, what does Perry's voice sound like these days? "Great, of course," says Miller. "More mature and with a defined 'intent'. There is a little 'rasp' in there, since the last time we heard him but a monster vocal talent, ageless and without stylistic confinements."[36]

Perry has the last word: "I'm not purposely keeping anybody waiting. It's taken me all this time to actually want to do this again. I'm not signed... Life is very short and getting shorter all the time, so we'll see what happens."[37]

1   Steve Perry quote, Craig Modderno interview, *Rock Magazine*, 1984.

2   Steve Perry quote, Dennis Hunt interview, *Faces Magazine*, 1984.

3   Bill Cuomo quote, author interview, 2010.

4   Randy Goodrum quote, author interview, 2010.

5   Randy Goodrum quote, author interview, 2010.

6   Bill Cuomo quote, author interview, 2010.

7   Bill Cuomo quote, author interview, 2010.

8   Steve Perry quote, Tarin Elbert interview, *Music Express*, 1984.

9   Bill Cuomo quote, author interview, 2010.

10 Randy Goodrum quote, author interview, 2010.

11 Michael Landau quote, author interview, 2010.

12 Michael Landau quote, author interview, 2010.

13 Randy Goodrum quote, author interview, 2010.

14 Steve Perry quote, Dennis Hunt interview, *Faces Magazine*, 1984.

15 Michael Landau quote, author interview, 2010.

16 Bill Cuomo quote, author interview, 2010 ("...Same thing happened to me on REO Speedwagon's *'Can't Fight This Feeling Anymore.'* I laid out the guitar licks in the intro on synth, and they ended up using them instead of the guitar – once again it was on the Chroma.")

17 Bill Cuomo quote, author interview, 2010.

18 Bill Cuomo quote, author interview, 2010.

19 *Street Talk* was reissued in 2006 and included the following bonus tracks: 'My My My,' 'Harmony,' 'Makes No Difference,' 'Don't Tell Me Why You're Leaving' and 'If Only For The Moment, Girl.'

20 Steve Perry quote, Rich Sutton interview, *Song Hits*, 1984.

21 Herbie Herbert quote, Andrew McNiece interview, *Melodicrock.com*, 2008.

22 Steve Perry quote, Howard Johnson interview, *Kerrang!,* 1984.

23 Steve Perry quote, interviewee unknown, *Rock Magazine*, 1984.

24 Steve Perry quote, Dave Reynolds interview, *Frontiers*, 1995. (Bettencourt and Perry crafted a song called 'Always.')

25 Steve Perry quote, Dave Reynolds interview, *Frontiers*, 1995. (Some reports suggested Perry had three albums worth of unreleased material.)

26 Steve Perry quote, Jorgen Holmstedt interview, *Boulevard Magazine*, 1984.

27 *For The Love Of Strange Medicine* was reissued in 2006 and included the following bonus tracks: 'If You Need Me, Call Me,' 'One More Time,' 'Can't Stop,' 'Friends Of Mine' and a live version of 'Missing You.'

28 Tim Miner quote, author interview, 2010.

29 Steve Perry quote, Jorgen Holmstedt interview, *Boulevard Magazine*, 1984.

30 Tim Miner quote, author interview, 2010.

31 Tim Miner quote, author interview, 2010.

32 Sass Jordan quote, author interview, 2010.

33 Steve Perry quote, Ross Cat interview, *Nightlife*, 2005(?)

34 Russ Miller quote, author interview, 2010.

35 Russ Miller quote, author interview, 2010.

36 Russ Miller quote, author interview, 2010.

37 Steve Perry quote, Rob Evans interview, *Powerplay*, 2006.

Acknowledgments

I am grateful to the following musicians, songwriters, producers, managers, PR personnel, photographers, and music writers for their help with this book: Phil & Sue Ashcroft, Russ Ballard, Geoff Barton, Jake Brown, Glen Burtnik, Joe Chiccarelli, Larry Crane, Bill Cuomo, Rob Evans, Robert Fleischman, Mike Fraser, Robert Galbraith, Randy Goodrum, Herbie Herbert, Mark Hoaksey, Jimi Jamison, Alphonso Johnson, Sass Jordan, Michael Landau, Dave Ling, Joel McIver, Andrew McNiece, Bruce Mee, Marco Mendoza, Russ Miller, Tim Miner, Marty Moffatt, Stanley Mouse, Derek Oliver, Keith Olsen, Ricky Phillips, Simon Phillips, Greg Prato, Jason Ritchie, Tony Saunders, Dave Shack, Roger Silver, Shelley Stertz, Jeff Scott Soto, Ryan Sparks, John Tucker, Danny Vaughn, Ron Wikso, Jeb Wright and Richard Zito.

Additional thanks are due to my agent Matthew Hamilton; Chris Charlesworth and David Barraclough at Omnibus Press; also special thanks to Emma Kilgannon, Robert McKenna and my family and friends.

Apologies if I have missed anyone out. It was not intentional.

Bibliography & Sources

BIBLIOGRAPHY

In terms of books there is not a great deal out there on Journey, so as well as those referenced in the footnotes, the author found the following printed and online publications especially helpful during the writing of this book. Special thanks goes to Andrew McNiece for letting me quote from his collection of interviews with the band published on his indispensible website www.melodicrock.com.

The author gratefully acknowledges permission to quote and use references from the sources as referenced in the footnotes and repeated in the bibliography. Every quote and reference taken from selected sources is fully acknowledged in the main text and in the following endnotes. However, it has not been entirely possible to contact every copyright holder, although every effort has been made to do so, and to clear reprint permissions from the list of sources. If notified, the publishers will be pleased to rectify any omission in future editions.

The author is openly indebted to every one of the following...

BAND BIOGRAPHIES

Christe, Ian, *Sound Of The Beast: The Complete Headbanging History Of Heavy Metal*. (London: Allison & Busby Limited, 2004.)

Monica Cucu, Laura, *Steve Perry – A Singer's Journey*. (North Carolina: Lulu.com, 2006)

REFERENCE BOOKS

Betts, Graham, *Complete UK Hit Singles 1952–2005*. (London: Collins, 2005.)

Betts, Graham, *Complete UK Hit Albums: 1956–2005*. (London: Collins, 2005.)

Larkin, Colin, *The Virgin Encyclopaedia Of Rock*. (London: Virgin Books, 1999.)

Roberts, David (ed.), *British Hit Singles & Albums*. (19th Edition) (London: Guinness World Records Ltd, 2006.)

Strong, Martin C., *The Great Rock Discography*. (6th Edition) (London: Canongate, 2002.)

MAGAZINES

16 Magazine / *BAM* / *Billboard Magazine* / *BOP* / *Boulevard* / *BW&BK* / *Circus* / *Classic Rock* / *Cream* / *Faces Rocks* / *Fireworks* / *Frontiers* / *Guitarist* / *Hard Rock* / *Hard Roxx* / *Hit Parader* / *Jam Magazine* / *Kerrang!* / *Kerrang! Mega Metal* / *Keyboard Magazine* / *Melody Maker* / *Melt Down* / *Metal Edge* / *Metal Forces* / *Metal Hammer* / *Metal Maniacs* / *Modern Drummer* / *Modern Guitars* / *Modern Recording* / *Music Express* / *Night Rock Magazine* / *NME* / *Powerplay* / *RAW* / *Record Collector* / *Record Mirror* / *Record Review* / *Rock Hard* / *Rock Magazine!* / *Rockline Magazine* / *Rolling Stone* / *Song Hits* / *Sounds* / *Super Rock* / *Voice Magazine*

NEWSPAPERS/NON–MUSIC PUBLICATIONS

Boston Globe / *Calgary Herald (Canada)* / *Entertainment Weekly* / *Faces Magazine* / *FactorX* / *Fort Worth Star-Telegram* / *GQ* / *LA Daily News* / *Pittsburgh Press* / *St. Louis Dispatch*

MUSIC WEBSITES

http://www.allmusic.com

http://www.antimusic.com

http://www.artistdirect.com

http://www.backstageaxxess.com

http:// www.bassguitarmagazine.com

http://www.billboard.com

http:// http://blogcritics.org/music

http://www.classicrockmagazine.com

http://www.classicrockrevisited.com

http://www.thedrumninja.com

http://www.getreadytorock.com

http://www.guitarnoise.com

http://heavymetaladdiction.com

http://houseofrockinterviews.blogspot.com

http://www.keyboardmag.com

http://www.komodorock.com

http://www.melodicrock.com

http://mixonline.com

http://www.moderndrummer.com

http://www.modernguitars.com

http://www.musicmight.com

http://www.music.msn.com

http://www.musictap.net

http://www.music.yahoo.com

http://www.premierguitar.com

http://www.roadrunnerrecords.com/blabbermouth.net

http://www.rocksbackpages.com

http://www.rockeyez.com

http://www.rocknworld.com

http://www.rocktopia.co.uk

http://www.rockunited.com

http://www.rollingstone.com

http://www.rushonrock.com

http://www.soundpress.net

http://www.techtrek.com
http://uk.launch.yahoo.com
http://www.ultimate-guitar.com
http://www.vh1.com
http://www.vintagerock.com

NON–MUSIC/ENTERTAINMENT WEBSITES

http://www.about.com
http://www.accesshowbiz.com
http://www.allaccessmagazine.com
http:///www.ap.org
http://www.bullz-eye.com
http://www.entertainment.ie
http://www.ew.com
http://jam.canoe.ca
http://www.livedaily.com
http://www.salon.com
http://www.variety.com

NEWS WEBSITES

http://www.bbc.co.uk
http://www.guardian.co.uk
http://www.independent.co.uk
http://www.independant.ie
http://www.latimes.com
http://www.mckinneynews.com
http://www.nytimes.com
http://www.peagususnews.com
http://www.time.com
http://www.timesonline.co.uk
http://www.usatoday.com
http://www.usaweekend.com

JOURNEY ON THE NET

http://www.journeymusic.com

http://www.journeyrock.co.uk
http://arnelpinedarocks.com
http://aynsleydunbar.com
http://www.deencastronovo.net
http://www.greggrolie.com
http://jeffscottsoto.com/news
http://www.myspace.com/sewtoe (JSS)
http://www.jonathancain.com
http://www.myspace.com/jonathancainmusic
http://www.schonmusic.com
http://www.myspace.com/nealschon
http://www.robertfleischman.com
http://www.rossvalory.com
http://www.myspace.com/rossvalory
http://www.prairieprince.com
http://www.steveaugeri.com
http://steveperryonline.net
http://steveperryfanclub.homestead.com
http://steveperryfans.com
http://www.vitalinformation.com (Steve Smith)